Rethinking Crime And Deviance Theory

Rethinking Crime and Deviance Theory

The Emergence of a Structuring Tradition

FRANCIS T. CULLEN

ROWMAN & ALLANHELD
PUBLISHERS

ROWMAN & ALLANHELD

Published in the United States of America in 1984
by Rowman & Allanheld, Publishers
(A division of Littlefield, Adams & Company)
81 Adams Drive, Totowa, New Jersey 07512

Library of Congress Cataloging in Publication Data

Cullen, Francis T.
  Rethinking crime and deviance theory.

  Bibliography: p.
  Includes index.
  1. Deviant behavior.   2. Criminal psychology.
I. Title.
HM291.C86 1983   302.5'42   83-17796
ISBN 0-86598-073-X

83 84 85/ 10 9 8 7 6 5 4 3 2 1

Printed in the United States of America

For Bruce, John, Terry, Dick, and John

Contents

Acknowledgments

The central ideas underlying this endeavor were initially formulated in classes and many helpful discussions with Richard A. Cloward at Columbia University throughout the latter half of the 1970s. During this time, I benefited as well from the insights and suggestions of Frances Fox Piven.

Over the course of the past several years, a number of other people have kindly provided critical readings of various portions of the manuscript. These include David Greenberg, Gresham Sykes, Francis Ianni, Sloan Wayland, Dale Mann, and Stephen Messner. Special thanks must be extended to Edward Sagarin, whose direction, editorial advice, and encouragement are largely responsible for whatever merits this book may possess.

I would also like to extend my appreciation to Fran Floyd, Irene Dahl, and Carol Skiles, all of whom showed much dedication and good humor when I asked that burdensome typing deadlines be met. It is necessary as well to express my gratitude to the editorial staff at Rowman and Allanheld for their faith in this project and for making the process of writing a pleasant task rather than an onerous chore.

I must also acknowledge the assistance of my former colleagues in the Department of Sociology and Anthropology at Western Illinois University and of my current colleagues in the Criminal Justice Program at the University of Cincinnati. I would be equally remiss if I did not recognize the diverse and invaluable support given to me by Barry Gold, Roger Sherman, Ros Tichen, Helen Miller, Beverly Conn, Craig Polanzi, Bo Ryan, Steve Hunter, Dave Lewis, Terry Delorto, Michael Tony, Mark Myrda, and in particular, Kathryn Golden. My deepest gratitude goes to my parents, Francis T. and Justine C. Cullen, to my aunts, Irene and Lillian Brooks, and to my dearest friend and companion, Robin Grover. In many special ways, they have made this endeavor possible.

Finally, I am pleased to dedicate this book to Bruce Link, John Wozniak, Terry Magel, Dick Fink, and John Cullen—my older and occasionally wiser brother. I hope they can understand how much they have helped.

PART I

Understanding the Structuring Perspective

chapter 1

The Structuring Perspective

This book rests on the assumption that an adequate theory of the origins of deviant behavior must address two distinct questions: (1) What conditions motivate or predispose people to violate social and legal norms? and (2) What conditions account for the specific form that a deviant response takes? It is suggested that theorists have been far more preoccupied with the first question of why someone becomes deviant than with the latter issue of why a person becomes deviant in a particular way. As a consequence, we have gained considerable insight into the factors that move individuals to transgress social standards, but we have been less successful in demarcating the forces that "structure" or regulate the exact nature of the deviant activity that emerges.[1]

The purpose of this work is thus to illuminate the theoretical importance of giving more systematic study to the structuring of deviant behavior. Toward this end, the first three chapters attempt to provide a general understanding of what is meant by a "structuring perspective" by outlining the perspective's central tenets, origin, and application within the field. The later chapters are devoted to a reconsideration of prevailing sociological models of crime and deviance. It will be argued that the integration of the structuring perspective into the core of deviance theory may potentially result in the enrichment of those traditions that have long guided thinking in the field.

Accounting for Form: Implications for Deviance Theory

In their quest to solve the puzzle of why people become deviant, social commentators have not been hindered by a lack of imagination. Indeed, a distinguishing feature of the field is that it continues to be marked by a wide diversity of theoretical perspectives, each trumpeting the causal significance of a separate set of social circumstances. Such conditions as anomie, status deprivation, social disorganization, differential association, and societal reaction—to name only the major ones—are said to motivate, predispose, drive, or encourage people to engage in socially disapproved behaviors. For the purposes of this discussion, these motivational variables and their corresponding explanations will be referred to as motivational theories (cf. Hirschi 1969 : 31–34, Briar and Piliavin 1965, Gibbons 1971).

Even though analysts differ significantly in their thinking about the origins of deviant behavior, it is nevertheless possible to group the field's competing theories of deviant motivation into two general categories: (1) those in which a particular motivational condition is said to cause a particular form of social deviance, and (2) those in which a particular condition is said to cause virtually all forms of deviance. Notably, each of these brands of theorizing is marked by an assumption of a fixed relationship between a motivational state on the one hand and the type of response that is made to this condition on the other. As will be argued, this contention is based on tenuous logic and has ramifications for the capacity of such theories to account for the specific form which a deviant adaptation takes. These matters are considered in greater detail below.

MOTIVATIONAL THEORIES OF ONE FORM OF DEVIANCE

Different forms of deviance have for any number of reasons proven of interest to different scholars. Thus, some analysts choose to study mental illness, while others prefer to focus on crime, delinquency, homosexuality, prostitution, alcoholism, drug abuse, or suicide. Once they have decided to study a particular form of deviance, analysts then proceed in a similar manner: they try to uncover the factors which create the desire to engage in the particular behavior under observation.

The classic, and perhaps most influential, example of this approach is Durkheim's *Suicide*. In his efforts to demonstrate the viability and distinctiveness of sociology as a discipline, Durkheim selected one of the most individual and personal of all behaviors—suicide—as the deviant phenomenon to be explained. He then embarked on a search for the factors producing differential rates of suicide under varying social conditions. Of greatest importance—at least if measured by its impact on subsequent deviance theorizing—was Durkheim's assertion that conditons of anomie and egoism precipitate suicide in modern, Western, industrial societies. Quite broadly, Durkheim argued that the torment of unfulfilled expectations (anomie) and the generalized tension of a meaningless existence wrought by lack of structural integration (egoism) drive people to take their lives.

Though in widespread use today, this approach to the study of deviance— one of starting with a single form of nonconformity and working back to uncover the factors producing deviant motivations—is nevertheless marked by a core difficulty. It often leads authors to operate, however implicitly, on the assumption that there is a direct one-to-one correspondence or *determinate* relationship between the mode of deviance under consideration and the motivational condition held to produce the deviance. That is, analysts seek to uncover a single motivational state which accounts solely for one particular deviant form. This notion had been referred to critically by Cassell as the fallacy of "etiological specificity"(1975 : 539). By contrast, it may prove more useful to proceed with the alternative assumption that the condition identified may cause not only the form of deviance being studied but other forms as well. It can thus be argued that there is an *indeterminate* and not a determinate or etiologically specific relationship between motivational variables on the one hand and any particular form of deviant behavior on the other hand. This, in short, is the *problem of indeterminacy*.

A reluctance to consider indeterminacy has potentially profound implications for the adequacy of the models of deviance that are typically constructed. Specifically, once we assume that a given social circumstance can predispose a person to engage in more than one form of deviant behavior, then the task remains to explain why one course of action is selected over another. Yet the very approach of endeavoring to link a specific motivational variable to a single form of deviance obscures the importance of systematically confronting this problem. As such, students of crime and deviance have been hestitant to demarcate the conditions that intervene between motivational states and deviant outcomes, and thereby have the effect of structuring the direction that an adaptation takes. Their analyses are thus at times less than complete because of the absence of "structuring variables"—factors which are distinct from motivation-producing variables and which determine when a specific form of deviance rather than another will transpire. In short, many analysts have not fully considered the implications of the *concept of structuring variables* (see Figure 1).

Durkheim's study of suicide, the exemplar of a motivational theory of a single form of deviance, well illustrates the issues at hand. One of Durkheim's central theses is that during anomic times rising expectations "surpass the means at their command," expose people to stress, and result in suicide. The question that arises is: why must rising expectations and the stress they engender lead specifically to suicide? In this light, it is clearly pointed out in Durkheim's work that, whereas large numbers of people are exposed to socially-induced stress, only a few "choose suicide." Yet the alternative ways in which the vast majority of people who do not take their lives might adapt to pressures are virtually neglected. It is of interest that other early theorists pointed out that differing responses to Durkheim's etiological state were possible. For instance, Alexis de Toqueville posited that rising expectations could trigger revolution, while Edward Jarvis, a nineteenth-century psychiatrist, maintained that the condition could produce mental illness.

Figure 1.
Motivational and Structuring Paradigms

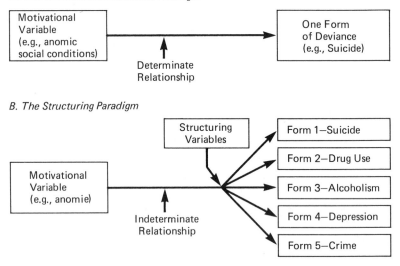

A. The Traditional Motivational Paradigm

B. The Structuring Paradigm

Durkheim's analysis thus implies that rising expectations lead inexorably to suicide. By passing over the problem of indeterminacy, he was able to remain largely silent on the issue of the conditions under which the stress produced by frustrated ambition will precipitate self-destruction rather than other deviant outcomes. As a result, while Durkheim succeeded in uncovering a variable (stress due to unfulfilled expectations) which may explain the general predisposition to violate social norms, he did not account for the form or content of the resulting deviant adaptation. To complete his model, one would have to delineate those "structuring variables" that shape the response a person makes to deviant impulses.

A similar commentary can be made about the explanations offered by many other students of wayward conduct. Indeed, the major deviance paradigms generally lack a *systematic* consideration of the conditions that socially structure adaptations to circumstances generating deviant motivations. The work of social disorganization theorists such as Shaw and McKay well illustrates this point. These analysts argued that the attenuation of control exercised by conventional society, coupled with exposure to the evils of the city (both products of social disorganization), predispose youths to delinquency. Yet theorists have blamed the disorganized conditions of urban life for a wide range of individual pathologies (e.g., mental illness, suicide) as well as group deviations (e.g., riots). If social disorganization and the motivational states it engenders are related to multiple forms of deviant behavior—that is, if there is an indeterminate relation between social disorganization and any given adaptation—then clearly the analyses of these commentators are in need of further elaboration. It is thus a theoretically important task to isolate the circumstances which guide youths in disorganized milieus along one deviant path as opposed another.

In a similar vein, Sutherland's views on the origins and distribution of criminal involvement do not fully confront the issue of explaining the specific form that an actor's deviance takes. Sutherland contended that people would be predisposed to engage in crime if their exposure to definitions "favorable to violation of law" outweighed those reinforcing conformity. He then offered the valuable insight that "differential association" is the common social process that creates the criminal motivations for all varieties of offenders— whether they are poor or wear white collars. However, Sutherland's overriding concern was to evolve a general theory of criminality, that is, to uncover the singular source of what inclines people, regardless of the mode of crime they manifest, to break the law. As such, his attention was focused in a less systematic way on why it is that one person with a criminal orientation becomes a robber, another a professional thief, and still another a white-collar criminal.

The more recent approaches of labeling and control theory are also restricted in their capacity to specify the form that deviant adaptations assume. For instance, labeling theorists have frequently proposed that a criminal identity engendered by societal reaction constrains a person to engage in a life of crime. These same theorists, however, do not question whether the stigma attached to a criminal identity might propel a person into a mental depression or cause a person to consider such retreatist adaptations as alcoholism, drug use, or suicide. In this light, it might prove fruitful for theorists to begin to consider two possibilities. First, thought should be given to how societal reaction may serve as a motivational variable which precipitates divergent lines of deviant activity. Second, analysts should examine how features of societal reaction itself may structure the ways in which actors break social rules.

The work of control theorists is also often characterized by an avoidance of structuring issues. Authors in this tradition have posited that motivational states do not differentiate deviants from conformists. Instead, deviance is held to occur only when society's controls over an actor are abrogated. Under this condition of deregulation, actors will either be driven to deviance by previously pent-up impulses (cf. Hirschi 1969 : 31–34) or, in a manner consistent with the images of the classical school of criminology, be in a position to exercise their will to deviate (Matza 1964). Thus, Hirschi has maintained that youths engage is delinquency when their bonds to conventional society are loosened (1969). Yet Hirschi's perspective could be fruitfully extended by explaining the conditions under which the weakening of control leads to a given variety of delinquency or perhaps to some other deviant response. In short, to the extent that control variables do in fact share an indeterminate relationship with the many forms of deviant behavior, it is likely that the integration of structuring variables into the works of control theorists would provide further insights into the origin and specific content of deviant behavior.

MOTIVATIONAL THEORIES OF MULTIPLE FORMS OF DEVIANCE

Not all theorists have assumed that a given motivational condition leads ineluctably to a given outcome. Some make quite a different assumption, namely, that a single motivational state can cause most, if not all, forms of deviance. These theorists thus believe that a particular set of social circumstances produces deviant motivations that are ostensibly so powerful and so pervasive in a social system that they can generate a great range of disapproved behaviors. Merton's anomie paradigm is perhaps the most notable of such theories. Here, Merton argued that the pressure growing out of a disjunction between socially approved goals and socially approved means to the attainment of these goals leads to virtually all forms of deviation. Another example is Parson's work on the sources of aggression in Western life, which asserts that the strain engendered by role malintegration gives rise to behaviors ranging from juvenile delinquency among males to war among nations. Similarly, conflict theorists have on more than a few occasions asserted that the tension of lower-class existence can result in a wide array of individual pathologies.

If analysts of single forms of deviance downplay the important notion that a motivational state can eventuate in a variety of adaptations, this insight obviously is not lost on the theorists we are considering here. At first glance, then, these theorists would seem to be aware of the problem of indeterminacy and the implications this idea holds for theory construction. But this is not always the case. For while they demonstrate that a given motivational condition can lead to multiple adaptations, they do not systematically spell out the circumstances under which one form or another of deviance is evidenced. Thus, they embrace the determinacy assumption insofar as they imply that a single motivational condition can "determine" or account for the specific form of all deviant adaptations. To say that a given predisposition is linked to all varieties of deviance, however, does not allow us to determine the exact way in which people will respond to the deviant drives they endure. As suggested, complete understanding of this issue can only be achieved by integrating structuring variables into the analysis. A brief consideration of

Merton's anomie hypothesis should prove useful in making these ideas more concrete.

Merton, of course, never stated that pressure may result in only a single type of nonconformity. Indeed, much of the apparent theoretical power of his framework rests on the very contention that people can make multiple deviant adaptations (innovation, ritualism, retreatism, rebellion) to the intense pressure generated by the inablility to attain a desired goal through legitimate means. Yet Merton never undertook the task of systematically delineating the conditions under which any one adaptation would occur. By omitting a full discussion of structuring variables, Merton largely reduced his paradigm to arguing that an actor under pressure will either conform or deviate in one of four logically exhaustive ways. Hence, while his theory offered an account of the pressures toward deviance in the social structure that would fascinate a generation of scholars to follow, it has proved to be less than successful in improving our insight on how features of the social structure constrain actors to pursue one adaptation but not another.

Indeterminacy and Structuring Variables: Further Notes

The weight of the discussion thus far suggests that motivational and structuring variables perform quite distinct theoretical functions. Motivational variables explain why people are moved to violate social norms. Structuring variables, on the other hand, explain why an actor who is intent on deviating will engage in a particular form of nonconformity and not another.

Underlying this analytical distinction in types of variables is the ''problem of indeterminancy'': a specific motivational condition is not believed to regulate the form or content that an actor's adaptation assumes. Stated a bit differently, there is an assumption that any given motivational state will not lead to or ''determine'' any one form of deviance more than another. For example, the argument presented here suggests that the stressful condition of unfulfilled goals (the central thesis of anomie theory) may increase a person's propensity to deviate, but that this stress state is no more likely to predispose the person to engage in suicide than in mental illness, drug use, crime, or alcoholism. As such, structuring variables are needed to explain the form of deviance that emerges.

But how tenable is this indeterminacy assumption, that is, the notion that motivational conditons do not account for the particular form an adaptation takes? Unfortunately, the empirical evidence needed to answer this question is less than adequate. Since analysts only on occasion entertain the full implications of the indeterminacy issue, their research typically measures the relationship between motivational variables and only one form of deviance.

As a result, their research does not endeavor to answer the question of whether a motivational condition is equally related to various forms of deviance, or whether it is unequally related and thus directs people toward a particular deviant form more than to alternative adaptations.

One notable exception which sheds light on the indeterminacy issue is the recent work of Linsky and Straus (1982). Their goal was to investigate the relationship between "stressful life-events" and "rates of violence and non-violent criminal behavior, and several other forms of maladaptive behavior." When control variables were introduced, they discovered that negative life-events were related, often similarly, to many different forms of deviance. Thus, consistent with the notion of indeterminacy, the partial correlations of the stress index to rates of deviance was .42 for crime, .51 for suicide, .36 for cirrhosis deaths, .74 for accidental deaths, and .38 for vehicular accident deaths. Faced with these findings, Linsky and Straus saw the need to incorporate additional "structuring" (nonstress) variables into their analysis to account for the specific "direction" of the response people make to stressful experiences. For instance, they "hypothesize that the level of stress will have a high (or higher) correlation with crime in regions characterized by a culture of violence." In the same vein, they offered the conclusion that "tight social control and high social cohesion" will preclude aggression and will encourage "such reactions as clinical depression or suicide" (1982 : 15–16).

While the work of Linsky and Straus is instructive, it nevertheless constitutes only an initial exploration of the indeterminacy issue. Consequently, in the absence of a definitive test of this thesis, the possibility of a pronounced determinate or etiologically specific relationship between one motivational condition and one form (or a limited category) of deviance cannot be ruled out. Indeed, based on common sense, it seems plausible that motivational states may exert some degree of determinacy on specific deviant types. It would thus appear likely that the stress or pressure emanating from marital discord would be more apt to give rise to certain adaptations (e.g., suicide, alcoholism, depression, child abuse) than others (e.g., property crimes). Similarly, it seems evident that "differential association" with criminal definitions would predispose a person toward some form of crime but not toward other kinds of wayward conduct.

However, even if a specific motivational condition were found to be closely correlated with and thus to explain a large part of the variance of one particular form of deviance, this would not mean that structuring variables could be safely ignored. For unless the motivational variable in question accounted for all of the variance, the specification of structuring variables would still be required to account for the remaining variance and to achieve a more complete explanation of this particular adaptation. As Cloward and Ohlin have remarked:

> All too often, a theory that explains the origin of a problem of adjustment is erroneously assumed to explain the resulting deviant adaptation as well. . . . We do not argue that there is no relationship between problems of adjustment and the resulting deviant adaptation, but we contend that there is no necessary deterministic relationship between them. The problem of adjustment may limit the range of satisfactory outcomes, but which alternative will emerge remains problematical. As long as there are at least two conceivable deviant outcomes to a given problem of adjustment, the problem of adjustment cannot be said to determine the outcome.[1960 : 41]

Similar insights can be found in the writings of Albert Cohen. In his noted theory of the emergence and character of lower-class delinquent subcultures, Cohen argued that the nature of the stressful conditions or "frustrating problems" youths experience limits or "determines" the kind of deviant adaptations that may arise. As he remarked, "to different problems the conceivable alternatives may be different" (1955 : 73). Yet he also recognized that other (structuring) variables still must be delineated for an explanation of the choice of a deviant solution to be complete. In this regard, he observed that "the range of alternatives may be further narrowed and the ultimate solution *more completely determined by other circumstances* that vary with social class, such as the conditions of communication, the facilities at one's disposal and other interests and values which might be jeopardized by certain of the solutions" (1955 : 73–74, emphasis mine).

It will become apparent in the chapters ahead that numerous other authors have also understood that deviant motivations do not fully account for the form and content of ensuing adaptations. In their efforts to make their explanations more complete, other researchers have likewise seen the need to supplement the important task of uncovering the unusual stresses and distinctly deviant cultural contexts that predispose people to violate social and/or legal norms. As such, these authors have attempted to delineate qualitatively different variables that shape the response that individuals make when negotiating deviant impulses. Most often, they have focused on the way in which social circumstances expose actors to particular values, skills, material resources, and social controls that make certain deviant options possible while precluding others. To be sure, such analyses have yet to provide us with a means of specifying sufficient conditions for the occurrence of a form of deviant conduct. Nevertheless, these works give us confidence that a structuring perspective will permit us to increasingly comprehend the complex of conditions that are necessary for a deviant form to occur, and hence to increase the probability that we can better account for the specific form a wayward act manifests.

Finally, it should be noted that arguing that a motivational condition does not fully account for or determine when any one adaptation transpires is *not* tantamount to suggesting that investigating sources of deviant motivations is a misguided theoretical enterprise. Indeed, it may very well be the case that the traditional deterministic approach to the study of deviance, as opposed to a structuring perspective, is more likely to lead authors to underestimate the true causal significance of these variables and to prematurely reject motivational theories.

To be more specific, when researchers find a negligible association between a motivational condition and a form of deviance, they naturally report that these factors have no "significant" impact and in turn surmise that the theory being assessed is of little etiological importance. Such a fate, for instance, is often suffered by the status frustration paradigm fathered by Merton (Cole 1975, cf. Hirschi 1969). Yet some caution should be exercised before such a sweeping conclusion is accepted. To the extent that the assumption of indeterminacy is viable, a general low relationship between a motivational state and any *one* adaptation would not be unanticipated. While such a state may not specifically "determine" or be closely associated with any particular type of nonconformity, however, it may be an important determinant of a person's *overall* propensity to violate norms. That is, while motivational variables do not regulate the form or content that a person's adaptation assumes, they may increase the likelihood that an actor will be moved to deviate in some undetermined way.

Since empirical studies invariably measure the relationship between only one motivational state and one adaptation, this more general causal effect of these variables is necessarily left unmeasured. More specifically, to adequately assess whether motivational variables influence an actor's overall propensity to deviate (as opposed to deviating in a given way), it would be necessary to study the relationship between a motivational conditon and the frequency with which actors deviate (regardless of form) or conform. Of course, in order to assess whether actors deviate, the researcher would have to survey as wide a range of adaptations as possible and not simply one adaptation, as is now common practice. Otherwise, it is likely that an actor's participation in some form of deviance would be overlooked and the relationship between a specific motivational condition and the general propensity to deviate artificially weakened. In this vein, House and Harkins have commented that "since most empirical studies have attempted to link status inconsistency [a motivational variable] to a given outcome (e.g., prejudice or psychological symptoms) *without specifying any of the intervening or conditioning variables which are necessarily involved*, it is not surprising that such studies find few significant status inconsistency effects" (1975 : 396 emphasis mine). Similarly, Cassell has observed that this same kind of error is made by researchers who assume that psychosocial stress is linked in a determinate manner to one, specific physical disease:

As far as research is concerned it would suggest that attempts to document that certain social processes are stressors, capable of producing disease, *by examining their relationship only to specific clinical entities* (coronary heart disease, hypertention, or various forms of cancer, for example) or even to subsets of diseases labeled 'stress diseases' *are unlikely to be too useful*. If the formulation is correct, certain people exposed to these stressors will develop the clinical entity under investigation. *Others however will not, but will develop some other manifestation which will not have been recorded or used as evidence as to the importance of the postulated stressor*. A more logical approach would be . . . to examine all disease outcomes related to exposure to the postulated stressor. [1975 : 541, emphasis mine]

Conclusion

As we have seen in this chapter, the major deviance paradigms prevailing in the field have largely focused on the problem of why people violate social and legal norms. Preoccupation with this important issue has often led to less consideration of the alternative, yet complementary, question of how to account for the specific form a deviant adaptation takes. At the same time, it would be too much to leave the impression that the theoretical inclinations of the authors of the dominant paradigms have led them to fully neglect this latter issue. Indeed, as will become apparent in the second half of this volume, a careful reconsideration of these prominent works indicates that they have much to tell us about the structuring of deviant choices. Equally important, a review of existing deviance research reveals a rather large body of writings that falls broadly within the conceptual framework outlined in our initial discussions. This "structuring tradition" will next occupy our attention.

Notes

1. A number of definitions of deviance are offered by scholars: normative, control, labeling, ethnomethodological, human rights (Becker 1963, Black and Reiss 1970, Gibbs 1972, Glaser 1974, Hirschi 1969, Rodgers 1975, Schwendinger and Schwendinger 1975, Warren and Johnson 1972). A normative definition of deviance will be employed in the present research: deviance is behavior which violates a norm. Similar to other conceptions of deviance, this definition has its strengths and shortcomings. Its major strength is that it is used by most deviance scholars; employing this definition thus allows for continuity in concept usage and in research. The prime deficiency of this definition is that it assumes that the norms whose violation constitutes deviance are readily known. Research on this empirical question is clearly not far advanced. The present study will attempt to circumvent this problem by using the concept to refer to norm-violative behaviors which deviance scholars have traditionally viewed to be deviant and to behaviors which, according to some researchers (e.g., Cullen et al. 1982, Rossi et al. 1974), are regarded as deviant by a large proportion of the American populace (e.g., crime, alcoholism, suicide, mental illness, drug addiction). Because of this usage, the present study will tend to be biased toward the explanation of the more "serious" forms of deviant behavior. I suspect, however, that this is true of most deviance theorizing. Thus, in reference to theories of crime, Toby (1974 : 86) has suggested that "the intellectual tools of the criminologist are better suited for

explaining crimes supported by a value-consensus of the population, that is, for explaining crimes that are also deviance, such as violent rape or premeditated murder.'' Finally, it should be noted that, because the definition of deviance employed here is not exact, it is best to view the definition as a ''sensitizing'' (Blumer 1969) or ''orienting'' (Homans 1967) concept, that is, a concept which gives a sense or feeling, more or less, for what the nature of the phenomenon being inspected is.

chapter 2

The Structuring Tradition: Past and Present Approaches

At first glance, the existence of a theoretical tradition that seeks to account for the form deviance assumes is not easily detected. By permitting the structuring perspective presented in the previous chapter to focus one's vision, however, it becomes readily apparent that the sociological literature is replete with studies illustrating how social conditions channel deviant actions in one direction rather that another. To be sure, the authors of these various works have not seen themselves as falling within a common paradigm. This has meant that their insights have remained largely independent of one another and have not yet coalesced to form the underpinnings of a clearly articulated structuring perspective of deviant behavior. Nevertheless, when these diverse analyses are taken together, they serve to illuminate how the structuring idea has been a persistent, if often unrecognized theme, informing both past and present approaches to the study of wayward conduct.

Examples of research which highlights the structuring of behavior in various realms of deviance are reviewed below. Such writings reveal that the structuring perspective is a longstanding tradition within the field of deviance theorizing. Further, it can be anticipated that research such as this will furnish an invaluable starting point in future attempts to build a structuring paradigm that is at once theoretically and empirically more adequate than the initial statement attempted in this book.

Sociological Illustrations of the Structuring of Deviant Behavior

CRIME AND DELINQUENCY

As we shall see in greater detail in the chapter ahead, the contributions of theorists of the Chicago School tradition constitute a fertile source for thinking about the structuring of criminal and delinquent behavior. Indeed, the writings of such commentators as Thrasher, Shaw and McKay, and Sutherland all point to the conclusion that differential access to deviant opportunities and learning environments exerts a crucial impact on the kinds of criminal and delinquent options available to people situated at different junctions in the social structure.

Examples of the structuring of criminal behavior are equally apparent in the work of those embracing very dissimilar theoretical assumptions. For instance, structuring ideas are clearly evident in the classic Marxist work of Willem Bonger, *Criminality and Economic Conditions*, first published in 1916. Anticipating modern-day Western radical theorists (Taylor et al. 1973, Quinney 1977) as well as Eastern social thinkers (Cullen and Cullen 1977), Bonger asserted that the exploitive economic relations of capitalism inevitably give rise to crime. He argued that the strains generated by capitalist arrangements promote an egoistic orientation in people that is essentially criminogenic. Further, while Bonger believed that the demoralizing conditions of working-class life certainly engender much crime by hindering the "development of social feelings on the part of the proletariate" (1969 : 48), he also held that criminal activity was far from alien to the bourgeoisie. The competitive and parasitic dimensions of bourgeois existence are fertile grounds for the growth of egoism and, in turn, of crime (1969 : 40–46). Consistent with his Marxist posture, Bonger concluded that a socialist and thus nonexploitive system would cultivate an altruistic spirit in its members and thereby eliminate the basic cause of criminal behavior, the egoism created by capitalist arrangements.

While Bonger devoted much effort to developing the thesis that the strain of egoism predisposes people to violate the law, he was aware that egoism does not determine the form of crime that will be pursued. Hence, he observed that the skills and opportunities a person possesses regulate how egoistic tendencies will be manifested:

> A man who knows how to make counterfeit bank-notes will commit this crime, whenever he wishes for any reason to enrich himself in a dishonest fashion, but he will become neither an incendiary nor a procurer. A former prostitute, on the contrary, will not think of making bank-notes, but will become a procuress. The kind of economic crime committed by the person who has a mind to commit such a crime, depends principally upon chance (occupation, etc.). [1969 : 90]

Similarly, Bonger observed that the social status a person occupies structures the criminal path that is followed. He was one of the first theorists to study how the status of sex exerts an influence on the type of offense committed. He noted, for instance, that because "the average woman of our time has less strength and courage than the average man . . . women participate less in crimes which require strength and courage" (1969 : 60). Also, "women take small part in sexual crimes." This occurs because "the role of women in the sexual life (and thus in the criminal sexual life) is rather passive than active" (1969 : 60). And, female political crimes are few due to "the almost wholly negligible participation of women in political life" (1969 : 63).

Bonger also went on to suggest, if only briefly, that not only is egoism related in a nonspecific fashion to different forms of crime, but that this etiological state can potentially lead to noncriminal adaptations as well. In this regard, he indicated that such factors as opportunity and personality regulate the particular kind of deviation that transpires:

> Three expedients offer themselves to one who has fallen into the blackest poverty: mendicity, theft, and suicide. It is partly chance (opportunity, etc.), and partly the individual's predisposition which fixes what anyone under the conditions named will become. . . . Generally those who have still some intelligence and energy become thieves, the rest vagrants. . . . Those who have recourse to suicide are either those who have known better conditions and find that the miserable existence that mendicity procures is not worth the trouble of living, or those who have lost all energy. Sometimes persons commit suicide to escape the shame of begging or stealing . . . These have been born with a very strong moral disposition and have lived in an environment where this disposition has been developed. [1969 : 96–97]

Lottier is another crime theorist who early on understood that stress or tension does not result exclusively in one form of crime. At first glance, this might not seem to be the case. Lottier was primarily concerned with depicting the origins of a single type of crime, embezzlement, and at times suggested that tension leads directly to this one wayward act. Thus, he commented that "the present theory is that the individual embezzler is a member of a competitive society who commits embezzlement as a consequence of tension-producing conflicts in the organismic, psychic, inter-personal, and cultural conditions of adjustment" (1942 : 842). However, at other points, Lottier made explicit mention of the indeterminate relationship between deviant motivations and criminality. He noted that "tension" may be a source of "offenses other than embezzlement which constitute departures from routine systems of behavior such as, for example, many thefts, most homicides, rapes and other assaults" (1942 : 848). This line of reasoning led Lottier to specify two factors that play an important role in regulating whether an actor will adapt to an existing state of tension through embezzlement or some other form of deviance. First, he argued that a person must be situated in "a particular position in the division of labor which allows the possibility of embezzlement as an accommodation to conflict" (1942 : 843). And second, an actor must possess a "lack of subjectively available alternatives to embezzlement" (1942 : 843).

It is instructive as well to consider Albert Cohen's widely read *Delinquent*

Boys (1955). This theoretical endeavor is important here not so much because it has become a classic statement of the origin of delinquency, but because it is typically reduced by deviance authors to nothing more than a motivational theory of youthful misbehavior falling within the Mertonian tradition (cf. Akers 1968). Yet it is much more than this. To be sure, Cohen's work contains deterministic statements linking deviant motivations directly to delinquency. For example, he readily adopted Parsons' thesis that middle-class, male delinquency is "primarily an attempt to cope with a basic anxiety in the area of sex-role identification" (1955 : 168). Further, he devoted most of his efforts to developing the idea that status frustration is a major problem of adjustment and ultimately the source of delinquency for lower-class Americans.

Nevertheless, it is equally clear that at various junctions in *Delinquent Boys*, Cohen was well aware that deviant motivations generated by status frustration do not lead exclusively to a subcultural delinquent solution. This adaptation is not available to all; certain social conditions, such as the opportunity to interact and communicate with youths possessing identical problems, must be present for the emergence of a group solution as opposed to alternative styles of delinquency. In this same vein, Cohen made clear statements on the theoretical necessity of explaining why an actor participates in a given deviant response. Thus, he remarked:

> Neither sociologists nor psychiatrists, however, have been sufficiently diligent in exploring the role of the social structure and the immediate social milieu in determining *the creation and selection of solutions. A way of acting is never completely explained by describing, however convincingly, the problems of adjustment to which it is a response, as long as there are conceivable alternative responses. Different individuals do deal differently with the same or similar problems and these differences must likewise be accounted for. . . .* Here we shall explore some of the ways in which the fact that we are participants in a system of social interaction affects the ways in which we deal with our problems. [1955 : 55–56, emphasis mine]

Structuring ideas are also present in the "group process" perspective initially advanced by Short and Strodtbeck (1965) and later developed by other students of delinquency (cf. Horowitz and Schwartz 1974). A major thrust of this perspective is to specify the types of conditions that precipitate certain episodes and forms of delinquent activity among gang members. While factors in the "external environment" of the gang are accorded some causal importance (e.g., neighborhood variations in social organization and social controls), the central emphasis is placed on interactive processes that occur in the context of everyday gang life that structure the behavioral alternatives available to youths. Special attention, for instance, is given to the importance of status management within the gang, and to how existing subcultural norms and the vivid reality of peer evaluations constrain gang members to respond to prestige challenges by erupting in aggressive acts aimed at reaffirming personal or group honor.

Similar insights have been offered by Gibbons. He has suggested that general predispositions produced by such conditions as status frustration or differential association do not invariably eventuate in criminal behavior. Instead, situational events which involve the dynamics of interpersonal exchanges "may often be the crucial, final element in a value-added process that ends in lawbreaking. Without the presence of situational correlates, the necessary and sufficient causes of at least some kinds of criminality fail to occur"(1971 : 275). Thus, as Gibbons has noted, growing up in a subcultural setting where violence is a common theme may inculcate a general predisposition or motivation to be aggressive. Whether this tendency is manifested in homicidal behavior as opposed to other specific instances of violence, however, will be determined by the presence of situational contingencies— for example, a marital dispute while drinking—which structure a given criminal alternative.

Gibbons is also a leading figure in another line of theorizing that argues for the importance of examining the causal processes underlying specific forms of criminality: the typological approach. Gibbons has offered the observation that if there is not a "sharp break . . . with the traditional approach which looks upon offenders as a relatively homogenous class, little progress is likely to be made toward explanation and prediction of crime and delinquency" (1981 : 40). As an alternative, he has suggested that scholars would evolve more complete explanations if they first developed offender classifications or typologies, and then proceeded to explore the specific complex of factors that makes one criminal pattern more probable than another. Toward this end, Gibbons noted that among the more influential conditions which shape the particular illegal roles chosen are social class, family background, peer association, personality dynamics, and the nature of contact with social control agencies.

Structuring ideas appear once again in the analyses of students of organized crime. Ianni's attempt to account for the increasing emergence of the "black Mafia" provides a good illustration. Ianni converged with the Mertonian tradition in proposing that blacks and other minorities turn to socially disapproved means when blocked from employing legitimate avenues to attain the goal of economic success (1974 : 322). He also realized, however, that the deviant motivations generated by frustrated ambitions do not determine the form of crime that will be "turned to." He noted that for some time blacks had been largely excluded from all but the lowest echelons of organized crime and thus had been limited to engaging in street crimes. By contrast, recent times have seen the heightened participation of blacks in the "Mafia." Ianni has attributed this changing offense pattern to a number of emerging factors that have coalesced over the past decade to create fresh opportunity structures for blacks in the underworld. Important in this respect are (1) the close social bonds that blacks are now acquiring in childhood gangs and in prisons which serve as functional alternatives for the ethnic/familial ties that bind members of the Italian Mafia together, and (2) the increasing control blacks are exerting over their neighborhoods. In short, then, Ianni has specified a set of structuring variables (and, significantly, not stress variables) that has altered the type of crime selected by blacks.

Of further interest is Ianni's observation that race/ethnicity not only regulates the availability of an organized crime adaptation but the kind of organized crime that can be pursued as well. He thus presented data revealing that the structure of the organization and the types of enterprises that are established differ according to whether the group in question is Italian, Cuban, Puerto Rican, or black.

This same theme is apparent in the work of Light. In his article, "The Ethnic Vice Industry," Light observed that traditional interpretations of organized criminality (such as anomie theory) are deficient because they do not appreciate that the characteristics of an ethnic group determine the form of vice enterprises which may possibly be established (1977 : 466–67). He thus concluded that "a more mature view begins with the insistence that American society thrusts opportunities for lucrative deviance upon the disadvantaged but acknowledges that sociocultural and demographic characteristics determine the manner in which providers respond" (1977 : 476).

Humphreys has also presented insights on how involvement in the vice activity of "tearoom trade," impersonal sex in public restrooms, is socially regulated. Based on his participant observation research, Humphreys was able to discern four different types of participants in tearoom encounters: trade, ambisexual, gay, and closet queens. Notably, he asserted that all of those engaging in the sexual exchanges are "acting in response to a variety of pressures toward deviance." Yet Humphreys also observed that in their efforts to resolve such strains, "these men . . . are able to choose only among the limited options offered them by society." Indeed, the particular "sets of alternatives, which determine the modes of adaptation to deviant pressures, are defined and allocated in accordance with major sociological variables." More specifically, Humphreys illustrated that knowledge of occupational and marital status allows us to "predict the styles of adaptation for men who are pressed toward sexual deviance" in the tearoom (1970 : 130).

Illustrations of the social structuring of criminal behavior are also common in the work of researchers examining the topic of women and crime. One of the earliest and most vivid examples of how sex structures adaptations in the criminal world can be found in Giallombardo's attempt to explain why the content of deviant inmate cultures differs markedly in male and female prisons.

The thrust of Giallombardo's study is that the type of inmate system that develops is not determined by the deprivations or stresses of prison life. Instead, a set of social conditions located in the "external culture" and associated with the sex status is held to regulate the form that an inmate culture assumes:

> However, when we consider that the deprivations of imprisonment were found to be present in the female prison studied and keenly felt by the female prisoners—yet the typical cultural system which emerges in the adult male prison is not present—we must conclude that the differences in structural form found in the two prison communities are inadequately explained by current functional analysis solely as a response to the deprivations of imprisonment. The deprivations may provide necessary conditions for the emergence of an inmate system, but they are *not in themselves sufficient to account for the structural form* that the inmate social system assumes in the male and female prison communities. . . . The evidence presented here suggests that the male and female inmate cultures are a response to the deprivations of prison life, but the *nature of the response* in both prison communities is influenced by the differential participation of both males and females in the external culture. The culture that emerges within the prison structure may be seen to incorporate and reflect the total external social structure; that is, the way in which roles are defined in the external world influence the definitions made within the prison. General features of American society with respect to the cultural definitions and content of male and female roles are brought into the prison setting and they function to determine the direction and focus of the inmate cultural system. [1966 : 286–88, emphasis mine]

More recent theories have devoted attention to explaining the distinctive crime patterns manifested by women as opposed to men. The empirical regularities have been amply established: females show high rates of petty shoplifting and prostitution but evidence only minimal participation in violent offenses, traditional property street crimes, and sophisticated criminal enterprises in which substantial resources can be accumulated (e.g., professional theft, organized crime, white-collar crime). Further, when women commit a "male" crime, they tend to do so in a feminine way; thus women who murder are likely to kill helpless or incapacitated loved ones in the home rather than strangers confronted on the street.

What is significant, however, is that analysts have not typically sought to locate the sources of sex variations in crime types in the differential exposure of women to conditions generating criminally deviant motivations. Instead, they have been far more inclined to highlight the ways in which sex roles function to structure female involvement in crime by restricting the illegal options available to women (Adler 1975, Simon 1975, Smart 1977). For instance, it is often asserted that the social position of women in the home or in less advantaged segments of the labor force limits opportunities for participation in property offenses traditionally committed by males. Similarly, socialization patterns that inculcate passivity rather than aggressiveness and which provide little exposure to the use of weapons lessen the chances that women will engage in crimes requiring force (assault) or threats (robbery). Alternatively, those criminal forms that women do pursue in considerable numbers are largely an outgrowth of the traditional female sex role. As Weis has commented, "Instead of denying 'femininity' and becoming more masculine, they are validating their 'femininity' illegally. They engage in role expressive and role supportive criminal behavior . . . which are extensions of their female role. . . . In short, female criminal behavior is an illegitimate expression of legitimate female role expectations and opportunities" (1976 : 18–19). Thus, the prototypical female offense of shoplifting can be anticipated to occur because going shopping is an acceptable female activity and hence women are comfortable operating in this social setting. As Smart has observed, shoplifting is "an extension of the female role, it is 'role expressive' both in method and in its object, unlike other forms of deviance which appear to contradict the traditional, stereotyped, female sex role" (1977 : 10). Similarly, the availability of prostitution as a criminal option reflects the nature of the conventional social role allocated to women. In the course of conventional socialization, women learn that it is appropriate for females to barter sexual favors for other rewards. Becoming a prostitute only requires applying these "normal" skills and information in an "illicit" fashion. In Rosenblum's words:

> Neither the call girl nor the non-deviant woman have high expectations about receiving sexual gratification (though to differing degrees) and both expect some type of "pay off" for their desirability (though the prostitute's payment is generally more tangible). The difference between the utilization of and the expectations regarding sexuality is only one of degree. The decision to become a call girl simply requires an exaggeration of one aspect of the situation experienced as a non-deviant woman. [1977 : 180]

Further, it appears that cultural stereotypes define appropriate "feminine" offenses (Cullen and Link, 1980), and in turn serve to channel women along certain criminal paths but not others. In this regard, Harris has proposed that there are "type-scripts" associated with the sex status that function to specify the "classes of criminal behavior it is likely, possible, unlikely, and impossible for particular types of actors to perform" (1977 : 11). This insight parallels Epstein's observation that job choices in the conventional work sphere are structured by "occupational images and values which help define some kinds of work as appropriate for women, and thus figure both in the selection of a profession and in the recruitment patterns of the professions. . . . Specific types of work are encouraged, tolerated, or tabooed. This early conditioning is nearly always crucial to later occupational decisions" (1970 : 18–19).

Structuring ideas are also at the center of the ongoing debate over whether there is a "new female criminal." Stimulated by the provocative writings of Adler, social commentators have contended that changing female sex roles are now providing women with the opportunities to engage in forms of crime previously reserved for men; just as women are increasingly becoming doctors, lawyers, and truck drivers, so too are they becoming robbers, burglars, and white-collar offenders. As Adler has suggested:

> What we have described is a gradual but accelerating social revolution in which women are closing many of the gaps, social and criminal, that have separated them from men. The closer they get, the more alike they look and act. . . . In the final analysis, women criminals are human beings who have basic needs and abilities and opportunities. Over the years these needs have not changed, nor will they. But women's abilities and opportunities have multiplied, resulting in a kaleidoscope of changing patterns whose final configuration will be fateful for all of us. [1975 : 30]

Research that questions the validity of this perspective is emerging, however. It is argued that changes in sex roles have been minimal in recent times and hence that the circumstances that have channeled women into a limited range of criminal adaptations have not been substantially altered. In short, sex status continues to structure participation in criminal ventures much as it has in the past. As Steffensmeier has concluded, "sex differences in adult criminality show very little change over the past decade and half. . . . Female experiences are not moving beyond traditional roles, either legitimate or illegitimate" (1980 : 1099, 1102; cf. Steffensmeier 1978, Steffensmeier and Steffensmeier 1980, Steffensmeier and Cobb 1982, Norland and Shover 1977, Hindelang 1979, Leonard 1982 : 42–43, Wolfe et al. 1982, and Wilson 1981).

Finally, two studies have appeared in recent years that offer innovative ideas on how we might improve our understanding of the social production of criminal forms of behavior. The first is the "routine activities approach" advanced by Cohen and Felson. These authors depart from traditional theories of crime by assuming the existence of individuals motivated to break the law. While agreeing that it is essential that the sources of illegal inclinations be delineated, they have nevertheless argued that an exclusive focus on the origins of such motivations is insufficient to account for the incidence of particular forms of crime. Instead, Cohen and Felson have suggested that theorists must also consider how routine or everyday activities furnish the criminally motivated with specific illegal opportunities by "providing a suitable target for the offender, and absence of guardians capable of preventing violations" (1979 : 590). To illustrate this structuring principle, they propose that increases over the past several decades in "direct-contact predatory violations" (e.g., rape, robbery, household burglary) cannot be attributed merely, or perhaps mainly, to the existence of more people willing to operate outside the confines of legal norms. Rather, Cohen and Felson report empirical evidence revealing that the escalation of ''predatory'' offenses is better understood as a reflection of changes in the daily activities of citizens which now place increasing numbers of Americans in circumstances where victimization is more possible.

> It is ironic that the very factors which increase the opportunity to enjoy the benefits of life may increase the opportunity for predatory violations. For example, automobiles provide freedom of movement to offenders as well as average citizens and offer vulnerable targets for theft. College enrollment, female labor force participation, urbanization, suburbanization, vacations and new electronic durables provide various opportunities to escape the confines of the household while they increase the risk of predatory victimization. . . . Rather than assuming that predatory crime is simply an indicator of social breakdown, one might take it as a byproduct of freedom and prosperity as they manifest themselves in the routine activities of everyday life. [1979 : 605]

A fresh perspective has also been set forth by O'Malley in his study of the politically-oriented crime of ''bushranging in nineteenth century Australia.'' Criticizing prevailing paradigms for their microsociological and ahistorical bias, O'Malley has observed that while scholars are ''much concerned with social pressures on individuals to adopt or maintain socially proscribed behaviors, there has been remarkably little work on the appearance, maintenance or disappearance of the forms of behavior'' (1979 : 271). Similar to that part of the Chicago school tradition which linked the growth and changing context of the city to the evolution of specific kinds of delinquent and criminal roles, O'Malley has contended that participation in any form of crime ultimately depends on broad, macro-level transformations of the social order that create new opportunity structures and hence allow activities to ''become possible modes of behavior'' (1979 : 271). In this light, O'Malley's investigation of ''bushranging'' reveals that two conditions coalesced to permit this criminal form to emerge and flourish: the presence of chronic class conflict and the absence of a legitimate political organization to represent the interests of the rural working class farmers. Alternatively, as political parties arose that ostensibly spoke for the disadvantaged and gave them a legitimate voice in policy-making, community support (e.g., warnings of police whereabouts, the hiding of offenders) for the individualistically-oriented and predatory conduct of the bushrangers against the affluent soon eroded. As a result, this category of crime experienced a ''sudden and virtually complete extinction'' (1979 : 279).

SUICIDE

Similar to students of crime, theorists concerned with suicide have also demonstrated that different aspects of self-destructive behaviors are socially structured. Two traditions of structuring analysis have emerged over the years. One group of authors has sought to investigate the question of why suicide takes a particular form. A second group has endeavored to understand why suicide, and not an alternative deviant response, is chosen.

Writing in 1881, Thomas Masaryk was one of the earliest theorists intrigued by the issue of why individuals choose one method of suicide over another. In his chapter "The Kinds and Forms of Suicide," Masaryk noted generally that "the choice of means" used in self-destruction "is determined by the situation in which the person finds himself" ([1881] 1970 : 120). He then went on to remark that status characteristics such as sex, age, nationality, and occupation condition the type of suicide that occurs. For example, Masaryk argued that "occupation determines the choice of means in that it often supplies means with which one can commit suicide; the chemist poisons himself; the soldier shoots himself; the miner throws himself into the coal mine, etc." (1970 : 122).

Throughout the years, numerous other theorists (including Durkheim, as we shall see in Chapter 4) have also commented on the factors that account for the content of a suicidal act. In recent times, Marks has presented the most thorough analysis of how social conditions structure the form a suicide takes (Marks 1977–1978, Marks and Abernathy 1974, Marks and Stokes 1976). Significantly, Marks pointed out that the factors which create the motivation to deviate do not regulate the content an adaptation assumes: the "methods of suicide are basically independent of reasons for suicide" (Marks and Stokes 1976 : 628). Having made this claim, Marks was able to set aside the question of why people commit suicide and instead address the issue of why people commit suicide in certain ways. Marks's central thesis is that an actor's social location patterns the kind of suicide pursued by regulating (1) the physical availability of as well as the skills needed to employ a given method, and (2) whether the use of a method is viewed as appropriate or normative for occupants of a particular status. For instance, Marks's research suggests that women rarely kill themselves with firearms because such a method of self-destruction would be inconsistent with cultural conceptions of femininity (i.e., it is seen as too messy or painful). Instead, women are far more likely to commit suicide by ingesting prescription drugs, both because drugs are easy to obtain and use, and because women know that suicide by overdose is viewed as normative for females.

While scholars like Masaryk and Marks have made a valuable contribution to our understanding of the way suicidal behavior is socially structured, they did not seek to build upon their insights about structuring by addressing the problem of why deviant motivations result in suicide rather than in alternative deviant forms. Other theorists within a second tradition of suicide research have focused on this issue.

Tocqueville is an early social commentator who illustrated that the choice of suicide is structured. Much like Durkheim, Merton, and other status frustrations theorists, Tocqueville observed that "inhabitants of democratic countries . . . can easily attain a certain equality of condition, but they can never attain as much as they desire. . . . At every moment they think they are about to grasp it; it escapes at every moment from their hold." And the price of this continuing lack of fulfillment is high. "The constant strife between the inclination springing from the equality of condition and the means it supplies to satisfy them harasses and wearies the mind." However, Tocqueville went on to recognize that the "disgust at life" generated by blocked aspirations would not necessarily result in suicide. Rather, the strength of religious beliefs in democratic nations would ultimately determine whether these stressful circumstances would lead to self-destruction or foster insanity. Thus, "Complaints are made in France that the number of suicides increases; in America suicide is rare but insanity is said to be more common there than anywhere else. These are all symptons of the same disease. The Americans do not put an end to their lives, however disquieted thay may be, because their religion forbids it" ([1835] 1945, vol. 2 : 146–47).

A number of other theorists have also long considered the question of why some people commit suicide while others direct their aggression outward and murder. Contemporaries of Durkheim such as the Italian positivist criminologists Ferri and Morselli dwelled upon this issue. More recently, the interest in this question has not waned. Though the literature is extensive, it is fair to say that the most studied of modern sociological treatises on the subject is *Suicide and Homicide* by Henry and Short (1954).

Henry and Short began their analysis with the premise that frustration or stress can elicit either of two "aggressive reactions": one directed against oneself—suicide, and one directed against others—homicide. Which adaptation is made cannot be discerned from knowledge of the pressure state alone. Instead, the nature of the response to frustration can only be gathered by "isolating the variables which determine the choice between suicide and homicide" (1954 : 16). The crucial factor seen to regulate the selection of an adaptation is whether or not the frustrated actors can "legitimize" the expression of aggression toward their others. When legitimation is possible, murder is held to transpire; when it is not possible, suicide is the likely outcome. In turn, the authors maintained that the ability of actors to legitimize other-oriented aggression is itself contingent on the extent to which their "behavior is required to conform to the demands and expectations of other people" (1954 : 17). For "when behavior is subject to strong external restraint . . . it is easy to blame others when frustration occurs. But when the external restraints are weak, the self must bear the responsibility of frustrations. . . . Others cannot be blamed since others were not involved in the determinations of behavior" (1954 : 18, 103).

Arthur L. Wood has sought to advance the traditional analysis of the suicide-homicide question by also considering the structuring of a third adaptation, economic crimes. In his study of these three modes of noncomformity in Ceylon, he argued that focusing solely on structurally-induced stress will not allow us to discern which deviant form will occur. He maintained that it is also necessary to delineate "intervening variables" that either "facilitate or inhibit certian types of deviance" (1961 : 753). In relation to this conception, Wood contended that a person's normative orientation is the key intervening condition regulating the occurrence of one or another adaptation. He proposed that actors possessing an alienated and demoralized orientation are likely to commit murder, while those strongly oriented toward cultural norms tend to be suicidal. He further suggested that those who engage in economic crimes appear to have attitudes favoring both "immoral conduct" and "achievement as opposed to apathy" (1961 : 752). One final theme developed by Wood is his assertion that the distribution of these normative orientations in turn determines the distribution of forms of deviance throughout the social structure.

Lastly, Phillips has considered the novel possibility that newspaper publicity given to suicides might have an "imitation" or "suggestion" effect which leads others to resolve problems through self-destruction (1979; cf. Bollen and Phillips 1981,1982). Phillips explicitly recognized the principle of indeterminacy (discussed here in Chapter 1) and the need to account for the deviant form that arises. Thus, at one pont in his analysis, he was able to state that "many different behaviors have been thought to result from anomie." He then continued:

> A central question in this literature has seldom been broached and has never been resolved: Given that so many behaviors are thought to result from anomie, what makes an individual respond to anomie with one type of behavior rather than another? Why do some individuals respond to anomie by committing suicide, while others turn to alcohol and still others join anomie-reducing social movements? [1979 : 1170]

Noting that the work of Merton and Cloward and Ohlin can "be shown to provide an incomplete answer to the question under discussion," Phillips asserted that "the concepts of suggestion, imitation, and modeling may provide a partial answer." Specifically, "an anomic individual may choose suicide rather than some other solution if a model individual has recently committed suicide—thus bringing suicide to the forefront as a salient solution to anomie" (1979 : 1170).

It is of further significance that the empirical data accumulated by Phillips tend to confirm his insights. Hence he discovered that after a publicized suicide in the mass media, motor vehicle fatalities suddenly escalate. Moreover, he found that murder-suicide stories are followed by increases in multiple vehicle accidents involving passenger deaths, while pure suicide accounts are followed by single-vehicle accidents. Taken together, these results indicate that news publicity may serve as an imitative mechanism that in large part determines the selection of suicide as a deviant response as well as the specific content this adaptation assumes.

In recent years, theorists have shown such a growing uneasiness over the simple formulation that stress leads directly to deviant behavior that this relationship has become a question of emerging importance in the field of deviance. One senses this uneasiness, for instance, among control theorists like Hirschi (1969) and Toby (1974), both of whom have asserted that stress will not be actualized into deviant behavior unless society's power to regulate an individual's behavior breaks down. Nowhere is this feeling more apparent, however, than in the work of authors researching the association between stressful life-events and mental illness. Here, a myriad of authors have argued that variables such as social supports intervene between a life-event and mental illness either to prevent the event from producing stress or to help a person under stress to avoid expressing psychiatric symptomatology (cf. Askenasy et al. 1977, Eaton 1978, Gore 1978, Liem and Liem 1978, Pearlin and Radabaugh 1976, Pearlin and Schooler 1978, Webb and Collette 1977).

While control and stressful life-events authors, among others (cf. Blake and Davis 1964, Becker 1963), have appreciated the problematic relationship between stress and deviant outcomes, they have often hesitated to explore the further possibility that the variables which intervene between stress and outcomes regulate not simply the occurrence of deviance, but the *type* of deviant response as well. However, others in the field have made clear inroads in this direction. The research of House and Harkins is notable in this regard (1975; cf. House 1981). In their article "Why and When is Status Inconsistency Stressful?," they initially offered the contention that variables intervene between status inconsistency and stress to determine when such inconsistency is experienced as stressful. More significantly, they went on to propose that numerous "conditioning variables" intervene between stress and a full complement of deviant responses (including forms of mental illness) to regulate when any given adaptation will transpire. Though the development of this latter insight is less than systematic due to the authors' greater concern for the problem of when status inconsistency produces stress, the thesis that circumstances intervene to impact on a range of outcomes is still present.

A number of other scholars, both past and present, have similarly perceived that psychiatric symptomatology is structured and thus have endeavored to investigate how various conditions determine the .type of disorder that emerges. In research conducted over two decades ago, Singer and Opler indicated that the "fantasy and motility" patterns of Italian- and Irish-American schizophrenics differ markedly as a result of the divergent "cultural frameworks and family constellations" associated with each group. Similarly, Langner and Michael observed that forms of mental illness vary by class position, with psychosis being characteristic of the lower classes and neurosis of the upper classes (cf. Hollingshead and Redlich 1958). As a consequence, Langner and Michael did not limit their analysis to inspecting "how social class might be conducive to different rates of impairment," but also saw the importance of addressing the distinct problem of how class is related to "different types of disturbances" (1963 : 439). This perspective prompted them to examine how social class influences such nonstress factors as mode of child rearing, self-esteem, and superego development which in turn shape the content of the symptomatology manifested by each class.

An equally clear example of the structuring of mental disorders has been provided by Dohrenwend and Dohrenwend (1976). In their critique of Gove and Tudor's stress theory (reviewed in Chapter 4), the Dohrenwends contended that sex differences in types of psychopathology "cannot easily be explained by role theories arguing that at some time and place one or the other sex is under greater stress and, hence, more prone to psychiatric disorder in general" (1976 : 1453). They suggested that the search for the answer of which sex has a higher overall rate of mental illness is unlikely to be a productive one. Instead, "the important question is, What is there in the endowments and experiences of men and women that pushes them in these different deviant directions," that is, into different forms of mental illness (1976 : 1453). As a starting point for understanding how sex structures mental illness, they urged researchers to pay attention to the empirical regularity of "the relatively high female rates of neurosis and manic-depressive symptomatology, and the relatively high male rates of personality disorders with their possible common denominator of irresponsible antisocial behavior" (1976 : 1453).

The finding that women are overrepresented in more passive forms of mental illness should not be unexpected. It is often suggested that the socialization that women undergo typically leads them to be channeled into passively oriented activities in other realms of deviance (e.g., crime). Carol Smart has aptly captured this insight:

> It has already been shown that personality disorders are not the most common psychiatric complaint among women, rather they are likely to be defined as schizophrenic, depressive or neurotic. This tendency for the majority of disturbed women to become (or to be diagnosed as) depressed and anxious may be related to the socialization process of girls which encourages them to repress their aggression and to find satisfaction vicariously through others and not on their own initiative. This perhaps has parallels in sex-related criminal activities where women can be seen to adopt deviant behavior which is

more closely related to their traditional feminine roles (i.e., prostitution or shoplifting). [1977 : 166]

ALCOHOL ABUSE AND ALCOHOLISM

The belief that people enduring life-stresses attempt to alleviate their difficulties through excessive alcohol usage has long possessed much appeal in both professional and popular literature. Pearlin and Radabaugh have thus concluded that "the view that consumption of alcohol may serve as a mechanism for coping with anxiety aroused by economic conditions has a variety of conceptual and empirical underpinnings in the vast literature on drinking" (1976 : 652). At the same time, there has been a fairly widespread awareness among alcohol theorists—perhaps more so than among students of other types of nonconformity—that deviant motivations such as stress or anxiety do not lead exclusively to the adaptation of interest to them, alcohol abuse.

The influential writings of Bales are undoubtedly responsible for sensitizing many theorists to the notion that stress and insobriety are related in an indeterminate fashion. To be sure, Bales did not discount the role played by stressful conditions in the etiology of alcoholism; socially-induced inner tensions are the forces that move people to seek relief through deviant means. But Bales also recognized that not everyone could adapt to such tensions through the use of alcohol. He argued that, quite independently of stress, cultural attitudes toward drinking as well as the availability of functionally equivalent alternatives to alcohol (e.g., drugs) influence whether an alcoholic response is made. To support his reasoning, Bales pointed to the way in which religio-ethnic affiliation structures alcohol usage and, ultimately, its abuse. In particular, he observed that aspects of Jewish culture preclude insobriety, while central value orientations of the Irish promote it.

Following Bales's lead, subsequent students of alcoholism have continued to note the importance of ethnicity in structuring alcohol usage. Snyder (1956, 1958, 1962) has been a prominent figure in providing additional support for the existence of Irish-Jewish differentials in alcoholism. Scholars have also demonstrated that membership in other ethnic groups, such as French and Italian, patterns alcohol consumption (Lolli et al. 1953, Sadoun et al. 1965). And, on a broader level, the ethnicity research has prompted Lisansky to assert that "the most promise lies in a sociopsychological theory of etiology. One needs to know not only about individual tensions and frustrations but also about the group's methods of coping and its attitudes toward the perception of alcohol" (1968 : 266).

Just recently, Glassner and Berg have dwelled on the issues outlined by Lisansky and have offered an important update on the relationship between being Jewish and alcohol abuse. Glassner and Berg note that, despite apparent decline in religious orthodoxy among Jews, the Jewish rate of alcoholism continues to be far below the national average (1 percent versus 7 percent). Yet in contrast to what commentators a decade ago predicted, why has this heightened secularization not precipitated a convergence of the Jewish rate of abuse with other religio-ethnic groups? That is, as religious attachments and hence corresponding controls have weakened, why has alcohol abuse as a response to psychic strain not increased among Jews?

Based on a three-year study , Glassner and Berg have learned that despite a secular trend, informal social controls against abusive alcohol consumption persist within the Jewish community. In all, they were able to discern four mechanisms that inhibit Jews from establishing a stable pattern of intoxication. The first is the existence of stereotypes or status-specific norms that define alcoholism as a non-Jewish problem and thus as inappropriate conduct for someone with their religio-ethnic status. Hence, just as we have seen that women would not see themselves as possibly becoming a burglar or robber, Jews find it inconceivable that they could be a problem drinker; it is simply something that "Jews do not do." Secondly, socialization experiences continue to link moderate drinking to special occasions and to invest such consumption with symbolic meanings. As such, Jews do not develop a "belief that problems can be alleviated through" alcohol usage, nor do they learn "how to use the substance to solve problems" (1980 : 655). Third, they tend to select peers, in particular other Jews, that are moderate drinkers. They are as a result largely insulated from those who would encourage more extensive substance abuse. Lastly, Jews frequently develop an "avoidance repertoire" (e.g., nursing a drink throughout the evening, joking about being a nondrinker) so as to blunt social pressures to become intoxicated. "Consistently utilizing an avoidance repertoire" is significant, as Glassner and Berg have pointed out, because "one misses opportunities to learn the deviant uses of alcohol, which is one of the crucial moves in development of alcohol problems" (1980 : 661).

Apart from those analyzing the relationship between stress, ethnicity, and insobriety, other alcohol theorists have also on occasion voiced structuring ideas. For instance, Rubington examined how the selection of a skid-row adaptation is structured by social conditions. Rubington noted that theorists have traditionally argued that people become skid-row alcoholics in response to the stresses generated by their alienation from conventional society. He realized, however, that these formulations are too deterministic :

> Where the attribute theorists argue that absence of rewarding social relationships *necessarily leads to* further withdrawal and ultimate dependence on alcohol, the contention here is that the absence of rewarding relationships creates the search for a primary group. Ultimate dependence on alcohol is a possible consequence of this search, *but it is neither the most likely nor the only consequence.* [1958 : 68, emphasis mine]

Having made the insight that "not all of the people alienated from dominant cultural traditions find their way into skid-row subculture," Rubington then explored the question of what pushes an alienated person into skid-row as opposed to an alternative adaptation (1958 : 68). As part of his answer, Rubington pointed to the role primary-group ties play in structuring the choice of deviant adaptations:

> The establishment of new primary-group ties would seem to be, then, the most satisfactory hypothesis to account for the selection of subcultural alternatives. Given two individuals subjected to similar stress and strain in their social relationships, one avoids the skid-row alternative because a different system of interpersonal relations binds the prospective deviant to major value-patterns. [1958 : 68–69]

Rubington finally went on to observe that a person's social position not only influences access to a skid-row subculture but also conditions the content that such an adaptation takes. He thus contended that the "social strata from which recruits have been alienated shapes the different modes of orientation for and induction in skid-row subculture. These differences bear heavily upon the different ways men participate in the culture once they have become introduced to it" (1958 : 69–70).

It is interesting to note that aspects of the female status continue to condition or structure the behavior of women who attempt to survive in a predominantly male skid-row setting. Thus, research indicates that the drinking patterns of skid-row women are unique in several respects. Reflecting general drinking patterns among women in our society, female alcoholics on skid-row consume less alcohol than men, are less likely to drink beer (17 percent to 35 percent for males), attempt to use their femininity to obtain free alcohol, and do not frequent bars and taverns (Garrett and Bahr 1973). Similarly, as the passage set forth below explains, alcoholic women on skid row remain sensitive to the pressures of social disapproval of drinking in public that females in our society typically experience:

> Oddly enough, these women go through a "predrinking" ritual before every drink. For example, Miss R., who usually drinks in the park, takes a drink if—and only if—there is no one in the immediate vicinity. Typically, she looks around, first looking up the street, then down, and occasionally even behind her bench; if no one is near she "sneaks" a drink from her wine bottle (disguised in the proverbial "brown bag") by holding her coat up around her face. Even more interesting is the drinking behavior of Mrs. D., who hides her drinking from public view by squatting near some bushes near the playground. [Garrett and Bahr 1973 : 1239]

Another clear example of the application of the structuring perspective is found in the writings of Pearlin and Radabaugh. These authors proposed that excessive alcohol use can arise from the "high level of anxiety" precipitated by economic hardship. Unlike many motivational theorists, however, they recognized that not everyone utilizes alcohol to alleviate their anxiety. Further, since drinking is not the only method to mitigate the discomfort generated by stressful circumstances, "it is necessary to take into account conditions that serve to make drinking an attractive coping technique for some distressed people but not for others" (1976 : 658). In this regard, Pearlin and Radabaugh asserted that some "intervening conditions . . . influencing the ways people attempt to cope with anxiety are rooted in personality" (1976 : 658). Specifically, "the relationship between anxiety and the coping functions of alcohol is mediated by sentiments of personal efficacy . . . and self-esteem" (1976 : 659–60). The authors concluded their analysis with the insight that factors which produce stress may also perform the distinct function of structuring the deviant solution a person adopts. They thus remarked that "it is equally apparent that there is an interlocking set of economic, social, and psychological conditions that both contribute to the arousal of anxiety and channel behavior to drinking as a means of coping with it" (1976 : 663).

COLLECTIVE FORMS OF DEVIANCE

Structuring ideas are also apparent in the work of theorists of collective behavior. Much of the activity (e.g., riots, revolutions, panics) that is of interest to these theorists involves a departure from existing social standards and hence can be considered as appropriate subject matter for those within the field of deviance. Several of the more vivid illustrations of the structuring of collective forms of deviance will be highlighted below.

The "value-added" framework of Neil Smelser (1962) continues to be a dominant paradigm within the area of collective behavior. What is of special interest to us here, however, is less the specific content of his analysis and more the logic that runs through his theorizing. To begin with, Smelser recognized that the questions of why deviant actions transpire and why a particular form emerges are distinct theoretical problems. He thus proposed that a satisfactory explanation must address not only "what determines whether an episode of collective behavior of *any sort* will occur," but also "what determines whether one type *rather than another* will occur" (1962 : 12). Further, he clearly perceived that there is an indeterminate relationship between structurally induced strain—"ambiguities, deprivations, conflict, and discrepancies"—and the kind of collective response that takes place. Hence, commenting on the efforts of a theorist to locate the origins of messianic movements in the deprivations of social life, Smelser observed that these circumstances can engender "several responses besides messianism. This is what is meant when we say there exists a residue of indeterminacy in the connections between determinants and outcomes in the field of collective behavior" (1962 : 13).

Smelser went on to suggest that certain social conditions must be "added in" for structural strain to result in a specific mode of collective behavior. For instance, unless the "structural characteristics" of a social setting are "conducive" (that is, provide the opportunity for) a given collective activity, "strain cannot be a determinant" of this response "however important it may be as a determinant of some other kind of behavior" (1962 : 16). Consider Smelser's remarks about the example of financial panic.

> Let us assume that property is closely tied to kinship and can be transferred only to first-born sons at the time of the death of the father. Panic under such conditions is ruled out, simply because the holders of property do not have sufficient maneuverability to dispose of their assets upon short notice. Under conditions of economic pressure, certain responses are possible—for instance, a movement to change the customs of property transfer—but not in a panic. The structure of the social situation does not permit it. [1962 : 15]

Similarly, "generalized beliefs" in a society are of causal significance in structuring the direction of collective adaptations because they "identify the source of strain, attribute certain characteristics to this source, and specify certain responses to strain as possible or appropriate" (1962 : 16). Also of importance is the "operation of social control" which may "prevent the occurrence of an episode of collective behavior" or, if "moblilized only after a collective episode has begun to materialize . . . determine how fast, how far, and in what direction the episode will develop" (1962 : 17). Finally Smelser argued that situational contingencies such as "precipitating factors" and the availability of leadership to "mobilize participants for action" regulate the specific time and place that an occasion of collective behavior will arise.

It is significant that Smelser concluded his work by briefly calling attention to the fact that strain may precipitate not only modes of collective behavior, but other forms of deviance as well. Observing that suicide, for instance, may be triggered by the "same kinds of social malintegration" that is at the root of collective adaptations, the question becomes, "Given a certain type of strain, what conditions determine whether suicide or some other kind of behavior arises?" (1962 : 387). To address this problem of the structuring of deviant choices, Smelser perceived that it would be necessary to move beyond a knowledge of the origins of strain to a consideration of such variables in his framework as "conduciveness, the operation of social and individual controls, etc." (1962 : 387). Smelser did not, however, dwell further on the implications of these insights, nor did he see how his model converged with those of authors who had previously commented on the structuring of deviant responses to socially induced strain (cf. Cloward 1959, Cloward and Ohlin

1960). As a consequence, his contribution to the structuring tradition has not often been understood by subsequent theorists of crime and deviance (cf. Gibbons 1971).

Rose has recently outlined a comparable framework for understanding the emergence of particular forms of collective conduct. Rose noted that "collective behavior appears under conditions of social dislocation" which engender "deprivation, stress, threat, and crisis." Yet citing Cloward's critique of anomie theory (1959), Rose argued that uncovering the sources of "deviant motivations" does not "adequately explain deviance itself." Instead, the occurrence of a specific collective response depends as well upon the availability of the prerequisite means. In concrete terms, this involves the presence of "such necessary resources as an ideology to support or legitimate the action in question, a set of social organizations predisposed to engage in a line of action, the availability of prophets and organizers to articulate the ideology and coordinate the action" (1982 : 244–47).

Another example of the structuring of collective activity is apparent in Colvin's account of the New Mexico prison riot (Colvin 1982; cf. Stone 1982, Serrill and Katel 1980). This uprising achieved national notoriety because thirty-three lives were lost, a toll second only to that reached at Attica a decade before. This statistic is sufficient to earn the New Mexico riot a special place in the dark history of American correctional institutions. Yet what proved to be the truly distinguishing feature of the disturbance was not the appalling number of deaths which occurred, but rather how the inmates perished: at the hands of fellow inmates, often after being tortured and mutilated. This pattern is in marked contrast to previous episodes of insurgency in which the confrontation was between prisoners and the state. The critical issue that suggests itself is, why did the New Mexico riot assume this atypical form?

Colvin chose to address this very matter. His analysis begins with the observation that prior to 1975 patterns of accommodation had arisen between the custodial staff and the institution's population. In essence, order was sustained by inducing powerful offenders into administrative positions that enhanced parole prospects, and by allowing selected subgroups to traffic in drugs. In both instances, inmate elites had a stake in keeping the social peace so as not to threaten their advantaged status. Following 1975, however, a new prison administration was appointed which soon moved to eliminate the exchange relations that had previously bolstered the prison equilibrium. Inmates were removed from all administrative positions and efforts were made to end the flow of drugs into the institution. To maintain control, the warden instead adopted a custodial orientation that justified both more coercive responses to infringements of prison rules and the use of informants to catch and punish troublemakers.

The final result of these policies, as Colvin has indicated, was to remove inmate access to non-violent means of influence. The resulting power vacuum fostered the creation "of a new opportunity structure" that gave status to those who exercised dominance through violence. Consequently, "a self-reinforcing structure of violent competition emerged which further incited inmate violence." In this context, solidarity was eroded and "inmate society became increasingly fragmented into small and unstable self-protection cliques" (1982 : 456). This state of disorganization was crucial in shaping the content of the riot that subsequently transpired. As inmates rose up in revolt, they not only directed their anger at prison property but at vulnerable inmates and long-standing enemies (e.g., "snitches"). Unlike other uprisings, including Attica, an inmate elite capable of gaining control and of effectively negotiating a settlement was conspicuously absent. Instead, a "Hobbsian state of nature" reigned within the prison until it exhausted itself after thirty-six, terror-filled hours.

Finally, Piven and Cloward have attempted to determine how the emergence of protest movements is socially structured. They have asserted that stressful social conditions need not lead to the eruption of protest. The emergence of mass insurgency as opposed to other deviant responses is thus a phenomenon that requires explanation in its own right. They maintained further that a complete analysis must explore not only the origin of unrest, but also the reasons why a political protest, when it does occur, assumes a certain form:

> In contrast to the effort expended in accounting for sources of insurgency, relatively little attention has been given to the question of why insurgency, when it does occur, takes one form and not another. Why, in other words, do people sometimes strike and at other times boycott, loot, or burn? [Piven and Cloward]

Addressing these issues, Piven and Cloward proposed that a group's social location structures both the ability to protest as well as the content that a protest movement manifests:

> Just as quiescence is enforced by institutional life, and just as the eruption of discontent is determined by changes in institutional life, the forms of political protest are also determined by the institutional context in which people live and work. . . . The opportunities for defiance are structured by features of institutional life. Simply put, people cannot defy institutions to which they have no access, and to which they make no contribution. [1977 : 14,23]

THE PERVASIVENESS OF THE STRUCTURING THESIS

Thus far, we have seen that a myriad of sociological theorists have illustrated both that there is an indeterminate relationship between the conditions generating deviant motivations and actual deviant outcomes, and that a variety of social circumstances structure when participation in a form of deviance will be possible. It should be recognized, however, that these insights are not confined to the sociological literature; they are found more and more often in other disciplines as well. For instance, a study by social psychologists Kahn et al. suggests that stressful circumstances in organizations such as role conflict and role ambiguity engender different adaptations. Thus, "stress factors in the work environment" lead to "various responses—some behavioral, some attitudinal—intended to help the individual find an adjustment to the stresses in his work role" (1964 : 223). Psychologist Seymour Halleck, in his perceptive book *Psychiatry and the Dilemmas of Crime* (1967), made an even more forceful and systematic statement of the indeterminacy thesis when he commented that "the criminologist must explain why two people exposed to similar stresses and motivated by similar forces behave in different ways." Indeed, "it is difficult to imagine a stress which could be adapted to in only one way." As such, since crime "represents only one of several possible adaptations, the criminologist must grapple with the question of why the criminal solution is 'chosen'." Because of this, a "theory of crime must look beyond the immediate stresses in the environment and also attempt to describe conditions or traits which predispose a person to criminal behavior." That is, a theorist must explain how "motivations . . . become structured by experience" by specifying "which variables must be present before crime is chosen ahead of other adaptations." For it is only by attending to this theoretical task that we will begin to understand "why some people choose conformity, others activism, others mental illness and others crime" (1964 : 61, 63, 196–97).

Similar themes are apparent in the writings of anthropologist Anthony Wallace on the etiology of differing varieties of mental illness (1961,1970). According to Wallace, "it is evident that even if it is possible to identify a specific physiological variable as the precipitant of the overt symptomatology . . . details of the form of the symptoms themselves, must depend on evaluating other variables." This logic, he suggested, leads to the conclusion that "it is the interaction of these other variables with the immediately precipitating physiological variable which provides the necessary and sufficient conditions for a type of mental illness to occur in a particular group with a particular frequency" (1961 : 274).

Though operating on a different level of analysis by focusing more on biological deviance or disease than social deviance, Cassell has presented a sequence of ideas which approximates Halleck's. Cassell was interested in exploring the relationship between psychosocial sources of stress and physical and, to a limited extent, psychological disease. He was struck by the frequency with which researchers assumed a direct one-to-one link between stress and a single type of disease, and thus maintains that it is "most unlikely that any given psychosocial process or stressor will be etiologically specific for any given disease.'' As evidence, Cassell cited the fact that ''a remarkably similar set of social circumstances characterize people who develop tuberculosis, schizophrenia, multiple accidents, suicide, and alcoholism. Common to all these people is a marginal status in society.'' Yet the theoretical importance of this insight, Cassell argued, has often been overlooked. ''It is perhaps surprising that this wide variety of disease outcomes associated with similar circumstances has generally escaped comment.'' For Cassell, however, the significance of this observation was clear. It meant that stress does not lead ineluctably to any one pathological adaptation. Instead, nonstress variables determine the content of the symptomatology that emerges. With this in mind, Cassell posited that ''the clinical manifestations of this enhanced susceptibility will then not be a function of the particular psychosocial stressor but of the physio-chemical or microbiological disease agents harbored by the organism or to which the organism is exposed'' (1975 : 539–40).

The above examples thus suggest that the relationship between deviant motivations, particularly stress, and deviant outcomes is a question that is emerging in various disciplines. Moreover, these studies indicate that the logic underlying the concepts of indeterminacy and structuring variables is sufficiently compelling to capture the attention of diverse theorists and to hold the potential of exerting a significant theoretical impact in various fields of study.

Conclusion

A review of sociological literature from the past and present reveals that numerous theorists have illuminated the ways in which the deviant choices people make are structured or patterned by social circumstances. Yet the literature review set forth in this chapter represents only a sampling of the works that could have been discussed. Indeed, an analysis that swept across the multitude of research studies in the field would uncover near endless instances of the use of structuring ideas. The existence of these many observations is of no small significance. Though the authors of such insights do not generally see themselves as falling within a common tradition, the consistent convergence of their thinking strongly supports the proposition that the further development of a structuring perspective will enhance our understanding of the origins of criminal and deviant conduct.

chapter 3

Accounting for Form: Cloward's Theory of Illegitimate Means

Thus far, an effort has been made to identify a theoretical tradition whose distinguishing feature is that it focuses on the issue of accounting for the specific form deviant behavior manifests. As suggested, this approach to the study of deviant conduct has remained largely latent because authors have not always perceived how the principles informing their undertakings are shared by others in the field. This has in turn limited the occasions on which analysts have sought to explore the broader implications of their work by generalizing beyond the particular sphere of crime or deviance under investigation.

It is of interest, however, that one theorist, Richard A. Cloward, did endeavor to set forth a more general statement of the concept of structuring variables at the very start of the 1960s. At this time, Cloward advanced the view that theories of deviant behavior often assume an overly deterministic relationship between the motivational condition of socially induced pressure or stress and particular deviant outcomes. He argued that an additional theory was required—one that would enable us to begin to identify the intervening forces impinging upon actors under pressure which lead them to deviate in specific ways. He referred to this as the "theory of illegitimate means" or of "the selection and evolution of deviant adaptations."

In the pages to follow, an attempt is made to examine the central tenets of the illegitimate means perspective and to explore its intimate connection to the earlier, yet still influential, Chicago School of criminology. Following this discussion, our attention will turn to the interpretation Cloward's work has commonly received subsequent to its publication over two decades ago. In particular, consideration will be given to why many have yet to fully appreciate the relevance of Cloward's thoughts for the development of a structuring perspective of deviant behavior.

The Theory of Illegitimate Means

ILLEGITIMATE MEANS AND STRUCTURING VARIABLES

Two theses run through Cloward's theoretical formulations. First, he asserted that simply being subjected to socially generated pressure or stress does not enable a person to deviate in any way whatsoever. Instead, he offered the commonsensical but often ignored conception that people under stress can only participate in a given adaptation if they have access to the means to do so. Thus, regardless of the amount of pressure members of the lower class experience, they are effectively excluded from access to the means to engage in "white-collar" crimes (e.g., crimes of financial trust, political corruption) and hence cannot select these adaptations.

Building on this initial thesis, Cloward went on to set forth a second and more far-reaching insight: if access to illegitimate means and not exposure to stress determines whether a person may engage in a given adaptation, then the form or content of deviant behavior cannot be regulated by stress states or other motivational conditions. Instead, the availability of illegitimate means must perform this function. In concrete terms, this suggests that if access to a prestigious occupation is the "means" required to commit a crime of financial trust, it is the variable of occupational status and not the stress variable which determines if the breach of trust will occur as opposed to another sort of transgression.

Focusing on the major motivational perspective of his day, Cloward proposed that although theorists in the anomie tradition clearly saw the significance of legitimate means in deviance causation, they strangely neglected the concept of *illegitimate* means. As such, they were often placed in the position of erroneously, if implicitly, assuming that an explanation of the origins of socially induced pressures is sufficient to account for the form of deviance that emerges. In contrast, Cloward asserted that the development of a "theory of illegitimate means"—a perspective oriented toward specifying the circumstances that intervene between stress states and deviant outcomes and thus structure the form that a person's response to stress takes—would allow us to avoid this questionable logic.

The central theme of Cloward's work then is that, independent of deviant motivations, there is a set of variables that shapes the direction of deviant conduct by making certain options possible while precluding others. Such a variable may be a slum neighborhood marked by a symbiotic relationship between conventional and illegitimate worlds that in turn makes the evolution of a criminal delinquent gang possible. Or it may be a religious value system that eschews frivolous drinking and thus precludes an alcoholism adaptation. Or it may be confinement to a prison where new criminal skills (e.g., how to crack a safe) are learned and new criminal livelihoods made available. Or perhaps it may be early socialization experiences proscribing aggressiveness that eventually constrain a person under stress from acting out in a violent way. Indeed, quite a wide array of circumstances both within individuals and in their social surroundings may operate to structure deviance choices.

It appears that many, but certainly not all, within the field have only partially understood Cloward's proposition that an analytically distinct *class* of variables is required to account for the form of deviance that people manifest. Instead, theorists and researchers alike have tended to envisage "illegitimate means" as a single variable—usually operationalized as "opportunity"—that could be included in their analyses or regression equations. The reasons for this interpretation are varied, in part due to fuzziness in Cloward's statement of his ideas, in part due to factors which have shaped the treatment of his writing by subsequent authors. Whatever the reasons, it seems evident that Cloward's use of the term "illegitimate means" has served to mask the thrust of his theorizing. To avoid further confusion, the set of conditions that account for the form a deviant adaptation takes—which Cloward subsumed under the concept of illegitimate means—will be referred to here as *structuring variables*.

CONSOLIDATING TWO TRADITIONS

Cloward's ideas on stress and structuring variables emerged as a result of his reinterpretation of the two leading deviance paradigms of his day: anomie theory and the Chicago School's cultural transmission theory. Cloward was convinced that anomie theory, represented by Durkheim and Merton, provided a plausible thesis as to why people would deviate: the stress or pressure generated by the inability of people to use conventional avenues to satisfy their desired goals would lead people to seek a deviant solution to their difficulties. He came to realize, however, that explaining why actors are moved to violate society's norms does not allow us to know which form of deviance a person will select. That is, "once processes generating differentials in pressures are identified, there is the question of how these pressures are resolved or how men respond to them" (1959 : 167). On this question, the anomie tradition, with its theoretical concerns directed elsewhere, remained largely silent.

As discussed, Cloward eventually embraced the conclusion that the illegitimate means at a person's disposal structures the response or adaptation to pressure that is made. "Taking into account the conditions of access . . . to illegitimate means," he reasoned, allows one to "specify the circumstances under which various modes of deviant behavior arise" (1959 : 175). Now in part, Cloward arrived at this insight by taking Merton's concept of legitimate means and generalizing it to the deviant world. Yet it is notable that Cloward felt that the real underpinnings of the concept of illegitimate means were more fully embedded within the writings of Edwin Sutherland and other cultural transmission theorists.

In this regard, it was clear to Cloward that Sutherland and his fellow theorists were most concerned with formulating a theory of the origins of crime as such. Consequently, they never systematically or consciously addressed the theoretical problem of why any particular form of crime (or other type of deviant adaptation) would occur. Nevertheless, Cloward's reanalysis of this tradition led to his discovery that much of their work, particularly the life-histories they collected, provided important clues on this very issue. Indeed, numerous passages revealed that simply being pressured or wanting to deviate does not enable a person to engage in any criminal endeavor whatsoever. Instead, it was readily apparent that, depending upon one's social location in society, a person is provided with certain values, skills and opportunities—that is, with certain illegitimate means—which make some adaptations possible and others unlikely.

This was perhaps most dramatically illustrated in Sutherland's classic life-history, *The Professional Thief* (1937). Sutherland perceived that to become a professional thief, an actor must be selected by a thief for tutelage in the various skills required to carry out this professional criminal role. Unless such talents (or means) are acquired, entering the world of professional thievery is impossible—even if one possesses "an inclination to steal" (Sutherland 1937:212). Sutherland's *White Collar Crime* provides a similar example. Here, Sutherland's purpose in studying white-collar crime was to show that members of the upper class engage in crime as such for the *same* reason as members of the lower class: they are exposed to an excess of definitions favorable to violation of the law. To Cloward, however, Sutherland's work demonstrated quite a different point—namely, that only those in the upper class possess the means to commit white-collar offenses and, more generally, that class position accounts for the form of crime that an actor may select.

In short, for Cloward the chief contribution of the cultural transmission theorists was to show how individuals, depending on their social attributes, are more likely to adopt one form of criminal behavior rather than another (assuming that they are going to become criminal at all). In doing so, their work contained the beginnings of the theory of illegitimate means or of structuring variables. Cloward thus went on to propose that it was only by developing the insights of the cultural transmission theorists and consolidating the tradition with anomie theory that a truly adequate model of deviance was possible. As a stress or pressure theory, the anomie tradition explained why people are motivated to deviate. In contrast, by essentially illuminating the concept of illegitimate means, the cultural transmission tradition provided an initial perspective on "how men respond to pressure," that is, an explanation that accounts for the specific content of the deviant path an actor follows.

APPLICATIONS OF THE CONCEPT OF ILLEGITIMATE MEANS

Cloward's first statement of the concept of illegitimate means appeared in his article "Illegitimate Means, Anomie, and Deviant Behavior" (1959). In this essay, Cloward pointed out that anomie theory significantly advanced our insight into the social sources of deviant motivations but that it was less adequate in helping us to know the specific way in which such impulses will become realized in deviant action. Heavily influenced by the revelation of the cultural transmission school that access to stable criminal roles such as professional thievery, jack-rolling, and organized crime is not uniformly available to all, Cloward formulated the concept of illegitimate means as a beginning way of understanding when any particular adaptation to socially induced strain will occur. For Cloward,

> by the term 'means,' whether legitimate or illegitimate, at least two things are implied: first, that there are appropriate learning environments for the acquisition of the values and skills associated with the performance of a particular role; and second, that the individual has opportunities to discharge the role once he has been prepared. The term subsumes, therefore, both *learning* and *opportunity structures*. [1959 : 168]

Cloward proposed that, regardless of the pressure experienced, the type of adaptation that people could select was limited by the availabity to them of "illegitimate means"—an environment where deviant values and skills are learned, and where specific opportunities for wayward conduct are present. He then added the insight that illegitimate means, like legitimate means, are distributed throughout the social structure. Just as chances to learn and perform conforming roles are not the same at different locations in the social structure, chances to learn and perform deviant roles also vary from one location to another. As a result, by regulating access to various illegitimate means, a person's position in the social structure controls the form of deviance that may be chosen. More generally, this suggests that the distribution of illegitimate means in the social structure patterns the distribution of forms of deviance throughout society.

To illustrate these principles, Cloward furnished several examples of how different social statuses may pattern or structure deviant responses. For instance, after noting that "it is a familiar sociological idea that values serve to order the choices of deviant adaptations that develop under stress," he observed that ethnic groups "tend to engage in distinctive forms of deviance." Cloward thus suggested that the Jewish value system "constrains modes of deviance which involve 'loss of control' over behavior" and hence effectively precludes Jews from alcoholism. Rates of alcoholism for the Irish, on the other hand, may be more pronounced because "their cultural emphasis on masculinity encourages the excessive use of alcohol under conditions of strain" (1959 : 167). Similarly, Cloward argued that access to stable criminal roles is shaped by such statuses as sex, race, and class. Thus, he noted that few blacks rise to the upper echelon of the rackets, that women become prostitutes and not professional thieves, and that for those at the bottom of the class structure "white-collar modes of criminal activity are simply not an alternative" (1959 : 173).

In conjunction with Lloyd Ohlin, Cloward subsequently applied the theory of illegitimate means to account for the structuring of deviant subcultural adaptations. In *Delinquency and Opportunity* (1960), Merton's theory is again embraced and the argument is set forth that the origins of deviant behavior lie in the inability of people—in this case, juveniles—to attain socially approved success goals through legitimate means. Cloward and Ohlin also recognized, however, that even after having delineated the origins of the pressures to engage in delinquency, they still had not dealt with the second and typically unanswered question of why a particular mode of delinquency is selected over others.

> The pressures that lead to deviant patterns do not necessarily determine the particular pattern of deviance that results. . . . Several delinquent adaptations are conceivably available in any given situation; what, then, are the determinants of the process of selection? Among delinquents who participate in subcultures, for example, why do some become apprentice criminals rather than street fighters or drug addicts? These are distinctive subcultural adaptations; an explanation of one may not constitute an explanation of the others. [pp. 34, 32]

Cloward and Ohlin thus took up the problem of how features of neighborhood social structure might help us to understand the empirical fact that the kinds of delinquent gangs (e.g., fighting gangs, criminalistic gangs, or drug-oriented groups) vary from one neighborhood to another (and from one time to another in the same neighborhood). In particular, they focused on the fact that slum neighborhoods range along an "organized-disorganized" continuum. They argued that the degree of neighborhood organization or integration greatly influences the form of delinquent groupings that are likely to emerge by limiting some kinds of deviant learning environments and some kinds of deviant opportunity systems, but not others, thus channeling deviant responses in one direction or another. In short, the neighborhood social context was seen as a "structuring variable" that regulates the form of gang delinquency that emerges.

Finally, Cloward also utilized his theory of illegitimate means to account for different types of deviant inmate leadership roles that emerge in the penitentiary. In his essay "Social Control in the Prison" (1960), he began with the observation that inmates face "intense pressures for deviance" within the prison community. While some respond with "passivity and docility" and with "defeatism and resignation," others prove to be more defiant and rebellious. To make matters worse, the custodial staff is faced with the task of preserving social peace with few effective methods of control at their disposal. One by-product of this conflicting situation is that guards seek to accommodate potentially insurgent inmates by exchanging access to leadership positions for assistance in maintaining order. Thus, correctional officers provide selected inmates with highly desired contraband articles that can be peddled; they furnish other inmates with valued information (e.g., about an impending shakedown) which, when shared, can make fellow captives indebted to them; and they afford a few more an unusual amount of deference which bolsters their social standing in the convict subculture. In return, those occupying these illegitimate elite positions are expected to ward off any disruptive tendencies among their inmate brethren that might upset the prevailing order within the prison social system. Cloward thus suggested that an unanticipated consequence of prison organization is the creation of deviant opportunity structures as well as the performance of these illegitimate roles within the society of captives.

The Legacy of the Theory of Illegitimate Means

Despite the consideration the illegitimate means concept has received (Cole 1975), many deviance theorists have not fully appreciated its central message, namely, that deviant behavior is socially structured. To be sure, some in the field have clearly understood this. DeLamater, for instance, grasped the structuring implications of the concept when he stated that "given some motivating condition, the deviant alternatives which are available are culturally determined." Consequently, "as Cloward points out, not all possible alternatives are equally available; the individual's access to illegitimate means may be limited" (1968 : 44). Similarly, Stein and Martin noted that "Cloward and Ohlin's . . . approach emphasizes that the range of deviant behavior which an individual can select is not limitless. . . . The chances of his reacting to psychological and social pressures by one means or another will then tend to vary with the range of outlets learned by and available to him, and to the extent to which any of these are better learned or more readily available than others" (1962 : 57). And more recently, Steffensmeier observed that "Richard Cloward's concept of illegitimate means . . . provided an initial perspective on how actors, depending on their social attributes, are more likely to adopt one form of criminal behavior rather than another (assuming that they are going to be criminalistic at all)" (1983 : 1027).

Nonetheless, such interpretations remain in the minority and have not prevented Cloward's work from typically being seen as a theory of why people deviate as opposed to a theory which accounts for the form such behavior takes.[1] Below, two possible reasons for this occurrence are suggested: the dominance of the logic informing the stress paradigm, and the limitations that characterize Cloward's initial presentation of his ideas.

THE DOMINANCE OF THE STRESS PARADIGM

Since the time of Durkheim, stress theory has been a major school of thought within the sociology of deviance (Hirschi 1969). Moreover, such theorizing has been clearly present in other disciplines as well. For instance, in their review of stress research, Rabkin and Struening remarked that research relating stressful life-events to physical and psychiatric disorders "appear with re-markable regularity in the major psychological, psychiatric, psychosomatic, and sociological journals, and to a lesser extent in those of clinical medicine and epidemiology" (1976:1013). The very prevalence of explanations for stress suggests that the stress perspective frequently functions as an important "paradigm" (Kuhn 1962) or "research programme" (Lakatos 1970) within the field, guiding both theory construction and research methodology. Above all, the paradigm instructs scholars to operate on the assumption of "deter-minacy": every form of deviance is determined or produced by a correspond-ing stress state (or set of stress variables). The task of the theorist is thus to hypothesize exactly what stressful condition is producing a specific deviant outcome; in turn the prescribed research methodology is to select one particular form of deviance and then work back to find the stress variable related directly to it.

As Szasz has observed, the ways we explain deviant behavior are often derived from the ways we explain physical anomalies of disease (1960, 1970). Szasz has suggested that this has occurred in large part because a convergence with a disease or medical model provides deviance perspectives with added prestige and contributes to their acceptance in both academic and public circles. In this context, it seems likely that the stress paradigm and its core assumption of determinacy were also inspired by, or at least reinforced by, the mode of analysis that has long been applied in the study of diseases.

Cassell has provided the clearest support for this contention. Commenting on research linking stress produced by psychological and social sources to disease outcomes (both physical and nonphysical, such as mental illness and suicide), Cassell has argued that these formulations mirror the disease research that seeks to relate specific biological states to specific disease outcomes. Notably, Cassell has questioned the viability of "etiological specificity," that is, of assuming determinacy, in either the physical or social realms:

> Stated in its most general terms, the formulation subscribed to (often implicitly)
> by most epidemiologists and social scientists working in this field is that the

relationship between a stressor and disease outcome will be similar to the relationship between a microorganism and the disease outcome. In other words, the psychosocial process under investigation is envisaged as a stressor capable of having a direct pathogenic effect analogous to that of a physico-chemical or microbiological environmental disease agent. The corollaries of such a formulation are that there will be etiological specificity, each stressor leading to a specific stress disease, and there will be a dose response relationship, the greater the stressor the more likelihood of disease. There is serious doubt as to the utility or appropriateness of either of these notions. [1975 : 358]

It would seem, then, that the deterministic logic underlying the stress paradigm is pervasive and potent. It not only informs stress explanations (as well as other motivational theories) offered by social scientists, but models of physical disease as well. In light of the potency of the stress paradigm, it is perhaps not surprising that Cloward's central message that nonstress variables regulate the nature of the deviant outcome has been overshadowed and has gone largely unrecognized by deviance theorists. Indeed, the stress paradigm has been so dominant that many authors not only tend to pass over Cloward's ideas on the structuring of deviant behavior but also interpret his contributions as constituting a stress or motivational theory (cf. Briar and Piliavin 1965 : 32, Gibbons 1971 : 269, Quicker 1974, Eve 1978). That is, Cloward is seen as falling within the very tradition that he sought to extend when he proposed the concept of illegitimate means. In particular, Cloward is frequently regarded as part of the more general Mertonian anomie tradition that locates the source of nonconformity in socially induced pressures to deviate. Thus Gould has remarked:

The idea that *frustrated* ambition leads to deviant behavior, and to delinquency as one form of deviant behavior, has been stated forcefully by Robert Merton and has been reiterated and elaborated in what are two of the most important theories of delinquent gangs [Cohen and Cloward-Ohlin are cited here]. The proposition states that delinquency (as a special class of deviance) results from a social situation in which certain persons are induced to hold aspirations which the social system is not geared to fulfill. [1969 : 710–11, emphasis mine]

Similarly, Akers has noted:

The structural theories contend that more people in certain groups, located in certain positions in, or encountering particular *pressures* created by the social structure, will engage in delinquency than those in other groups and locations. . . . Although there are now a number of variations on the disorganization-*anomie* theme, they all derive ultimately from Durkheim. The following are among the more careful and systematic statements on variants of this approach: Merton, . . . Cohen, Cloward and Ohlin. [1968 : 457–58, n.15, emphasis mine]

All of this is not to assert that the dominance of the stress paradigm is fully responsible for the lack of attention shown Cloward's thoughts on the structuring of deviant behavior. It is equally apparent that his statement of the structuring perspective lacked the clarity and persuasiveness required to counteract the dominating force of the paradigm and capture the attention of authors in the field. To be sure, Cloward's writings are replete with remarks that explicitly set forth the indeterminacy thesis as well as the idea that nonstress variables regulate the selection of deviant forms. Nevertheless, his work contains three shortcomings that almost certainly have served to direct attention away from the notion of structuring variables and impede its theoretical advance.[2]

THE LIMITATIONS OF CLOWARD'S STATEMENT OF THE CONCEPT OF
STRUCTURING VARIABLES

Cloward did not with sufficient force make clear that his insights on illegitimate means or structuring variables were applicable not only to the preeminent stress perspective of his day—Merton's anomie paradigm—but to *all other stress and motivational theories*. Throughout his work, Cloward embraced Merton's explanation of the origins of deviant motivations and then sought to extend Merton's theory with the notion of illegitimate means. As a result, Cloward became intimately identified with the anomie tradition. While this undoubtedly contributed to his visibility in the field, it also had the unanticipated consequence of obscuring the principle significance of the concept of illegitimate means. Caught in the shadow of the dominant stress paradigm of his day, Cloward's concern for the explanation of forms of deviance—the very problem which the concept of illegitimate means sought to address—is easily overlooked. At best, Cloward is viewed simply as another theorist who falls within the anomie tradition; at worst, as we have seen, he is reduced exclusively to a Mertonian stress theorist.

In attempting to demonstrate the structuring of forms of deviance, Cloward also focused extensively, though not exclusively, on the criminal world. Many of his substantive analyses were oriented toward explaining participation in different forms of delinquent subcultures or stable criminal roles. While Cloward intended his ideas to apply to a wider range of deviant behaviors (e.g., alcoholism, 1959 : 167), the bulk of his work masks this point. Moreover, later evidence failed to confirm his most popularized application of illegitimate ideas: the contention that distinct subcultural forms of delinquency exist in specific neighborhood contexts (Short and Strodtbeck 1965, Gibbons 1979 : 107; cf. Spergel 1964). In the absence of more diverse examples of the structuring of other modes of deviant behavior, theorists have tended, I suspect, to throw the baby (the more general perspective of structuring variables) out with the bathwater (the unvalidated empirical instance of how delinquent subcultural adaptations are socially structured).

A final factor that has served to limit the development of the notion of structuring variables is the terminology that Cloward employed. Again, the core thesis conveyed by Cloward is that there are two analytically distinct classes of variables: those that create general motivations to deviate (e.g., stressful social conditions), and those that regulate when a particular form of deviance will occur. Thus, with Lloyd Ohlin, Cloward warned that "an explanation of the forces that lead individuals to depart from conventional norms does not necessarily explain the form of deviance that will result. . . . Some variables help us to explain why predispositions to deviance from norms arise; other variables tell us why delinquent rather than other types of deviance are selected" (1960 : x, 43). Yet it can be imagined that this crucial point is missed by many theorists, because the terminology that Cloward used— "illegitimate means" and "differential opportunity structures"—is not thought to connote a distinct class of variables. Instead, as suggested earlier, theorists typically interpret illegitimate means to be simply one variable, usually operationalized as "opportunity," which can influence why people deviate.[3] One can debate whether theorists have tended to give only a narrow reading to Cloward's work or whether Cloward was guilty of ambiguously stating his position—but this is not the important issue at hand. What is of consequence is the compelling theoretical point that Cloward's concept of illegitimate means was meant to highlight, namely, that a wide array of social conditions, which intervene between stress or other motivational states and deviant outcomes, account for the form of the ensuing deviation by making certain adaptations possible while precluding others.

Conclusion

In setting forth the theory of illegitimate means, Richard Cloward was endeavoring to shift the focus of theorists from the problem of explaining the origins of deviant motivations to a consideration of the ways in which disapproved behaviors are socially structured. While his statement was perhaps more systematic than those made before and after him by analysts who shared this theoretical concern, Cloward's efforts nonetheless are best seen as falling within a broad and continuing tradition that has attempted to account for the form of deviance that individuals come to embrace.

In this light, the goal of the first three chapters has been to furnish an understanding of what this structuring tradition is and to demonstrate that it has indeed occupied a persistent, if at times only implicit, place in the writings of deviance analysts over the years. The remaining chapters in Part II undertake a diffferent but related task. Through the eyes of the structuring perspective, the major theories of crime and deviance will be rethought. Special attention will be given to stress (or strain) theory and the Chicago School, two theoretical orientations that have long shaped views about crime and deviance causation. The more recent "revisionist" approaches of labeling theory, control theory, and conflict theory will also be reviewed and their relationship with the structuring perspective articulated.

In "rethinking" the prevailing theories in the field, it will be suggested both that the architects of these dominant paradigms have been largely preoccupied with answering the question of why someone becomes deviant and that subsequent scholars have tended to focus exclusively on this portion of their writings. More important, it will then be argued that nearly all of the major theorists have nevertheless integrated structuring ideas into their theorizing. By bringing these insights to the fore, it is hoped that the value of entertaining the merits of a structuring perspective will be reaffirmed and that our ability to account for the form and content of deviant adaptations will be advanced.

Notes

1. This contention is well supported by citational data. Following the method employed by Cole (1975 : 188–89) and extending his analysis from 1973 through to the end of 1981, I examined the manner in which Cloward's writings were referenced by the authors of deviance articles contained in four leading sociological journals: *American Sociological Review, American Journal of Sociology, Social Forces,* and *Social Problems.* The primary aim was to determine whether an author referenced the illegitimate means portion of Cloward's theorizing and if the author comprehended the implications of the concept for the explanation of forms of deviance. When doubt existed about an author's comprehension of the illegitimate means thesis, the author was counted as understanding the concept. This was done to avoid underestimating the general understanding of Cloward's work in the field. In all there were 128 articles in which Cloward's deviance writings were referenced. Of these 128 articles, 89 or 69.5 percent make absolutely no mention of the concept of illegitimate means. By contrast, 39 or 30.5 percent of the articles sampled cited the illegitimate means portion of Cloward's work. Of these citations, 18 or 46.2 percent did not explore how the concept might be linked to the explanation of forms of deviance. Twenty-one or 53.8 percent evidenced a fairly complete comprehension of the central thrust of Cloward's theorizing. Even here, however, the majority (14) of these authors sought only to apply the concept of illegitimate means in a limited fashion. For example, they used the concept to specify why actors choose one of two forms of deviance (e.g., suicide over homicide) and not why actors engage in a certain type of deviance as opposed to one of a range of alternative forms. Quite significantly, only seven authors, 5.5 percent of the entire sample, referenced Cloward for the concept of illegitimate means—the major contribution of his theorizing—and clearly perceived the full implications of this concept.

2. The commentary here pertains to Cloward's original and most prominent formulations of the concept of illegitimate means. More recently, however, Cloward has joined with Frances Fox Piven to elaborate upon his earlier ideas and to apply them to the structuring of political protest and female deviance (Piven and Cloward 1977, Cloward and Piven 1979, Cloward and Piven et al. 1977).

3. Cloward focused on the concept of "opportunity" in two different (but not necessarily inconsistent) ways in his work. First, he considered opportunity to be the simple chance to perform a deviant act (for example, to rob a bank, a person must be in a locality that has a

bank). Second, and more broadly, Cloward wished to study how structuring variables such as religious values, class position, and neighborhood integration limit an actor's deviant opportunities or possibilities and thereby regulate the form of deviance that transpires. In this latter usage of opportunity by Cloward, it is not clear whether employing the concept always serves a necessary theoretical function. For instance, the proposition: "because Jews possess values that eschew nonceremonial, frivolous drinking, they do not possess the opportunity to become alcoholics and thus do not engage in the adaptation of alcoholism" could be more concisely formulated: "because Jews possess values that eschew nonceremonial, frivolous drinking, they do not engage in the adaptation of alcoholism." Similarly, Gibbs and Short (1974) have argued that occupational experiences influence the range of opportunities which in turn regulate the type of crimes that are committed. Again, it would be more economical to state simply that occupational experience is a structuring variable that regulates the type of crime committed. In both these propositions then, it would seem possible (though not essential) to reduce the proposition from the logic, structuring variables (e.g., religious values, occupational experiences)—opportunity—form of deviance, to the logic, structuring variables—form of deviance. One possible advantage of including the concept in such propositions is that it may serve as an added reminder to deviance theorists of a reality that they commonly overlook: actors cannot freely choose to perform any deviant role whatsoever, or, alternatively, social constraints operate to limit the possibilities that actors predisposed to deviate may consider and pursue. For further comments on the concept of opportunity, see Nettler (1978 : 229–30).

PART II

Rethinking Theories of Crime and Deviance

chapter 4

Stress and Deviant Behavior: The Durkheimian Tradition

It is common wisdom in sociology today—passed on since the time of Durkheim—that deviant behavior is an expectable, necessary, and thus normal feature of social life. At the same time, it is perhaps equally agreed upon that departures from social standards do not occur under normal circumstances. Analysts of deviant behavior typically assert that it is only when people are subject to special influences that they are sufficiently moved to violate society's norms. Quite frequently, analysts locate these special, deviance-producing influences in the unusual stresses, pressures, strains, frustrations, or tensions that social life on occasion engenders.

The very ubiquity of stress or "strain" theories of deviance makes it of little surprise that they are not all of a piece (cf. Empey 1982, Hirschi 1969, Kornhauser 1978). Some theories maintain that the stress leading to deviant behavior arises from the failure to fulfill expectations; others point to lack of structural integration; others to the demoralizing conditions of working-class existence; and still others to the shock of such life-events as marital discord or the death of a loved one. Yet despite this diversity, stress theorists have often evidenced considerable consensus on the issue of how to go about explaining the origin of socially disapproved behaviors. Two general "procedural rules" (Hirschi 1973) typically guide their efforts: first, they select a single form of deviance to examine; second, they attempt to delineate the stressful social condition that determines or is etiologically specific to this particular deviant form. By following these rules, theorists inevitably end up formulating explanations that link stressful conditions to a single type of nonconformity; that is, they are led to construct "stress theories of one form of deviance."

Such an approach seems at first glance to be a reasonable one. After all, Durkheim employed this mode of analysis with apparent success in his classic study of suicide, and the same could be said of generations of deviance theorists who have followed his example. When the diverse theoretical formulations based on the procedural rules listed above are viewed together, however, a potential shortcoming in this traditional approach to the study of deviance and in the explanations this approach generates becomes manifest.

To be specific, theorists operating within this tradition have at one time or another linked stress with nearly every conceivable kind of deviance. Thus, the analysis of one theorist will conclude that stress engenders alcoholism, a second theorist will present evidence suggesting that stress is related to mental illness, and other theorists will hypothesize that stress elicits suicide, or perhaps crime, drug use, or homosexuality. Moreover, theorists have frequently asserted that the *same stressful condition* can produce a myriad of deviant adaptations. For instance, a quick review of the deviance literature will reveal that the stress held to be generated by such conditions as status frustration or social disorganization has been associated with every major type of nonconformity. And here is where the shortcoming that characterizes particular "stress theories of one form of deviance" becomes clear. How can any theorist legitimately proceed on the assumption that a stressful condition determines or is etiologically specific to only the single adaptation under investigation, when the research of their fellow theorists indicates that the same stressful condition can result in a variety of alternative deviant outcomes? Further, if stress does indeed produce many different forms of deviance, how can it be said to determine when any particular form occurs? Is it not thus essential for theorists to specify those conditions that intervene between stress and deviant outcomes and regulate when any given outcome will transpire?

Thus, the potential flaw with stress theories of one form of deviance is that they are based on the "assumption of determinacy," the questionable idea that stress leads ineluctably to one and only one form of deviance and therefore determines the form a deviant response takes. It has been hypothesized that a more reasonable assumption is that deviant motivations such as socially induced stress are related in an "indeterminate" fashion to deviance, that is, that stress can lead to a variety of adaptations and therefore does not account for the specific form of a deviant response. Instead, the form of the adaptation is shaped more fully by those circumstances which structure the adaptation to stress that people may choose. This set of conditions, as discussed previously, I have termed "structuring variables."

By this point it should be clear that the determinacy assumption flows directly from the procedural rules that theorists typically follow when constructing explanations of deviant behavior. By starting an analysis by selecting a single form of deviance and then working back to uncover the stressful state related to this one form, the possibility that this state could elicit other responses simply is not raised. In contrast, a structuring approach to the study of deviance, sensitive to the indeterminate relationship of stress to deviance, would follow a vastly different set of procedural rules. These would include: (1) starting with a stressful condition, (2) uncovering the different adaptations that can arise from this condition, and (3) specifying the structuring variables that regulate the occurrence of a particular adaptation.

As stated above, Durkheim's analysis of suicide is the exemplar of a theory that seeks to link specific stressful circumstances to a specific deviant outcome. Yet, while this deterministic mode of analysis intimately influenced Durkheim's work, he nevertheless on occasion escaped the constraints imposed by this logic and furnished clear insights on the structuring of deviant choices. What is perhaps most notable is that these aspects of his thinking have been virtually ignored by subsequent authors. Indeed, as detailed later in this chapter, those falling within the stress theory tradition have more often embraced the more dominant logic in Durkheim's paradigm which suggests that the etiology of each deviant form rests in a specific stressful condition.

With these remarks in mind, an important caveat should be noted. It might be argued that theorists who link a condition like status frustration to a single deviant form such as suicide or crime, are actually quite aware that this is not the only response engendered by this motivational state. That is, if questioned, these authors would readily agree that, "of course," other outcomes are possible. While nearly all may acknowledge the potential existence of indeterminacy, however, it is less common for authors to take the next step of thinking through what the implications of this idea might be for their causal models. As such, there is a distinct tendency to proceed "as though there were" etiological specificity between a particular stressful condition and the form of deviance they are studying. In turn, this "working assumption" obscures the possible explanatory power of structuring variables and may result in causal statements that are less than complete.

Suicide: Durkheim's Anomie Theory

While numerous scholars have published explanations of the origin of the act of suicide, it is fair to say that no statement has attracted more attention or exerted such a pervasive impact on the thinking of deviance theorists than the one set forth by Emile Durkheim in his sociological classic *Suicide*. Within this work, Durkheim distinguished four social conditions that he believed generate suicide: anomie, egoism, fatalism, and altruism. Durkheim's thoughts on each of these circumstances constitute a distinct theory of the single deviant form of suicide. Below, his most noted stress theory of suicide, that of anomie, is reviewed and the place of structuring notions within Durkheim's theorizing is related.[1]

THE THEORY

Durkheim's conception of human nature formed the underpinning for much of his sociological work (Simon and Gagnon 1976 : 374). Nowhere is this clearer than in his analysis of anomic suicide (however, cf. Durkheim 1961). Any account of Durkheim's anomie theory, therefore, must begin by focusing on his view of the human condition.

According to Durkheim, it is possible to distinguish between a human being's "organic" and "moral" or social needs. Organic needs are automatically regulated by the human organism. In contrast, social wants, such as love and ambition, are "insatiable and bottomless" by nature and cannot be governed by his "organic constitution." For "it is not human nature which can assign the variable limits necessary to our needs." Instead, only an external force, one which can "play the same role for moral needs which the organism plays for physical needs," can effectively rule social desires. In Durkheim's view, "society alone can play this moderating role" (pp. 247–48).

One problem deserves attention at this point. It is unclear if Durkheim conceived of social or moral needs as being innate or culturally produced. Clinard apparently has opted for the former view in stating that Durkheim's "idea of the nature of man, while questionable, reflected the prevailing view of the time that man was filled with certain innate desires which needed to be fulfilled" (1964 : 7). In contrast to this position, Giddens has argued that Durkheim held that "human faculties are both produced and sustained by society. . . . Man's needs are socially created" (1976 : 715). Pope has also commented that, for Durkheim, "needs are not given by man's biological, psychological, or individual nature. Rather, they are social products that vary from one social context to the next" (1976 : 25). And Nisbet maintained that "Durkheim sees in man a duality of nature, the first side physical, inherited through germ plasm, the second and more important the social, acquired through acculturation and socialization" (1974 : 229). Regardless of which assessment of Durkheim's conception of social needs is more accurate, theorists in both camps agree on one point: assuming that a social need is possessed, Durkheim believed that these needs would spiral unendingly unless controlled by society.

Durkheim contended that suicide is the ultimate by-product of the inability of society—to be more exact, the normative structure of society—to regulate social needs. He reasoned that, when normative constraints were lacking, that is, under conditions of deregulation or anomie,[2] a person's appetites would rise to unattainable heights. "His needs would not be sufficiently proportioned to his means" (p. 246). The tragedy of being caught in this bind is that the ever-striving person is destined to eventually fail in the attempt to grasp a cherished end. And when failure does occur, "how painful it is to be thrown back'' (p. 257). Durkheim maintained that the ''pain,'' ''torment,'' and ''suffering'' engendered by the experience of ''being thrown back'' pressures or motivates the commission of suicide. As Pope has noted:

> Durkheim introduced a second variable, regulation, and named low regulation, ''anomie.'' Anomie is the consequence of social change resulting in a dimunition of social regulation. . . . Free from social control, passions and appetites are subject to no restraint, since only the collective moral authority of a group can perform this function. People's desires quickly outstrip their means. The result is frustration, exasperation, and weariness leading to high suicide rates. [1976 : 12]

Significantly, the problem of the motivation to deviate (to commit suicide) was not the major explanatory obstacle for Durkheim. Indeed, his conception of the human condition allowed him to easily dispose of this question: by their very nature people will experience the pressure to deviate if they are placed in a social environment lacking proper normative constraint. The more difficult task that confronted Durkheim was to explain the conditions which produced deregulation or anomie. To the extent that the primary focus of Durkheim's work is on specifying the conditions under which normative control is deficient, his ''anomie theory'' converges with the ''control theory'' tradition (see Chapter 7). Hirschi, recognizing this intellectual linkage, thus commented that ''Durkheim's theory is one of the purest examples of control theory: both anomie and egoism are conditions of 'deregulation,' and the 'aberrant behavior' that follows is an automatic consequence of such deregulation'' (1969 : 3, n. 2; cf. van den Haag 1975 : 75).

What, then, are the social circumstances that Durkheim held to foster deregulation? To begin with, he found the greatest cause for concern in the economic sector of society. Indeed, he proposed that good times and bad times, as well as the current economic state of Western industrial society all contribute to the breakdown of prerequisite normative regulation. For Durkheim, periods of prosperity allow people to enjoy financial rewards that were previously beyond their reach. Yet, good times are not without their dark side. Prosperity strains or attenuates traditional normative standards governing what an actor should desire. No longer are such standards reasonable to people who are experiencing newfound success, and, as a result, the standards lose the power to regulate a person's wants. For those freed from the guidance of traditional norms, ''the limits are unknown between the possible and impossible. . . . Consequently, there is no restraint upon aspirations. . . . Appetites, not being controlled by a public opinion become disoriented, no longer recognize the limits proper to them'' (p. 253). And as these unregulated ''appetites'' rise unabated, they inevitably outstrip the means available to satisfy them. Their ''very demands make fulfillment impossible. Overweening ambition always exceeds the results obtained, great as they may be, since there is no warning to pause here. Nothing gives satisfaction and all this agitation in uninterruptedly maintained without appeasement'' (p. 253). For those caught in the web of ''agitation,'' suicide is a likely path of escape.[3]

A sense of irony pervades Durkheim's analysis: while prosperity breeds tragedy, poverty has the ''positive function'' of preventing this consequence. The needs of the poor are regulated by their very condition. As Durkheim observed, ''Poverty protects. . . . Lack of power, compelling moderation, accustoms men to it'' (p. 254). Consequently, the goals of the poor remain commensurate with their means; the poor experience no ''agitation,'' and hence are effectively insulated against the impulse to take their lives.

The protection of poverty, however, extends only to those persistently trapped in its clutches. Less fortunate are the prosperous who are suddenly made poor, those, according to Durkheim, who experience ''declassification.'' When cast into a lower economic position, these people face the difficult task of adjusting their desires to the means now available. ''They must reduce their requirements, restrain their needs, learn greater self-control'' (p. 252). However, ''society cannot adjust them instantaneously to this new life and teach them to practice the increased self-repression to which they are unaccustomed'' (p. 252). As such, ''they are not adjusted to the condition forced on them, and its very prospect is intolerable'' (p. 252). For some, relief from this ''intolerable'' circumstance is only attained through suicide.

The isolated cases of declassification and sudden prosperity were of little import to Durkheim. Rather, he was most concerned by periods of major economic changes, such as a depression or ''abrupt growth.'' For it was then that society suffered from a significant rise in the suicide rate. Yet, while the gravity of these times did not escape Durkheim, his analysis is characterized by the promise of societal readjustment. The effects of economic crises are only temporary: society adapts either by returning to its original state when the crisis subsides or by evolving normative standards that ''reclassify men and things'' and thus effectively constrain man's ''appetites'' once again (p. 253). When society readjusts into a state of ''equilibrium,'' the suicide rate declines.

The sense of optimism evident in Durkheim's thesis of societal readjustment does not pervade all of his work on anomie and suicide. Thus, Durkheim asserted that ''one sphere of social life—the sphere of trade and industry—is actually in a chronic state'' of anomie (p. 254). Durkheim maintained that, ''for a whole century, economic progress has mainly consisted in freeing industrial relations from all regulation. Until very recently, it was the function of a whole system of moral forces to exert this discipline'' (p. 254). With the emergence of modern industrial society, however, traditional institutions—such as the church and occupational group—have lost their regulatory force. As a result, actors' ''appetites . . . have become freed of any limiting

authority'' (p. 255). Even more troubling than this condition of anomie—
that is, of the breakdown of controls—is that normative standards have developed that actually encourage actors to constantly raise their expectations.
''These dispositions are so inbred,'' Durkheim believed, ''that society has
grown to accept them and is accustomed to think them normal'' (p. 257).
And since expanding desires inevitably induce the torment of insatiability
and, in turn, suicide, it should be of little surprise that suicide has become a
permanent feature of the economic sector of modern society.

Durkheim's thesis of chronic anomie signifies a marked departure from his
earlier view of society. In *The Division of Labor*, the pathological aspects of
society are underplayed and a near unending faith that organic solidarity will
insure societal stability is affirmed. In *Suicide*, however, Durkheim gives a
far more pessimistic picture of society: anomie in general and chronic anomie
in particular are ever-present forces that threaten the stability of society. As
Stephen Marks has suggested, much of Durkheim's work following *Suicide*
was devoted to developing solutions to the problems of anomie and, consequently, to the problem of social order (1974).[4]

While the economic bases of anomie constitute the heart of Durkheim's
anomie theory of suicide, researchers often err by failing to note that Durkheim
held that ''economic anomy is not the only anomy which may give rise to
suicide'' (p. 259). Durkheim thus believed that a number of marital conditions
(e.g., being single, married, divorced, widowed) could influence the rate of
suicide. For instance, referring to ''conjugal anomie,'' Durkheim contended
that marriage could function to regulate the ''appetites'' that man had for
love: ''By forcing a man to attach himself forever to the same woman marriage
assigns a definite object to the need for love, and closes the horizon''
(p. 270). With his desires effectively constrained and the risk of unfulfillment
reduced, the married man is less likely to commit suicide than his unmarried
counterpart (cf. Pope 1976 : 27–28, Tiryakian 1981).

To summarize, Durkheim asserted that when society is in a state of dise-
quilibrium and controls break down, desires will rise beyond the point of
satiation through the means available, thus engendering ''torment'' and eventually suicide. More generally, the suicide rate will be higher among those
populations that experience deregulation and its by-products.

The above account of Durkheim's anomie theory of suicide conforms, at
least on major points, to the interpretations of his work usually set forth in
the literature.[5] It is important to recognize, however, that the common account
of Durkheim's theory typically does not attend to the full range of causal
propositions contained in *Suicide*. This occurs because analysts generally draw
their interpretations from his ''Anomic Suicide'' chapter, while largely ignoring a later section of *Suicide*—''The Social Element in Suicide''—in which
anomie is also discussed. As a result, there is a tendency to overlook the

causal significance of a factor which appears mainly in the later chapter and which is central to Durkheim's analysis: "currents of anomy."[6]

Durkheim did not specify the exact nature of a social current with a great deal of clarity. In general terms, though, it appears that he was referring to "common ideas, beliefs, customs, tendencies," (p. 302) and "opinions" (p. 321). These phenomena were seen to have reality of their own in that they are external to and independent of individual consciousness. Yet, while external and independent, these "ideas, etc.," are able to direct or constrain an individual's activity (including suicide).[7] According to Durkheim, "currents of anomy" are responsible for the production of suicide. These anomic currents vary in nature and strength from nation to nation, from community to community. It is this variability in the currents which regulates the variability in the suicide rates among differing localities.

Durkheim's position on how anomic currents cause suicide is not consistently stated. He links this phenomenon to suicide in at least two ways, each constituting a separate causal proposition. First of all, the logic of Durkheim's analysis in the chapter "Anomic Suicide" supports the thesis that such events as sudden prosperity and divorce are likely to engender suicide. Actors experiencing these events would suffer the deregulation of appetites, the torment of unfulfilled desires, and the impulse to seek relief through suicide. In his later chapter, however, Durkheim suggests that this thesis is incomplete because it does not confront the issue of why "these desperate situations are identically repeated annually, pursuant to a law peculiar to each country." That is, "how does it happen that a given, supposedly stable society always has the same number of disunited families, of economic catastrophies, etc.?" (p. 306).

This problem is crucial because it is these "situations" or events which eventually produce suicide and, more significantly, it is the distribution of these events that regulates the distribution of suicides (the suicide rate) among various populations. To explain why populations are marked by a given proportion of suicide-provoking events, Durkheim invoked the concept of social currents:

> The regular recurrence of identical events in proportions constant within the same population but very inconsistent from one population to another would be inexplicable had not each society definite *currents* impelling its inhabitants with a definite force to commercial and industrial ventures, to behavior of every sort likely to involve families in trouble, etc. [p. 306, emphasis mine]

In short, social currents direct actors to engage in courses of action that are likely to lead to deregulation and suicide. The degree to which a society or sector within a society is characterized by such suicide-producing currents determines the locality's suicide rate.

This explanation by Durkheim does not entail a challenge to his deregulation hypothesis presented in the "Anomic Suicide" chapter. For Durkheim does not argue here that social currents are a separate causal factor that directly produces suicide. Rather, the implication is that the effects of social currents on suicide are indirect: they simply produce those behaviors which then set in motion the processes delineated in the deregulation hypothesis (i.e., currents—behaviors that induce crisis—lack of control—unfulfillment of appetites—suicide). As a result, social currents are best viewed as a set of variables which expands but does not alter the causal scheme earlier set forth by Durkheim.

Durkheim's second proposition regarding the causal role of social currents represents a more significant departure from his discussion of deregulation. Social currents are now seen to exert an independent effect on suicide. The attempt, then, is not to expand the causal scheme contained in the deregulation hypothesis but to present a different explanation of suicide.[8]

Durkheim asserted that "currents of opinion" can "bend men's inclinations" in the direction of suicide. He maintained that currents of anomie "contaminate" a certain proportion of a given population just as epidemics do and thus determine the population's suicide rate. Indeed, the "stronger" the current is, "the more agents it contaminates" (p. 321). Further, it is the variability in the potency of the current which is responsible for the differing rates of suicide in differing localities. In turn, Durkheim argued that the strength of the currents is controlled by three "sorts of causes":

> 1. the nature of the individuals composing the society; 2. the manner of their association, that is, the nature of the social organization; 3. the transitory occurrences which disturb the functioning of the collective life without changing its anatomical constitution, such as national crises, economic crises, etc. [p. 321]

Thus, the causal scheme presented was: factors $\xrightarrow{\text{strength of current}}$ current $\xrightarrow{\text{number contaminated}}$ suicide rate.

"The role of individual factors in the origin of suicide" did not escape Durkheim's attention (p. 323). Such factors, he held, specify who will be "contaminated" by the current (Pope 1976 : 200). Thus, those whose "mental constitution, as elaborated by nature and events, offers less resistance to the suicidogenetic current," will be the suicide victims. However, individual factors have no effect on the overall rate of suicide; this is determined by the strength of the current. Durkheim thus asserted that "when an epidemic center appears, its intensity predetermines the rate of mortality it will cause, but those who will be inflicted are not designated by this fact. Such is the situation of victims of suicide with reference to suicidogenetic currents" (p. 325, n. 20).

This latter contention, however, rests on the tenuous assumption that the proportion of actors susceptible to suicide is the same in all populations. Otherwise, the strength of the "suicidogenetic currents" would not be the sole determinant of the suicide rate (as Durkheim hypothesized). For instance, if two populations were inflicted with currents of equal potency, yet one population possessed a greater proportion of actors with weak "mental constitutions," then the rates in the two groups would not be identical. The population which had a greater proportion of susceptible individuals would have a higher suicide rate, because more people would be "contaminated" by the current. The failure of Durkheim to test his assumption of equivalent susceptibility to currents in all populations by controlling for individual characteristics exposes his thesis to the charge that his conclusions are based on potentially fallacious ecological correlations (cf. Robinson 1950).[9]

DURKHEIM AND THE STRUCTURING OF DEVIANT BEHAVIOR

Throughout most of his writings, Durkheim failed to discuss how social conditions might structure deviant behavior. This omission would seem in large part to be an outgrowth of the methodological strategy or "procedural rules" that he followed. Durkheim first chose to study suicide and then set out to discover its causes. His approach, then, was to link specific etiological factors, such as anomie, directly to suicide. This orientation did not readily prompt him to wonder whether the torment or stress engendered by deregulation—which only relatively few people resolve by means of self-destruction—might lead others into alternative realms of deviant conduct.[10]

Even though Durkheim frequently hesitated to consider the implications of structuring notions, the logic of his thinking did not allow him to ignore such insights altogether. It is thus notable that structuring ideas appeared in three sections of *Suicide*. To start with, Durkheim observed that there were a number of ways in which to commit suicide (e.g., "strangulation and hanging, drowning, firearms, leaping from a high spot, poison, asphyxiation"), and that the forms utilized vary in frequency from society to society (pp. 290–91). He also noted that "social causes certainly determine the choice of means" (p. 290). More important, Durkheim also asserted that the variables which structure or pattern the method of suicide in a given locality differ from those which predispose an actor to commit suicide:

> The social causes on which suicides in general depend, however, differ from
> those which determine the way they are committed. . . . The causes impelling
> a man to kill himself are therefore not those determining him to do so in one
> way rather than in another. The motives which set his choice are of a totally
> different sort. [pp. 291–92, emphasis mine]

Durkheim believed that two "structuring variables" were particularly crucial in regulating the way in which a suicide is carried out. The first is the means of suicide that a person's social location makes available:

One factor is the totality of customs and usages of all kinds, placing one instrument of death rather than another at his disposal. Always following the line of least resistance so long as no opposing factor intervenes, he tends to employ the means of destruction lying nearest to his hand and made familiar to him by daily use. That, for example, is why suicides by throwing one's self from a high place are oftener committed in great cities than in the country: the buildings are higher. Likewise, the more the land is covered with railroads the more general becomes the habit of seeking death by throwing one's self under a train. . . . As the use of electricity becomes commoner, suicides by means of electric processes will become commoner also. [p. 292]

The second circumstance is the value system that prevails in a locality:

But perhaps the most powerful cause is the relative dignity attributed by each people, and by each social group within each people, to the different sorts of death. . . . This is why suicide by strangulation is much commoner in the country than in the city and in small cities than in large cities. It is because it connotes something gross and violent which conflicts with the gentleness of urban manners and the regard of the cultivated classes for the human body. [292–93]

An even clearer example of structuring ideas appears in Durkheim's examination of the relationship between suicide and homicide. In his attempt to refute the proposition of the contemporary Italian criminologists Ferri and Morselli that the two forms of deviance are a by-product of the "same psychological state," Durkheim suggested an alternative hypothesis: suicide and homicide are linked to one *social* condition—anomie. According to Durkheim, "anomy, in fact, begets a state of exasperation and irritated weariness which may turn against the person himself or another according to circumstances; in the first case, we have suicide, in the second, homicide" (p. 357). Notably, Durkheim then went on to observe that which adaptation transpires is not determined by the stress being endured but rather by the nature of a person's morality. Thus, "the causes determining the direction of such over-excited forces probably depend on the agent's moral constitution. According to its greater or less resistance, it will incline one way rather than the other. A man of low morality will kill another rather than himself" (p. 357).

Finally, the structuring concept is evident in Durkheim's brief discussion of the types of murder that women commit, that is, the "feminine forms of murder" (p. 342). Implicit in his analysis is that the availability of means is the central factor patterning the kinds of homicide women are constrained to choose. "Indeed," Durkheim remarked, "we are inclined to forget that there are murders of which she has a monopoly, infanticides, abortions and poisonings. Whenever homicide is within her range she commits it as often or more often than man" (p. 342).

Again, the very fact that Durkheim attempted to account for both the specific content of suicide and for the selection of self-destruction over other possibilities is of considerable significance. It reveals that he ultimately saw that he might make his explanation more complete by introducing social causes that are quite distinct from the stress generated by an anomic context. Such reasoning, to be sure, did not penetrate to the major areas of his paradigm. Moreover, his thoughts in this regard were not, as we shall see below, sufficiently comprehensive to compel many subsequent analysts to question their customary approach to the study of crime and deviance. Nevertheless, his initial insights into the social structuring of adaptations to stress at the very least lend credence to the proposition that a structuring perspective might furnish us with fresh understandings on the origins of deviant conduct.

The Durkheimian Tradition

Apart from his substantive contributions to our understanding of the social circumstances that predispose people to take their lives, the main thrust of Durkheim's writings also provided future students of deviant behavior with a powerful example of how to proceed with their research: select a form of deviance and then discover the stressful conditions that induce this one response. It has been suggested that such a methodology risks obscuring the possible indeterminacy that exists between stressors and specific outcomes as well as the theoretical significance of structuring variables. Now, as we have seen vividly in Chapters 2 and 3, not all theorists have failed to consider the potential significance of structuring principles; indeed, their numbers are plentiful and increasing. Nevertheless, it is equally apparent that others have more fully embraced the research strategy outlined by Durkheim and have thus formulated explanations largely bereft of structuring considerations. To illustrate this contention, the work of several stress theorists falling within the Durkheimian tradition to the study of deviant behavior is outlined below.[11]

One of the notable statements in this tradition is that presented by Gibbs and Martin (1958, 1964). Building more upon Durkheim's theory of egoism than his anomie ideas, these authors explored the relationship between status integration and suicide. At one point in their analysis, they make the important observation that status integration "should be correlated with the incidence of forms of deviance other than suicide" (1964 : 221). Gibbs and Martin did not pursue this idea further, however. They chose instead to confine their attention to a study of how status integration is etiologically specific to suicide. As a result, they stopped short of addressing the problem of when the stressful condition of status malintegration will produce any given adaptation.

Deterministic thinking has similarly characterized the efforts of those concerned with the origins of psychiatric symptomatology. Such theorists have long proceeded on the assumption that there is a direct relationship between the amount of stress people endure and rates of mental illness. As far back as 1850, Edward Jarvis suggested that "men were more prone to insanity than women" because of the "more stressful roles of men in the society of his day" (Dohrenwend 1975 : 368–69). Similarly, it is a popular conception in both academic and non-academic circles that "the stresses and strains of urban living lead to higher rates of psychiatric disorder" (Dohrenwend 1975 : 369). Further, differential exposure to stress is a prevalent explanation of why the lower strata experience higher rates of mental illness. In his review of classic studies on the relationship of social class to psychopathology, Dohrenwend thus concluded that "all of these theoretical positions are examples of social causation orientations. In each, psychopathology is viewed as in large part a consequence of environmentally-induced stress on the individual" (1975 : 371–72).

The idea that stressful social conditions generate disturbed behavior still has considerable support today. One of the more prominent sociological stress theories of mental illness is that of Gove and Tudor (1973). In "Adult Sex Roles and Mental Illness," they attempted to demonstrate that female rates of mental illness exceed those of males and to account for this apparent empirical fact. Central to their theoretical analysis is the thesis that "women find their position in society to be more frustrating and less rewarding than do men" (1973 : 816). They observed, for example, that, whereas a man has two "sources of gratification, . . . his family and his work, . . . a woman has only one, her family" (1973 : 814). Thus, "if a woman finds her family role unsatisfactory, she typically has no major alternative source of gratification," but "if a male finds one of his roles unsatisfactory, he can frequently focus his interest and concern on the other role" (1973 : 814). Similarly, women are likely to be unhappy with their usual role, being a housewife, because it is a position of low prestige, technically undemanding, and often inconsistent with a woman's level of educational attainment. Further, the "major instrumental activities" of the wife's everyday life, "raising children and keeping house," are themselves inherently "frustrating" (1973 : 814–15). The housewife role is also "relatively unstructured and invisible," a situation which allows the housewife "to brood over her troubles" (1973 : 815). The male worker, however, has far less time to become "obsessed with his worries" (1973 : 815). Yet even when adult women do work, they encounter more strain than males. Women in the occupational sphere are more likely to be employed in less desirable jobs that are not commensurate with their talents and to continue to "perform most of the household chores" at the same time (1973 : 815).

Significantly, Gove and Tudor argued that "more women than men become mentally ill . . . because of the difficulties associated with the feminine role" (1973 : 816). Due to their social position, women experience greater amounts of stress or frustration and, consequently, have more "emotional problems"

(1973 : 814). Gove and Tudor noted, however, that their thesis pertains only to married men and women. They asserted that, unlike the roles of their married counterparts, "the roles of unmarried men and women appear to be more similar" (1973 : 827). Not surprisingly therefore, there are only minimal sex differences in mental illness among the unmarried (cf. Fox 1980).

Finally, Gove and Tudor maintained that prior to World War II female mental illness was less pronounced than that of men (1973 : 826). Available data thus indicate a changing sex distribution of mental illness. Consistent with their theoretical scheme, Gove and Tudor accounted for the changing rates of female mental illness by pointing to the "recent changes in the women's role in industrial societies" (1973 : 816, 828). In earlier times women did housework that took more time, required more skill, and was thus "highly valued." Moreover, women often played a role in the family's business enterprise, did not receive an education inconsistent with their role demands, and were not exposed to ideologies of sexual equality. In short, "women previously had a more meaningful role" (1973 : 816). As a result, they experienced fewer role difficulties and concomitant role stress, and had lower rates of mental illness than either their male contemporaries or present-day Western women.

As is typical of commentators who set forth stress theories of one form of deviance, Gove and Tudor implicitly assumed that a one-to-one determinate relationship exists between the stress generated by role difficulties and mental illness. Their work is replete with statements such as the following:

> There are ample grounds for assuming that women find their position in society to be more *frustrating* and less rewarding than do men and that this may be a relatively recent development. Let us, then, at this point postulate that, because of the *difficulties associated with the feminine role* in modern Western societies, *more women than men become mentally ill* [1973 : 816, emphasis mine]

Notably, their concerns did not prompt them to ask why role stress leads exclusively to mental illness. For instance, it is quite conceivable that married women might make such alternative adaptations to stress as the excessive use of prescription drugs or child abuse. Indeed, Gove and Tudor even observed that suicide and attempted suicide also "reflect a high degree of distress"; they did not, however, explore the full implications of this insight (1973 : 238). Further, would we anticipate, as Gove and Tudor's logic suggests, that if changes in the male sex role exposed men to greater amounts of stress, there would be an equivalent increase in rates of mental illness? We could perhaps expect that more men would manifest this adaptation. Yet it would appear more likely that the most pronounced increases would be in forms of deviance more consistent with the male sex role—for example, alcohol abuse or episodes of aggression. That is, men would respond to rising stress with what are traditionally male adaptations. Moreover, whatever increases in psychiatric symptomatology that did occur among men would not be distributed in a uniform manner across all types of mental illness. We would less likely see a significantly larger number of men with depressive symptoms and far more likely find a greater incidence of aggression-oriented personality disorders (cf. Dohrenwend and Dohrenwend 1976).

Gove and Tudor's hesitance to consider fully the social circumstances that might structure responses to stress raises questions about the adequacy of their explanation. For example, do women experience higher rates of mental illness because they are exposed to more stress or because aspects of their sex roles largely preclude alternative adaptations (e.g., crime, alcohol abuse)? Is the social life of men really less pressure-filled or does it simply lead men along paths of deviance which do not fall under the rubric of mental illness? In short, are sex differentials in rates of mental illness more a function of factors that expose men and women to greater or lesser doses of stress (as Gove and Tudor suggest), or more a function of those conditions that structure the nature of their responses to stress in very different ways? While definitive answers to these questions await empirical confirmation, the logic of a structuring perspective at the very least forces us to pause before embracing the accepted wisdom that stress accounts in a direct and uncomplicated way for the rate of any form of deviance.

The notion that stressful social conditions move people to violate legal standards is far from new. Since the 1800s, many have thought that the frustrations and strains of urban slum life are responsible for a good portion of the crime problem in America. It is fair to say, however, that stress explanations of crime and delinquency, prevalent for some time (Reckless 1961 : 335), became particularly popular in the 1960s when Merton's paradigm of social structure and anomie exerted a major impact on crime theorizing. During this period, numerous authors sought to build upon Merton's stress ideas by exploring the direct one-to-one relationship between the stress generated by the inability to attain the goal of success through socially-approved means and a person's involvement in the single deviant form of crime/delinquency. Taken together, the efforts of these authors are often referred to as "status frustration theory."

A typical example of status frustration research is Quicker's "The Effect of Goal Discrepancy on Delinquency" (1974). In this study, Quicker challenged Cloward and Ohlin's thesis derived from Merton's writings that the blockage of occupational success goals pressures adolescents into delinquent behavior (Cloward and Ohlin 1960). Quicker maintained that his data "corroborate earlier speculation by Bordua and the empirical findings of Hirschi that frustrated occupational goals do not seem to be influential in producing delinquency" (1974 : 85). Unlike past critics, however, Quicker did not seek to discard the status frustration paradigm. Instead, he attempted to advance the model by suggesting that delinquency is generated when youths are blocked from achieving current goals, such as educational success. Future careers are so far-removed from a youth's everyday life that they do not assume great importance. As such, the perception that they may be excluded from a preferred job later in life apparently does not cause sufficient pressure to induce a juvenile to violate the law. Quicker contended that adolescents possess alternative goals that are of considerable meaning to them in their current life, and when these goals are frustrated, delinquency will arise:

> There do seem to be other goals more immediate than occupational goals, which can be influential in producing delinquency. Specifically, this study has shown that one of these goals, educational goals, will produce delinquency when they are frustrated. . . . Adolescents experience many situations that produce intense frustrations, sufficiently intense to produce the delinquency with which Cloward and Ohlin are concerned. But these frustrations stem from more immediate circumstances; they stem from what is happening now, tomorrow, not what may happen in the more distant future, if it ever comes. [1974 : 85]

While Quicker's writings contain novel insights on the origin of stress, his work nevertheless suffers from the assumption that the more pressure juveniles experience, the more delinquent they will become. While this may in part be an accurate appraisal, this theoretical equation implicitly suggests that the "intense frustrations" juveniles feel will uniformly precipitate delinquent conduct. It is certainly plausible, of course, that such stress could promote varied adaptations, perhaps suicide, drug use, or alcohol abuse. Indeed, other social commentators have warned that this is the case (cf. Phillips 1979). Given Quicker's orientation, however, this possibility did not emerge as a matter of immediate theoretical consequence.

Quicker might also have addressed the more limited issue of when a given form of delinquency will occur. Such an undertaking would not have been unanticipated since he was obviously familiar with Cloward and Ohlin's *Delinquency and Opportunity*, which emphasizes the importance of this very question. Quicker was preoccupied, however, with testing and expanding upon Cloward and Ohlin's thesis that the primary source of pressure to deviate among youths is the frustration of occupational success goals. It appears that Quicker viewed Cloward and Ohlin's contributions exclusively as a major stress theory of delinquency. As a result, Cloward and Ohlin's ideas on illegitimate means and the structuring of delinquent activity—the part they considered to be the more novel and significant message of *Delinquency and Opportunity*—did not serve to direct Quicker's research enterprise.

The belief that people enduring life-stresses attempt to alleviate their difficulties through excessive alcohol usage continues to possess much appeal in professional and popular literature alike. Pearlin and Radabaugh have thus observed that "the view that consumption of alcohol may serve as a mechanism for coping with anxiety aroused by economic conditions has a variety of conceptual and empirical underpinnings in the vast literature on drinking" (1976 : 652). One of the most widely debated formulations linking stress to alcohol abuse in a deterministic way is Horton's analysis of rates of insobriety among fifty-six "primitive" societies (1943). Horton maintained that the primary source of anxiety or stress for inhabitants of primitive societies is living in a subsistence economy. He also proposed that excessive alcohol use serves to reduce the strains that inhabitants experience. This reasoning in turn led to the conclusion that rates of alcoholism are largely determined by the level of stress characterizing a society; that is, the higher the stress in a given social location, the higher the alcoholism. The possibility, however, that rates of alcohol abuse are conditioned by other, nonstressful circumstances—such as the availability of alternative ways of lessening tension or the influence of ethnic orientations that encourage or preclude intoxication—was not elevated to the point of major theoretical significance. Of course, as discussed in Chapter 2, later alcohol scholars were to focus on precisely these kinds of considerations in detail.

Notably, if taken together, the studies of theorists in the Durkheimian tradition provide firm evidence in support of the indeterminacy thesis and against the logic typically underlying "theories of one form of deviance." For as seen above, this body of research convincingly indicates that stress states may be responded to in divergent fashions. Recall that the stressful condition of seeking unattainable goals or ambitions has been associated with a myriad of alternative adaptations. Thus, Durkheim proposed that the pressure generated by the frustration of spiraling needs leads people to take their lives. On the other hand, Edward Jarvis long ago contended that unsatisfied aspirations engender mental illness. For "status frustration" theorists such as Quicker, however, the strain arising from goal-blockage is the cause of criminal behavior; others have linked this stress state to revolutionary uprisings (cf. Davies 1962); and still others have located the source of alcoholism in the tensions created by a person's inability to achieve desired ends through socially-approved means (cf. Snyder and Pittman 1968 : 271). Of course, the question that each of these theorists does not systematically address is: when does a stressful social condition like frustrated aspirations result in the form of deviance the theorist is studying and not in one of the many other adaptations linked to this very condition by fellow investigators?

In this light, a structuring perspective suggests that the ways people adapt to deviant strains will be shaped less by the nature of the strains themselves and more by the possibilities encouraged or closed off by their social situation. Concretely, this means that an elderly, white woman living in a rural community will not be able to respond to intense pressures in the same way as a young, black man from a ghetto. Such an insight is, of course, based on little more than common sense. It is nevertheless the kind of "sense" that theorists neglect to entertain in a meaningful way when they assume that levels of a particular stress—and not the general circumstances people live in—account for involvement in the form of deviance they are endeavoring to explain.

Notes

1. Of Durkheim's four "theories" of suicide, three could be termed stress perspectives. Specifically, Durkheim argued that suicide is generated by three stressful conditions: (1) deregulation of needs or anomie, (2) excessive regulation of needs (e.g., among slaves) or fatalism, and (3) lack of structural integration or egoism. In his fourth hypothesis on the origins of suicide, however, Durkheim did not propose that stress is the source of self-destruction. Instead, suicide is viewed simply as the result of a person's socialization into "altruistic" cultural values that prescribe or at least encourage taking one's life. In this respect, Durkheim's ideas on altruistic suicide constitute a nonstress theory similar to the cultural-learning models of other forms of deviance, such as Sutherland's "differential association" theory of crime (see Chapter 6).

2. The concept of *anomie* is often translated as "normlessness." As some scholars have suggested, and I agree, a more accurate translation is "deregulation" (cf. Durkheim 1951 : 253). While the connotations of the two translations may appear to be substantially the same, an important distinction is present: normlessness refers to the total absence of norms, while deregulation refers to the inability of norms to control or "regulate" behavior. Further, *anomie* (or anomy, as it is spelled in the translation of *Suicide*) should not be confused with the term anomia, which refers to a psychological state of individuals and not to a social condition (cf. Srole 1956).

3. While Durkheim's data were group-level in nature, he utilized these data to make statements about individual behavior. As a result, his work may be characterized by an ecological fallacy (Robinson 1950). Thus, Durkheim's data show only that during times of prosperity the suicide rate increases. Durkheim assumed, however, that it is those who are the beneficiaries of prosperity that commit suicide and account for the rise in the suicide rate. Yet, an equally plausible hypothesis which can be drawn from his data is that it is those who remain poor and suffer from "relative deprivation" who become the victims of suicide. In sum, Durkheim's failure to control for individual characteristics places his interpretations in a questionable light.

4. Durkheim's concern with social order has led scholars to argue that his work is marked by a conservative bias, even though Durkheim himself was on the political left (Nisbet 1966). However, others have argued against this view (Giddens 1976; Taylor et al. 1973). While it is true, they argue, that Durkheim decried the evils of modern society and yearned for the stability of past eras, he did not simply desire to "turn the clock back" to past social arrangements. Rather, his desire was to achieve stability within the context of an equitable (meritocratic) social system.

5. Cf. Clinard 1964, Cloward 1959, Cohen 1966, Collins and Makowsky 1972, Gibbs 1966, Johnson 1965, Marks 1974, McClosky and Schaar 1965, Mizruchi 1964, Taylor et al. 1973.

6. A few authors have focused on Durkheim's concept of currents of anomie (Aron 1967, Benoit-Smullyan 1948, Nisbet 1966, 1974, Parsons 1937, Timasheff 1955). These authors, however, usually do not either specify the different ways in which Durkheim links social currents to suicide, or attempt to reconcile his usage of currents with the causal proposition set forth in Durkheim's chapter, "Anomic Suicide."

7. In short, for Durkheim, social currents constitute "social facts" (1938 : 3). Also, in *Suicide*, social currents appear to be "established" beliefs or customs. In *The Rules of Sociological Method*, however, Durkheim employs the concept in a different way:

> Since the examples that we have just cited (legal and moral regulations, religious faiths, financial systems, etc.) all consist of established beliefs and practices, one might be led to believe that social facts exist only where there is some social organization. But there are

other facts without such crystallized form which have the same objectivity and the same ascendancy over the individual. These are called "social currents." [1938 : 4]

8. It might be argued that Durkheim introduced the concept of social currents in order to elevate his level of analysis to that of the sociological: social currents—a social fact—produce another social fact, the suicide rate. This may be true. Nevertheless, his deregulation hypothesis also involves a thoroughly sociological explanation: social conditions such as the economic state of a society (a social fact) produce fluctuations in the suicide rate. Thus, while Durkheim's "Anomic Suicide" chapter depicts the psychological consequences of deregulation in detail, his deregulation hypothesis would appear to be on the same level of analysis as his social currents hypothesis.

9. This criticism can be directed at much of Durkheim's work (see note 3). It is also interesting to note that Durkheim's use of social currents here represents an early attempt at a "contextual" or "structuring effects" argument (cf. Blau 1960).

10. It should be mentioned that, while Durkheim does specify four different forms of suicide (anomic, egoistic, altruistic, and fatalistic), he does not employ structuring variables in this analysis. These four forms are not differentiated by the way the act is committed (i.e., the behavior); thus there is no "patterning of behavior" to explain. Instead, Durkheim separates his forms of suicide according to the hypothesized motivational factor that causes the commission of suicide.

11. In the pages to follow, much of the commentary will necessarily dwell on what many prominent authors did not do, namely, pay systematic attention to structuring considerations. This approach holds the unfortunate risk of appearing unduly critical, for it fails to attend to the very real contributions which these authors have made to the field. It seems essential, therefore, to disclaim any notion that such a negativistic intent informs the current endeavor. Indeed, to the extent that criticism is offered, it is done only to persuade readers that even the best of theorists have constructed deviance explanations which might have been fruitfully extended had they considered the merits of a structuring perspective.

chapter 5

Merton and Parsons:
General Deviance Paradigms

Not all stress theorists have been content to explore the relationship between stress and a single form of deviant behavior. Some theorists, most notably Merton and Parsons, have held grander designs. Their goal has been to explain how stress can cause most, if not all, forms of deviance. They have thus undertaken the task of specifying the origin of a "master stress"—a stress state that is ostensibly so pervasive in a social system and so powerful as to generate a great range of disapproved behaviors. They have, then, endeavored to formulate general deviance paradigms.

In this light, it is apparent that the major preoccupation of these authors has been to explain why people are moved to violate social standards. Much of their theorizing, therefore, has sought to account for the fluctuations in overall rates of deviance that occur over time and across the social structure. These important theoretical concerns have thus led them to concentrate on identifying and describing the origins of the master stress itself—for example, conflicts between cultural and social structures or conflict generated in the intrafamilial environment. Meanwhile, they have been less interested in studying the specific circumstances that structure the nature of deviant choices. Notably, because of their overriding focus on the question of why people deviate, master stress theorists have risked conveying the impression that the way in which people deviate is not a question of equivalent theoretical significance.

The very assumption underlying the master stress theory that a stress can engender a myriad of deviant responses is, however, not without consequence. To be sure, it has not always allowed authors to escape from deterministic thinking altogether; at times, analysts seem to assume that delineating the sources of stress is sufficient to explain the content of any ensuing adaptation. Nevertheless, the very notion of a master stress necessarily runs counter to the strict idea that stress states enjoy a specific relationship with a single form of nonconformity. It should thus not be surprising to discover that theorists in this tradition have frequently escaped the confines of deterministic logic and have attempted to cultivate our understanding of why people from different segments of the social structure are constrained to respond to a master stress in very different and socially patterned ways. Indeed, once a structuring perspective is utilized to reconsider their writings, it can be seen that they have provided vivid illustrations of the structuring of adaptations.

As with other deviance commentators, master stress theorists differ in the degree to which they integrate the concept of structuring variables into their investigations. This is apparent when one compares the work of Robert K. Merton and Talcott Parsons. Merton, whose paradigm of social structure and anomie is the most prominent of all sociological stress perspectives, often paid less systematic attention to the issue of why people deviate along certain lines and not others. In contrast, Parsons devoted considerable attention to the structuring of responses to aggressive impulses and other socially produced strains.

Despite the fact that Merton and Parsons grasped the need to address the question of the way in which people deviate, many students of their ideas have tended not to recognize this problem. Not sensitized to Merton and Parson's insights on the structuring of deviant behavior, later analysts have often taken a given master stress, such as status frustration, and considered it in relation to a single form of deviance. They have thus posed essentially deterministic questions, such as: Do disjunctions between goals and means produce juvenile delinquency? Do they produce drug addiction? Or white-collar crime? Master stress concepts, in short, have been treated as if they were statements about a deterministic relationship between a given stress state and a given disapproved outcome. To further explore these ideas, let us turn to a discussion of the master stress theories of Merton and Parsons.

Merton's Anomie-Stress Theory

Since Merton's initial statement in "Social Structure and Anomie" (1938), his anomie-stress theory has exercised a persistent influence on American deviance thought. His perspective achieved its greatest popularity during the 1960s, when it was the dominant theory in the field (Cole 1975, cf. Cole and Zuckerman 1964). More recently, the competing orientations of labeling theory and conflict theory have had greater success in capturing the attention of deviance authors (cf. Cole 1975, Sykes 1974, Wheeler 1976). Nevertheless, Merton's perspective still occupies a central position in the field. Research on anomie continues (Fischer 1973, Marks 1974, McCloskey 1976, Simon and Gagnon 1976, *Social Forces* 1981, Thio 1975), and Merton's approach is invariably treated in deviance and criminology textbooks (Clinard 1974, Empey 1982, Gibbons 1979, Sutherland and Cressey 1970).

In reviewing Merton's paradigm of deviant behavior below, it is argued that this paradigm contains two distinct theories of why people engage in disapproved behaviors. One theory, by far the more popular, locates the origin of deviance in the stresses or pressures generated by a disjunction between goals and means, while the other sees the root of deviance in the social condition of anomie. Following this analysis, Merton's thoughts on the concept of structuring variables as well as the fate of these remarks at the hands of subsequent students are considered.

STRESS AND DEVIANT BEHAVIOR

In "Social Structure and Anomie," [1] Merton launched a challenge to the notion popularized by Hobbesian and Freudian writings that deviant behavior is rooted in people's pent-up hostile impulses. Merton argued that such a view was based on a "fallacious premise" for it assumed that deviant motivations are integral to human nature and are not the very thing that must be explained. It thus seemed evident to Merton that Freud was wrong in suggesting, as he did in *Civilization and Its Discontents*, that deviance emerges when society becomes negligent in its efforts to suppress the evil that hides within each person. Instead, Merton proposed that wayward inclinations are imposed from without, that they are fresh creations of the social structure. "If the Freudian notion is a variety of the 'original sin' doctrine, then the interpretation advanced in this paper is a doctrine of 'socially derived sin'." (1968b : 185).

Scholars commonly group Merton and Durkheim into the same intellectual camp and emphasize (or assume) the existence of strong intellectual linkages between the two. The perspectives of Merton and Durkheim, however, differ as much as they converge. Thus, Merton's rejection of the Freudian-Hobbesian formulation is particularly significant because it also entails a rejection of a cornerstone of Durkheim's theory: Durkheim's conception of the human condition. For Durkheim shared with the Freudian-Hobbesian tradition the view that the motivation to deviate is ultimately given in human nature (Simon and Gagnon 1976). This is not to say that Durkheim's conception is identical to that of Freud and Hobbes. If a quick distinction is possible, the latter theorists tended to see drives as inherently hostile, evil, or deviant. In Durkheim's view, a person's (social) drives or needs were not deviant per se, but, if not regulated, they would inevitably spiral until they produce deviant impulses. This difference aside, Durkheim, Freud, and Hobbes concurred that the potential to deviate is characteristic of all individuals. It is interesting to note that this similar conception of the human condition had an important by-product: it led all three theorists to offer what could best be termed a control theory of deviance (Hirschi 1969). For once these theorists assumed that the motivation to deviate is given, they were forced to explain why actors are not deviant all the time. To resolve this problem, they placed the responsibility for nonconformity in society's failure or inability to control or regulate people's deviant impulses.

Not accepting this notion that deviant motivations are ultimately rooted in human nature, Merton argued instead that deviant desires are entirely a social product. It should be of little surprise, therefore, that Merton's own theory of deviance departs from Durkheim's model in significant respects. Merton's major proposition was formulated in the following way: When actors are socialized to hold a cultural goal but are blocked by the social structure from attaining this goal, they will experience stress or pressure (i.e., deviant motivation). In turn, they will be likely to attempt to alleviate this pressure by employing deviant means. In short, when people suffer a means-goal disjunction or gap, then deviant behavior is a probable outcome.

Durkheim also maintained that a discrepancy between available means and spiraling desires (goals) was integral to causing suicide. To this extent, Durkheim and Merton's formulations converge.[2] However, important differences remain. For Durkheim, social or moral needs, once internalized, are never permanently fixed; they always have the dangerous potential to rise indefinitely. Merton viewed goals as created in the process of socialization and as fixed or stable (though they could escalate or decline under certain social conditions, e.g., new socialization). Durkheim also contended that the major cause of deviance is society's failure to regulate people's needs. Society's *lack of presence* in actors allows needs to rise, outstrip means, and create deviance. Holding needs or goals to be fixed, Merton did not see society's lack of regulatory power as the factor most responsible for a means-goal disjunction. Instead, it is the very *presence* of society in actors which is crucial to the etiology of nonconformity. For it is only when society has the power to create goals that some individuals cannot attain that deviant behavior will transpire.[3]

To demonstrate the relevance of his framework, Merton looked no further than at American society. He observed that a large proportion of Americans are socialized to subscribe to the goal of economic success. At the same time, the social structure does not permit universal achievement of this end. For those deprived of success, participation in deviant behavior is quite probable, if not expected:

> It is when a system of cultural values extols, virtually above all else, certain *common* success-goals for the *population at large* while the social structure rigorously restricts or completely closes access to approved modes of reaching these goals *for a considerable part of the same population*, that deviant behavior ensues on a large scale.[1968b : 200]

Thus, building on his concern for unmasking unanticipated and ironic consequences (Merton 1936, 1968a), Merton remarked, "In this setting, a cardinal American virtue, 'ambition,' promotes a cardinal American vice, 'deviant behavior' " (1968b : 200).

Merton held that of the parameters of social structure, class status is the one most responsible for restricting access to success. Needless to say, those in the bottom rungs of society are seen to be most affected. Raised to embrace an open-class ideology and socialized into the goal of success, those in the lower class are the least likely to possess the educational or material resources to advance toward high economic attainment. The frustration engendered as status desires remain beyond reach in turn creates intense motivations to deviate—an experience which an advantaged position insulates against. A central proposition, then, that emerges from Merton's analysis is that the lower class disproportionately endures the rigors imposed by the master stress precipitated by blocked opportunity and thus manifests the highest rates of deviant behavior (Merton 1968c : 224–29).

Merton's selection of American society as a substantive example of his theory and, in particular, his highlighting of the etiological significance of the class structure, have had important implications for (1) the direction of research in the field of deviance, (2) ideological appraisals of his model, and (3) the range of empirical situations to which his model has been applied. As the dominant paradigm in the field of deviance during the 1960s, Merton's framework served, in a Kuhnian (1962) sense, to define which research puzzles deserved examination. One of the most important puzzles Merton's work suggested was the study of class differentials in deviance. The fact that a myriad of studies on this topic appeared in the 1960s is indicative of the impact Merton's paradigm exercised in directing research activity. Supportive of this line of thought, Cole has stated:

> The major latent function of theory is to provide puzzles for scientists to work on. From this point of view, Merton's decision to treat anomie as differentially distributed within the class structure turned out to be strategic. Although choosing the other alternative [anomie and deviance are equally distributed within the class structure] would have avoided much of the criticism the theory has faced, the theory would have been less useful in providing puzzles for sociologists to work on. There was much greater opportunity to study and greater interest in differential rates of deviance within the United States than there was in differential rates of deviance among societies. [1975 : 213]

Merton's concern for the influence of the contradiction between America's cultural and class structures on deviance has also generated divergent ideological appraisals of his work. On the one hand, Gouldner has suggested that:

Merton was always much more *Marxist* than his silences on that question may make it seem. Unlike Parsons, Merton always knew his Marx and knew thoroughly the nuances of controversy in living Marxist culture. Merton developed his generalized analysis of the various forms of deviant behavior by locating them within a systematic formalization of Durkheim's theory of *anomie*, from which he gained analytic distance by tacitly grounding himself in a Marxian ontology of social *contradiction*. It is perhaps this Hegelian dimension of Marxism that has had the most enduring effect on Merton's *analytic rules*, and which disposed him to view *anomie* as the unanticipated outcome of social institutions that thwarted men in their effort to acquire the very goods and values that these same institutions had encouraged them to pursue. In its openness to the internal contradictions of capitalist *culture* few Lukacians have been more incisive. [1973 : x–xi]

Similarly, the "radical" or "new criminologists" Taylor, Walton, and Young, though critical of Merton, have referred to him as a "cautious rebel. . . . Merton does take on the role of the rebel in the substantive analysis of American society. He does stand outside the system and make criticisms, which, if taken to their logical conclusion, would necessitate radical social change" (1973 : 101). On the other hand, however, scholars have accused Merton's work of containing a "class bias" (Taylor et al. 1973; Thio 1973, 1975; Simon and Gagnon 1976). The root of the bias is seen to lie in Merton's premise that the lower class has higher rates of deviance. It is held that Merton's theory "stands accused of predicting too little bourgeois criminality and too much proletarian criminality" (Taylor et al. 1973 : 107). As such, it fosters a "dangerous class" image of the lower stratum and obscures not only the rich's participation in deviant behavior but also their usage of deviant means to maintain or increase their advantage.

Merton's ability to link his model to the American experience has likewise been largely responsible for the popularity of his work. I suspect, though, that the very popularity of the success goal/class constraint example has served to limit the applicability of his framework. Nearly all attempts to test his work have studied propositions emanating from this example. Similarly, nearly all summaries or critiques of Merton's work assume that this substantive example is his theory. Merton has argued, however, that his model is not restricted to the success goal/class constraint example (1968c : 220). Instead, Merton has maintained that his work is applicable to a wide range of empirical situations. Deviance will transpire when a conflict exists "between cultural goals and the availability of using institutional means— whatever the character of goals" (1968c : 220). And, "we must emphasize again that the general theory of social structure and anomie is *not* confined to the specific goal of monetary success and of social restrictions upon access to it" (1968c : 235). An alternative empirical instance is Merton's 1957 analysis of scientists who utilize deviant means (e.g., falsifying experiments) to achieve the goal of prestige not available to them through legitimate channels (cf. Zuckerman 1977).

An important distinction between Durkheim and Merton yet to be mentioned concerns the scope of the two theorists' models. Durkheim sought to construct an explanation only of suicide. Merton was more ambitious; his aim was to formulate a general theory of deviance. In contrast to Durkheim, he argued that his proposed motivational state (pressure emanating from a means-goal disjunction) could give rise not simply to one form of deviance but to all forms (and perhaps conformity as well). To systematize this notion, Merton developed a "typology of modes of individual adaptation" (1968b : 194). In essence, he argued that the myriad of possible responses to pressure could be grouped into one of five categories (four deviant, one conformist). Merton intended these five categories to be logically exhaustive and consistent, though some scholars have disputed this claim (Dubin 1959, Harary 1966, Hill 1968, Parsons 1951, Simon and Gagnon 1976).[4]

Merton differentiated the adaptations within the typology according to whether they entailed an acceptance (positive valence, $+$) or rejection (negative valence, $-$) of (1) cultural goals and (2) institutional means. The acceptance of both means and goals Merton termed "conformity" ($+$, $+$). Here, Merton in effect contended that a means-goal disjunction does not necessitate a deviant response. Instead, some, if not the majority of people experiencing a means-goal disjunction will learn to live with the pressure their situation engenders (1968b : 195). Turning now to Merton's four deviant adaptations, "innovations" ($+$, $-$) transpires when a goal is accepted but the institutional means are rejected. An example of innovation is the "box man" who accepts the goal of economic success but tries to achieve this success by cracking open safes. The rejection of a cultural goal and acceptance of the means constitutes "ritualism" ($-$, $+$). Ritualists are actors who "go through the motions," even though they no longer maintain any commitment to a prescribed goal. As such, their deviance is not behavioral or overt but rather is attitudinal or internal. "Retreatism" ($-$, $-$) involves the rejection of both goal and means. Grouped under this category are such deviant modes as drug addiction, alcoholism, mental illness, and hoboism. "People who adapt (or maladapt) in this fashion are, strictly speaking, *in* the society but not *of* it. Sociologically they constitute the true aliens" (1968b : 207). Finally, Merton defined the rejection of both a goal and means and the substitution of a new goal and means as "rebellion" ($\pm$, $\pm$). An obvious example of this adaptation is revolutionary activity.

ANOMIE AND DEVIANT BEHAVIOR

While Merton is typically classified by scholars as an "anomie theorist," a close reading of his writings will reveal that the role attributed to the social condition of anomie (deregulation, normlessness) in causing deviance is relatively minor. Instead, as noted above, Merton's major proposition is that the (master) stress arising out of the gap between means and goals produces deviant behavior. Using Merton's own words, it is his "central thesis that aberrant behavior may be regarded sociologically as a symptom of dissociation between culturally prescribed aspirations and socially structured avenues for realizing these aspirations" (1968b : 188).

In light of this fact, it is not surprising that theorists typically assume that this master stress hypothesis constitutes the totality of Merton's paradigm. One common by-product of this interpretation is that many scholars then go on to label the discrepancy between means and goal and the stress it generates as "anomie." Maris, for instance, has commented that "anomie simply indicates that there is a disjunction of means and ends, of effort and attainment" (1969 : 253). Palmore and Hammond have stated that "our assertions are that lower strata generally, and Negroes and boys especially, face more barriers to legitimate goals. Their situation is more anomic" (1964 : 852). Similar remarks are found in Faia's work: "Merton's hypothesis on the structural sources of deviancy may be stated in the following form: the higher the degree of anomie, as defined in terms of the means-end discrepancy, the higher the rate of social deviancy" (1967 : 402).[5]

This interpretation has had two unfortunate consequences. First, since anomie refers to deregulation or normlessness and not to a means-goal gap, it has encouraged what appears to be a misuse of the concept of anomie in the deviance literature. Second, by in effect reducing his paradigm of social structure and anomie exclusively to a stress or pressure theory, deviance commentators have overlooked Merton's distinct, nonstress theory of the relationship of anomie to deviant behavior. In this regard, it is perhaps significant that, in contrast to the many empirical tests of Merton's master stress thesis (Cole and Zuckerman 1964, Cole 1975), few assessments have been made of the anomie portion of his general paradigm of deviant behavior. In sum, despite the impressions fostered by most scholars and despite the title of his influential article on the subject ("Social Structure and Anomie"), the concept of anomie is not applicable to the major thrust of Merton's paradigm. With this caveat in mind, it is possible to examine the exact fashion in which he did employ the concept.

To a certain degree, Merton drew his usage of anomie from Durkheim. Similar to his predecessor, Merton defined anomie as a condition of deregulation or normlessness. Further, he followed Durkheim in arguing that a lack of normative control can give rise to deviant behavior. Here, however, the convergence ends. Indeed, it might be remembered that for Durkheim deregulation unleashes escalating needs that outstrip means and ultimately pressure actors into committing suicide. By contrast, viewing needs or goals as fixed by the process of socialization, Merton did not believe that anomie allows needs to spiral and produce nonconformity. More significantly, Merton did not maintain that an unregulated individual has to experience any special stress or pressure to become deviant. It is instructive that Merton failed to insert his means-goal disjunction thesis at this point. Thus, once anomie sets in and controls break down, a person need not necessarily experience the frustration induced by blocked aspirations to violate moral boundaries that have been rendered impotent.

In taking this stance, Merton departed from the essentially positivist image of the pressured deviant that characterizes most of his work and which has led him to be designated a "strain" or "status frustration" theorist (cf. Hirschi 1969, Kornhauser 1978, Empey 1982). In place of this image, Merton substituted a thoroughly classical view of the deviant, arguing that the deregulated or anomic actor is free to choose any course of conduct. The only guide to the person's activity is the rational calculation of the costs and benefits of the various means available. Deviant behavior now occurs when illegitimate means are the "technically most effective procedure" that can be employed to secure a desired end (1968b: 188). As Merton has noted, anomie or "this attenuation of institutional controls" creates a "situation erroneously held by the utilitarian philosophers to be typical of society, a situation in which calculations of personal advantage and fear of punishment are the only regulating agencies" (1968: 211).

Unlike Durkheim, Merton failed to provide a systematic analysis of the conditions which produce anomie. In a number of disparate places in his writings, however, he did suggest several major causative factors. First, Merton contended that two polar, ideal-types of societies can be distinguished: societies that demonstrate an exclusive concern for the achievement of cultural goals, and societies that view adherence to institutional means to be of primary import. For Merton, societies which tend toward the former polar type, that is, which overemphasize the significance of cultural goals, are especially prone to anomie. For when the exultation of goals so weakens faith in institutionally legitimate means "as to have the behavior of many individuals limited only by considerations of technical expediency. . . .the society becomes unstable and there develops what Durkheim called 'anomie'" (1968b: 188–89). That is, as the "extreme cultural emphasis on the goal of success attenuates conformity to institutionally prescribed methods of moving toward this goal . . . norms are robbed of their power to regulate and the 'normlessness' component of anomie ensues" (1968c: 223). Another factor is the malintegration between a society's cultural and social structures. Here, it is not simply the overemphasis on cultural goals which eventuates in anomie, but the emphasizing of goals in a society whose social structure cannot permit universal goal attainment. To Merton, this situation creates a "strain toward the breakdown of the norms, toward normlessness" (1968c: 217). Finally,

Merton suggested that the very presence of successful deviant behavior in a social setting is a source of anomie. The flourishing of such wayward conduct tends "to eliminate the legitimacy of the institutional norms for others in the system. The process thus enlarges the extent of anomie within the system" (1968c : 234; cf. 1964 : 232, 235).

Of final interest here is the fact that scholars analyzing Merton's deviance writings almost invariably fail to attend to his final essay on anomie, "Anomie, Anomia, and Social Interaction: Contexts of Deviant Behavior" (1964). As such, several of the important additions or adjustments in the theoretical stance made in this essay are left unmentioned. First of all, as he had done previously (1968c : 215–16), Merton distinguished between *anomie*, a property of the social environment, and *anomia*, a psychological state of individuals. Here, however, he employed the term anomia in a novel fashion. On the one hand, he called the psychological condition emanating from a means-goal disjunction "anomia of deprivation." More important, he departed from a disadvantaged (and perhaps class-biased) image of the deviant by coining the concept of "anomia of success." This he held "arises from another kind of seemingly futile pursuit, when progressively heightened aspirations are fostered by each temporary success and by the enlarged expectations visited on them by associates" (1964 : 225). The intellectual debt to Durkheim's thesis linking prosperity to deviance can be readily seen here. Secondly, building in a sense on Durkheim's "currents of anomie" idea but more directly on the work of Kendall and Lazarsfeld (1950), Merton conceived of anomie as a contextual variable that can have an independent effect on deviance (cf. Hill 1968). Thirdly, Merton contended that, apart from experiencing a means-goal disjunction, who a person interacts with can cause deviant behavior. Of particular importance is the degree to which an actor encounters others who are anomic or nonanomic. Finally, Merton maintained that once in existence, deviant subcultures have the potential to commit someone to a deviant lifestyle, even though the person is not faced with a discrepancy between available means and a desired end. "There is, so to say, no special theory needed to account for continued, renewed, and elaborated deviant behavior by those who come into a subculture which is defined as deviant" (1964 : 223).

MERTON AND THE STRUCTURING OF DEVIANT BEHAVIOR

In his quest to construct a general theory of deviance, Merton was aware that a means-goal disjunction could potentially give rise to multiple forms of deviance. In fact, he argued that the master stress arising out of a disjunctive situation could foster all forms of deviance (which could be grouped into his typology of adaptations). One might expect, therefore, that Merton would have recognized the need to delineate the conditions under which a given adaptation would ensue—in short, the need to specify structuring variables. Notably, Merton did make inroads in this direction.

Merton's most detailed use of the structuring concept was presented in his analysis of innovation and ritualism. He observed that lower-class actors are more likely to make an innovative adaptation when experiencing a stress, while those of the lower middle class are more likely to engage in ritualistic behavior. Merton then argued that the differential selection of adaptations was regulated or patterned by the type of socialization members of each class received. Firmly socialized to hold the moral mandates of society, those of the lower middle class are constrained from utilizing illegitimate means when they lack legitimate means to attain a desired end. Moreover, they are admonished to adhere to institutional means. As a result, one of the few paths that remains to alleviate their pressure is to maintain conformity to institutional means but, at the same time, to lower their psychic investment in the cultural goal being sought—that is, to become ritualistic. In contrast, those of the lower class are more likely to experience defective socialization and thus are free to employ illegitimate or innovative means to satisfy their blocked aspirations (1968c : 205).

Along similar lines, Merton posited that socialization was involved in channeling actors into retreatism. Candidates for this adaptation experience constant failure in their striving for a prescribed cultural goal. However, they are unable to utilize "illegitimate routes," because their socialization has effectively laden them with "internalized prohibitions" (1968b : 207). The only way left to resolve this conflict is to abandon "both the precipitating elements, the goal and the means." By retreating, therefore, "the escape is complete."

Next, Merton converged with a rich tradition of sociological thought when he discussed, in effect, the structuring of the rebellious adaptation. Here, he postulated that rebellion is a probable response when actors cast off their false consciousness and blame the "system" for their unpleasant predicament. He thus observed that in the face of "thwarted" aspirations, "those who find its source in the social structure may become alienated from that structure and ready candidates for Adaptation V (rebellion)" (1968b : 201). Finally, in addition to employing structuring variables in these three substantive examples, Merton stated more generally that it is essential to study "the forces making for one rather than another type of adaptation" (1968c : 230), and that "deviant behavior itself is patterned" (1968c : 217).

From this discussion, it is clear that the idea of structuring variables informed Merton's theorizing. At the same time, it must be admitted that Merton hesitated to vigorously pursue the question of why people deviate in certain ways. Merton recognized this in the conclusion to "Social Structure and Anomie" when he cautioned that "this essay . . . has not included an exhaustive treatment of the various structural elements which predispose toward one rather than another of the alternative responses open to individuals; it has *neglected, but not denied the relevance of, the factors determining the specific incidence of these responses*'' (1938 : 682, cf. 1968b : 214, emphasis mine). Merton later declared that his previous discussion of the way in which class differentials in socialization led to ritualism among the middle class and innovation among those less advantaged did not prompt him to pursue this reasoning to its logical conclusion. He thus noted that ''pressures for deviant behavior are one thing; actual rates of deviant behavior quite another. I had made a slight and insufficient effort to distinguish the two and to bridge the gap by distinguishing socially generated pressures for deviance from . . . vulnerability to pressure for one or another type of deviant behavior.'' He then went on to observe that ''this is at best no more than a bare beginning. It is necessary to identify other sociological variables that intervene between structurally induced pressure for deviant behavior and actual rates of such behavior'' (1959 : 188).

In spite of the fact that he had illustrated several instances of the structuring of deviant adaptations in his work, it seems that Merton underestimated the full importance of specifying these ''intervening'' variables. As a matter of fact, Merton did not appreciate the significance of these variables until his student Richard Cloward evolved the theory of illegitimate means. Commenting on Cloward's contribution, Merton noted that he had not considered how the distribution of illegitimate means can regulate participation in certain adaptations. Merton had assumed ''by default that access to deviant and illegitimate means for reaching a valued goal is uniformly available, irrespective of position in the social structure.'' Cloward, however, ''corrects this unwitting and, it appears, untrue assumption by dealing with socially patterned differences of access to learning how to perform particular kinds of deviant roles and of access to opportunities for carrying them out'' (1959 : 188). Reflecting further on this point, Merton wrote that, though he had linked the idea of illegitimate means to the structuring of deviant behavior in an earlier essay (Merton and Montague 1940), he was not aware of his theoretical ''discovery'':

> I can add another example of this kind of blind-spot, in which the systematic implications of a general idea are not seen even though it is used in a particular instance. Some years ago, I collaborated on a critique of Hooton's work on ''the biological inferiority of criminals.'' We raised the question whether we were to ''assume biological determinants of the fact that there are proportionately five times as many Texas criminals [in Hooton's example] convicted of forgery and fraud as there are in the Massachusetts sample? . . . Possibly the 'glib and oily art' of stock-swindling is less a matter of bodily type than of petroliferous regions and an established pattern of promoting chimerical gushers.'' But this

offhand allusion did not lead us to see the general concepts of learning- and opportunity-structures implied on it, concepts which Cloward shows, can be methodically used to help interpret variations of rates of different kinds of deviant behavior. [1959 : 188, n. 25] [6]

In short, Merton's appreciation for the need to explore more fully why people make certain deviant choices in response to master stress did not become complete until Cloward clarified how attention to this issue might enrich the paradigm of social structure and anomie. This occurrence is of particular interest when one realizes that much of Merton's sociology outside the field of crime and deviance focuses on the very problem of the social structuring of behavioral adaptations. As Stinchcombe has argued in his over-view of Merton's theory of social structure, "the core process that Merton conceives as central to social structure is *the choice between socially structured alternatives*" (1975 : 12). One possible explanation for this blind-spot is that, similar to other theorists, Merton embraced or was limited by the positivist school's bias that deviance is a special kind of phenomenon fundamentally different from the conventional side of life (Ehrlich 1973). As a consequence, Merton was unable to utilize the sociological concepts that he would so readily apply to his study of "normal" behavior (cf. Cullen and Link 1980).

To further illustrate this point, it can be observed that much of the theoretical power of Cloward's work rested on his use of the concept of "means" in an innovative way. He argued that not only are there legitimate means, but illegitimate means as well, and that it is the availability of these illegitimate means which regulates when any particular form of deviance (e.g., a type of gang activity) is pursued. It seems odd, as it did to Merton himself in 1959, that he could have overlooked both the very existence of illegitimate means and their relationship to participation in unconventional activities. After all, the core of Merton's general sociological theorizing flows in large part from Parsons's scheme of action, the unit act, of which "means" is a central element. It would appear, however, that once Merton assumed that he was examining a special kind of behavior—deviance—his ability to analyze this behavior as he would any other normal social behavior was limited. To account for the origins of wayward conduct, he instead relied upon such special concepts as structurally induced deviant pressures and anomie. Meanwhile, the notion that "means" exist not only in the conventional world but in the criminal arena as well remained largely obscured.

In a similar vein, Merton has often been criticized for his thesis that the lower classes experience higher rates of crime and deviance (Taylor et al. 1973). Thio has asserted that Merton fell into the trap of formulating a class-biased theory because he saw deviance as a product of the strain of absolute deprivation which is more prevalent among the lower classes. In contrast, Thio maintained that it is primarily relative and not absolute deprivation that triggers nonconformity, and that nonconformity is thus located more heavily in the upper strata. Again, Merton did not consider this possibility even though he had utilized the very concept of relative deprivation extensively in his own sociology:

> For all the lengthy discussion on the concept of relative deprivation in the very same book where he presents his anomie theory (Merton, 1968 : 279–440), Merton does not see the connection between social class and relative deprivation or does not apply it to his anomie theory. Otherwise, he would have found untenable his assumption that lower-class persons are more likely than upper-class persons to experience obstacles to the realization of high aspirations. [Thio 1975 : 148]

SUBSEQUENT STUDIES OF SOCIAL STRUCTURE AND ANOMIE

As a master stress theory, it might have been expected that Merton's paradigm would have had the effect of challenging the view held by most authors that stress leads ineluctably to one form of deviance. It might also have been anticipated that the inroads which Merton made with regard to the concept of structuring variables would have led authors to focus on the way in which deviant behavior is socially structured. Many students of Merton's anomie-stress paradigm, however, have failed to come to grips with the fundamental problem of indeterminacy and build upon the structuring insights so clearly present in his writings. This is particularly true for the numerous authors who have attempted to study how Merton's master stress is related to a single form of nonconformity. Thus, it is common for an analyst to study the ways in which stress generated by a means-goal discrepancy is associated with juvenile delinquency, or to examine the link between Merton's stress state and alcoholism, or to test the impact of this condition on an adaptation like rebellion, suicide, or perhaps psychiatric symptomatology (cf. Clinard 1964). Given this deterministic application of Merton's ideas, it is of little surprise to find that many authors ignore the full implications of Merton's insight that social stresses can result in numerous adaptations and pass over his later comments (1959) on the need to identify those variables which "intervene" between his master stress and behavior and then structure the deviant choices actors make.

Faia's essay "Alienation, Structured Strain, and Political Deviancy: A Test of Merton's Hypothesis" (1967), illustrates this kind of analysis quite well. Faia centered on the problem of why certain academicians possess political attitudes that deviate from those of their colleagues. The major conclusion he offered was that "political deviance" among professors stems from efforts to deal with "perceived structural inadequacy," that is, "status anxiety arising from perceived obstacles to social mobility" (1967 : 401). (From Merton's perspective, this is the equivalent of a perceived means-goal disjunction.) More specifically, Faia hypothesized that political aberrance allows frustrated academicians to "displace" their aggression by providing a means "to express hostility toward his academic colleagues and the system they represent" (p. 412). Similar to Cohen's analysis of lower-class delinquency (1955), deviance in this case is seen to be a non-utilitarian or irrational reaction "against certain kinds of socially-induced strain" (p. 407).

Faia's otherwise thought-provoking essay errs in its unwitting assumption that a stress or pressure state is not only a necessary but also a sufficient condition for the causation of a solitary deviant response. Faia made no mention of the possibility that "perceived structural inadequacy" can lead to other forms of deviance, such as the utilitarian response of falsifying research findings in order to gain respect within the profession, a possibility which Merton had highlighted in his own research (1957). Consequently, the issue of why academicians seek to resolve their conflicts by manifesting deviant political attitudes as opposed to following alternative illegitimate options was not investigated.

A few students of Merton's work have recognized that a motivational state can give rise to a myriad of deviant behaviors. Even here, however, the problem of determinacy is not well addressed; if anything, it is compounded. One example is available in the work of Simon and Gagnon (1976). In "The Anomie of Affluence: A Post-Mertonian Conception," these authors developed a paradigm which challenges Merton's theory of deviance by building on Durkheim's concern for deviance among the prosperous. According to Simon and Gagnon, Merton offered an "anomie of scarcity" model, insofar as he postulated the *unavailability of means* to be crucial to the etiology of deviant behavior. Given the social context in which Merton formulated his ideas on deviance—"the late 1930's, years of only partial recovery from a major depression"—his stance is held to be understandable (1976 : 369). Yet while Merton's position is "not surprising," it is seen as theoretically limited. As a product of a depressed area, Merton's work "suffers from historically and culturally circumscribed imagery" (1976 : 357). Specifically, Merton fostered the imagery of the deviant as disadvantaged. In doing so, and unlike Durkheim, Merton neglected "the deviance of those in the higher economic and educational strata" (1976 : 369). In light of the persistent trend toward affluence in advanced industrial societies—an "expression of a cumulative and continuing technological revolution"—this omission ranks as a crucial one (1976 : 377).

In Merton's view, deviance is the solution to the problem of not having access to the institutional means required to achieve a cultural goal. For Simon and Gagnon, on the other hand, deviance can also be the solution to the difficulties posed by a privileged life-situation, in which institutional means are not scarce but readily available. What is quite problematic, however, is the response that the affluent make in relation to the prescribed goal (e.g., of success). Deviance occurs when an actor does not maintain an appropriate level of commitment to the goal and/or when the person does not secure an appropriate level of gratification from the goal.

It is interesting that Simon and Gagnon maintained that the anomie of affluence can give rise to a number of different responses. They contended that "to the degree that . . . the two dimensions of commitment and gratification can be conceived as being independent of one another, it becomes possible to create a typology of adaptations along the lines of Merton" (1976 : 369). By cross-tabulating these two dimensions with the valences of "plus," "minus," and "innovative," nine "adaptive responses" are obtained. One adaptation, "optimal conformist," is nondeviant in nature. The eight remaining deviant outcomes are: "detached conformist," "compulsive achiever," "conforming deviant," "detached person," "escapist," "conventional reformer," "missionary," and "total rebel."

In linking the anomie of affluence to multiple adaptations, Simon and Gagnon thus converge with Merton and remain apart from those in the Durkheimian tradition who assume etiological specificity between stress and a particular deviant form. And in so doing, they contribute much innovative thinking on the origins of a master stress capable of precipitating many varieties of deviance in the more affluent sectors of the social system. Their reluctance to pursue the logic of indeterminacy nevertheless seems to have prevented them from systematically specifying the conditions under which any given adaptive response would occur. Of note is that this failure to delineate variables which pattern the proposed typological adaptations has consequences for their paradigm. To the extent that their typology is meant to be complete, Simon and Gagnon essentially end up arguing that anomie of affluence will cause either conformity ("optimal conformist") or one of eight logically exhaustive deviant responses—in short, that it may cause any behavior. By relating their motivational conditions to all possible responses, but doing little more, they risk leaving all responses unexplained. As such, they are unable to present any falsifiable propositions on when any particular outcome will occur, and thus, in this respect, their model is of questionable scientific value (cf. Popper 1959, Braithwaite 1968).

Simon and Gagnon's paradigm is nonetheless successful in the sense that it fulfills their goal of furnishing an initial formulation in a theoretically underdeveloped area. They intended their "typology of adaptive responses" to serve a sensitizing function, to offer "an imagery (again like Merton's) for research" (p. 1976 : 370). At the same time, however, it is conceivable that their virtual neglect of the structuring concept may eventually cause subsequent researchers to overlook the empirical possibilities suggested by their paradigm. The absence of any discussion of the circumstances that determine when any one of their nine proposed adaptations will arise is likely to leave their work open to misinterpretation or the kind of criticism that is often leveled at Merton's theory, namely, that the theory is strictly typological and not meant to generate research hypotheses (cf. Dubin 1959).

Scholars have thus not always recognized that Merton's writings constitute a beginning point for the investigation of the social structuring of deviant choices. Instead, finding his insights on the sources of a master stress more fascinating, they have been more concerned with the issue of why people deviate than with the question of why people deviate in a certain way. In the following section, however, it will be seen that another stress theorist, Talcott Parsons, has taken up this latter question with greater resolve.

Talcott Parsons on Deviant Behavior

Considering Talcott Parsons's preeminent status within the sociological community, it is not surprising that his writings have exerted a perceptible influence on deviance scholars for nearly thirty years (cf. Cole 1975). In particular, Parsons's work on youthful aggressive behavior served as an important delinquency paradigm during the 1950s and laid the groundwork for such analyses as Cohen's notable *Delinquent Boys* (1955). More recently, Parsons's work on the "sick role" has enjoyed a renewed popularity among labeling theorists (1951). But given Parsons's large influence on other areas of sociological thought, his influence on the study of deviance per se has not been overwhelming. This is especially true of his comprehensive theory of deviance set forth in *The Social System* (1951 : 249–325). In contrast to Merton's paradigm, Parsons's scheme fostered little empirical research. This is readily understandable in light of his penchant for grand theorizing (cf. Smelser and Warner 1976 : 203–4). What is less understandable, however, is that, unlike most other aspects of his work, Parsons's deviance scheme has not received much attention from theorists. Not only has his framework rarely been summarized in books or chapters on theories of deviance (cf. Matza 1969, Sutherland and Cressey 1970, Taylor et al. 1973, Gibbons 1979), but it has also received only scant attention in volumes devoted to the analysis of Parsons's sociological contributions (Black 1961, Turk and Simpson 1971). In fact, I know of only one article (Smelser and Warner 1976) that systematically relates even a substantial portion of Parsons's thought on deviant behavior.

Yet Parsons's work should be of special interest because he showed much more awareness of the socially structured character of deviant behavior than many other deviance theorists. To be sure, Parsons was much more interested in the origins of deviant behavior as such than in the structuring of that behavior. Consequently, structuring notions do not possess the same level of systematic generality as his work on the stressful sources of deviant behavior. Nevertheless, the understanding that social and psychological conditions serve to channel deviant drives is integral to his thinking, and his insights in this vein lend much legitimacy to the proposition that stresses, however potent, do not account for the form a deviation takes.

Parsons made two major statements on the etiology of deviant behavior.[7] On the one hand, he addressed the more limited issue of the origin of different forms of aggressive behavior in Western societies. On the other hand, he sought, similar to Merton, to construct a general model of all types of deviance. Within each of these theoretical statements, Parsons not only delineated sources of stress, but also went on to discuss why certain kinds of deviant responses arise.

FORMS OF AGGRESSION IN WESTERN SOCIETIES

Perhaps the most popular of Parsons's endeavors in the field of deviance is his article "Certain Primary Sources and Patterns of Aggression in the Social Structure of the Western World" (1947). Though this essay did not focus exclusively on youthful aggressive behavior, it was Parsons's ideas on this particular problem that received most notice. In fact, these ideas formed the basis of a major paradigm of juvenile delinquency that prevailed during the 1950s.

In this statement, Parsons viewed youthful (and adult) aggression within a context of vast institutional change. Particularly consequential are the transformations in the occupational and kinship systems which take the father out of the home for much of the day and create the "relatively isolated conjugal family" (1947 : 170). This kinship arrangement undermines the traditional social supports provided by the traditional extended family (with the father present). As such, these transformations "favor high levels of insecurity structured in relatively definite and uniform ways and correspondingly a good deal of aggression" (1947 : 170).

Parsons held this arrangement to be especially stressful for boys, and thus likely to produce aggressive tendencies in them. With the father away at work, the mother assumes the task of the primary socializing agent in the home. In contrast to the father, she has considerable contact with the children. As a result, both boys and girls tend to emulate the mother, and, in turn, develop early feminine identification. In the course of the socialization-identification process, "good" behavior comes to be looked upon by the children as a feminine trait. This occurs because the mother, in her attempt to instill morality in her children, comes to symbolize "what is good behavior," what is in "conformity with the expectations of the respectable adult world" (1947 : 172). As the boys grow older, this developmental sequence causes difficulties.

Unlike girls who find a feminine identity consistent with societal role expectations, boys realize during the latency period that "it would be shameful for them to grow up to be like a woman" (1947 : 171, cf. 1954a). To alleviate the strain of having an inappropriate sex identification, the boys are compelled to reject their feminine leanings by compulsively asserting their masculinity. In the process of changing identities, the boys reject the feminine trait of "good" behavior, which has been associated with their former role-model, the mother. Hence, "when he revolts against identification with his mother in the name of masculinity, it is not surprising that a boy unconsciously identifies 'goodness' with femininity and that being a 'bad boy' becomes a positive goal" (1947 : 172). The final consequence of the socialization-identification process is that "there is a strong tendency for boyish behavior to run in antisocial if not directly destructive directions" (1947 : 172, cf. 1954b : 345).[8]

Parsons thus located the source of aggressive behavior among juvenile boys in the stress generated by intrafamilial conflict. He also recognized, however, that this "master" stress could give rise to other forms of aggression as well. Not only could this stress elicit direct aggressive outbursts such as those evidenced by juveniles; the aggressive impulses could also be repressed and then expressed later in life in more indirect ways—such as through out-group hostility. Parsons therefore saw the need to specify the nonstress factors that structure whether a direct or indirect aggressive response would result.

Parsons's "masculine-feminine identification theory" has received a good deal of attention, particularly as a theory of juvenile delinquency. What is often misunderstood, however, is that these ideas on the origin of youthful misbehavior represent only a segment of Parsons's explication of the etiology of different forms of aggressive behavior among all age categories in Western societies. In other words, the thesis presented in the 1947 essay was that the strain arising out of intrafamilial identification problems is a master stress that can be adapted to in various ways, of which delinquency is only one. Parsons's comments on the indeterminate relationship between deviant outcomes and general aggressive predispositions produced by stressful conditions have thus been largely overlooked. Consider, for example, the following excerpt from Parsons's essay:

> If it were possible to arrive at a statistically reliable estimate of the average strength of aggressive tendencies in the population of a nation, it would by itself be worthless as a basis of predicting the probability of that nation embarking on an aggressive war. The specific goals and objects to which these aggressive dispositions are attached, the ways in which they are repressed, deflected, projected, or can be directly expressed according to the forces which channel or oppose them and the structure of situations into which they come— *all these are equally important with any aggressive potential in determining*

concrete behavioral outcomes. . . . The present analysis therefore will be largely concerned with *the social structuring of aggression in Western society*, rather taking for granted that there is an adequate reservoir to motivate the familiar types of aggressive behavior. [1947 : 167, emphasis mine]

Parsons's theory thus is too often interpreted in a deterministic way. Stress is seen to cause only juvenile delinquency, and Parsons's ideas are evaluated according to whether his propositions on the origin of such stress can be substantiated (Cohen 1955, England 1960). In short, Parsons's work has typically been reduced to a theory of a single form of deviance—juvenile delinquency—and, in the process, his ideas on the structuring of deviant behavior have been obfuscated.

As noted above, Parsons maintained that the stress generated by intra-familial identification problems does not lead in every case to aggressive juvenile acts. Indeed, Parsons indicated that most youths do not engage in "antisocial" or "destructive" behavior, or do not engage in such activity for long. Instead, "the bulk of aggression generated . . . in the process of growing to adulthood . . . must in the nature of the case remain repressed" (1947 : 173). This occurs primarily because the force of moral norms precludes youths from directly expressing aggressive impulses. Moreover, the youths' eventual entrance into the occupational structure, despite exposing them to strains that further fuel aggressive predispositions, at the same time fosters the repression of impulses. For it is here that the workers in the competitive and often unfair struggle of economic life are subjected both "to a severe discipline" and to a strict normative code demanding that they take their "misfortunes and disappointments with outward equanimity" (1947 : 176). Thus, childhood and adult life-experiences have two opposite effects: they give rise to strains which eventuate in aggressive tendencies, yet they also serve to repress the direct expression of the very tendencies they produce. According to Parsons, these repressed tendencies are significant because they constitute a "large reservoir" of "free floating" aggressive impulses (1947 : 173–74). And, while "few direct outlets are provided for most types of aggressive impulses," opportunities do exist for the indirect expression of these impulses (1947 : 176). Most commonly, Parsons maintained, they obtain release through out-group hostility.

Following this line of reasoning, Parsons maintained that social circumstances "operate to structure the direction" of how these hidden aggressive tendencies are expressed (1947 : 178–79). To illustrate, he proposed that Nazism was perhaps the clearest empirical manifestation of the group expression of repressed hostile impulses (1954c, d, cf. 1971 : 130). According to Parsons, the process of Weberian scientific "rationalization" in Germany severely challenged traditional, conservative values. This set the stage for "a 'fundamentalist' revolt against the whole tendency of rationalization in the Western

world, and at the same time against its deepest institutionalized founda-
tions" in German society (1954c : 123, cf. Gusfield 1967). Integral to the
occurrence of such a revolt was the presence of a strong sense of rationalism,
which was "bound up with conservative tendencies" and "could be mobi-
lized . . . against all forms of radicalism" (1954c : 122–23, 1954d : 138–39).
Equally telling was the existence of "deep-seated romantic tendencies"
(1954c : 123) that fostered the expression of aggression by reinforcing mili-
tarism in general and the "heroic ideal of the fighting man" in particular
(1954c : 122).

In sum, Parsons manifested a general understanding that stress does not
regulate the content that a deviant adaptation assumes. He observed that such
factors as normative standards, participation in the occupational structure,
rationalization, nationalism, and romanticism determine whether a predisposition to aggression will be expressed in direct (antisocial destructive behavior) or indirect (out-group conflict) ways. In his paradigm on the origin
of all deviant behavior, Parsons applied this insight on a broader level: not
only is aggression socially structured, but so also are all other forms of deviant
behavior.

PARSONS'S GENERAL THEORY OF DEVIANCE

Parsons is typically categorized as a stress or "strain" theorist (Hirschi
1969 : 3, n. 1; cf. Cohen 1959 : 466 and Clinard 1964 : 23), an accurate but
perhaps incomplete appraisal. To be sure, the idea that strain leads to deviance
is central in his work on aggression. Moreover, in his attempt to develop a
comprehensive theory of deviance in *The Social System*, Parsons devoted
much attention to the sources of the master stresses that ostensibly underlie
all forms of deviance (1951 : 249–325). It is not often noted, however, that
Parsons's analysis in *The Social System* is not confined to the strains which
engender deviance. As a "structuring theorist" and not simply a strain theorist, Parsons did much more: he also addressed the question of why people
deviate in certain ways.

In *The Social System*, Parsons argued that the overriding cause of the
"motivation to deviance" was the strain produced when a disequilibrated
system does not permit its members to satisfactorily fulfill role expectations.
At the outset of his chapter on deviance, Parsons maintained that an actor
will experience strain when a role partner contravenes the obligations inherent
in their role relationship (1951 : 252). Using the ego-alter dyad as his focal
point, and assuming that mutual role expectations have developed, he
(1951 : 252) proposed that strain will arise when, "from whatever source, a
disturbance is introduced into the system, of such a character that what alter
does leads to a frustration, in some important respects, of ego's expectation-
system vis-a-vis alter."

Later in his analysis, Parsons turned his attention away from the strain or stress created by alter's failure to meet role obligations, instead focusing on ego's difficulty in living up to or managing his/her own role expectations. Here, Parsons detailed three situations likely to engender deviance-producing strain (Smelser and Warner 1976 : 191). First, he noted that the emergence of pressure is "a function of the kind of pattern with which he is expected to conform" (1951 : 267). That is, strain or pressure is forthcoming when an actor cannot live up to given normative expectations, particularly those demands which are at odds with the actor's need dispositions. Thus, in American society, strain is often induced because roles commonly require "an exceptionally high level of affectively neutral and universalistic orientations," both of which are inconsistent with the more emotional and particularistic inclinations people wish to exhibit (1951 : 268).

Second, Parsons observed that "normative patterns" in complex societies are usually quite "generalized" or "abstract" (1951 : 269). Applying such standards in any particular situation is no simple task. As a result, an "actor faces the problem not only of living up to the expectations of his role . . . but of knowing just what is expected of him" (1951 : 269). Such "role ambiguity" (Smelser and Warner 1976 : 191) can at times lessen conflict and contribute to the system's stability by functioning as a "safetly valve" which provides "an element of extra 'permissiveness' or license for behavior which on other occasions would not be tolerated" (1951 : 270). Yet the very "indefiniteness of expectations" created by role ambiguity can also foster anxiety and hence deepen the "motivation to deviance" (1951 : 170).

Third, Parsons proposed that the "conflict of rules" or "role conflict" is also involved in the genesis of strain. This occurs in two ways. Paralleling the phenomenon of role ambiguity, the generalized nature of expectations often creates a situation in which it would appear that two conflicting norms are "intrinsically applicable" (1951 : 272). The actor therefore lacks a "clear definition of what the expectations are" and of which expectations, if any, should take precedence. Such uncertainty in turn may result in strain. On the other hand, actors also confront situations in which role expectations are explicit yet at the same time incompatible to the extent that "complete fulfillment of both is realistically impossible" (1951 : 280). Not surprisingly, a person's exposure to this type of role conflict is "an obvious source of strain and frustration in that it creates a situation incompatible with a harmonious integration of personality with the interaction system" (1951 : 282).

Significantly, Parsons did not end his analysis once he had discussed the sources of stress or strain. Parsons apparently was aware that delineating the source of strain does not adequately account for the nature of the deviant response made to such strain; that is, he realized that explaining the "direction" (1951 : 257) or "structuring" (1951 : 288) of deviant behavior is a distinct and an important theoretical question. He thus attempted to address the question of the way in which deviant behavior is structured. To begin with, Parsons sought to specify the determinants of the "direction of deviant tendencies" (1951 : 256–67). His basic proposition was that the direction is structured by three, dual-faceted dimensions of the personality. The first parameter, "conformative and alienative dominance," requires a brief discussion. As stated earlier, Parsons postulated that ego will experience strain when alter violates role expectations. Under strain, ego can no longer positively cathect to either alter or the institutionalized expectations alter has transgressed. But past attachments to and gratifications derived from interacting with alter makes a complete rejection difficult. As a result, ego's usual response is one of ambivalence. Typically, however, one side of the ambivalence within the personality structure is "dominant." The "dominance" is "conformative" when ego continues to positively cathect to alter and, more significantly, continues to conform to the role expectations alter violated. Conversely, "alienative dominance" obtains when ego's primary inclination is to reject alter as well as "the established system of expectations" (1951 : 253–57).

"Activity-passivity" is a second dimension that structures deviant tendencies. For Parsons, actors with an "active" orientation "take a larger degree of control over the interaction process than role expectations call for," while those who are passive assume "less initiative and let alter control the situation and himself, to a larger degree than role-expectations call for" (1951 : 257, n. 3). In their extreme forms, activity manifests a "compulsive performance orientation," passivity a "compulsive acquiescence in status expectations" (1951 : 257).[9] A final parameter distinguished by Parsons is the aspect of the interaction on which an actor "focuses." An actor's major focus may be on a "social object" (i.e., alter) or on "norms" (i.e., "the normative pattern which integrates the interaction" of ego and alter) (1951 : 258).[10]

By cross-tabulating the dimensions of conformative/alienative dominance, activity/passivity, and focus on social objects/norms, Parsons arrived at eight "definitions of the direction of deviant tendencies."[11] These have been aptly summarized and illustrated by Smelser and Warner:

> (1) The compulsively active conformist with an emphasis on social objects is the "bossy" character who pushes others around. (2) The compulsively active conformist with an emphasis on norms is the rigid enforcer of rules, the taskmaster, who goes by the book. (3) The compulsively passive conformist who focuses on social objects is the meek type who puts himself in the position of continuously submitting to others. (4) The compulsively passive conformist who focuses on norms also lives by the book, but instead of demanding exacting performance from others, falls into the role of the functionary who lives by the letter of the rules. (5) The compulsively active alienated person who focuses on social objects moves through the world with a chip on his shouler, always trying to pick a fight whatever the cause. (6) The compulsively active alienated

person who focuses on norms is the individual who breaks rules for the sake of breaking rules, perhaps a "rebel without a cause." For this person, the very presence of a rule excites the impulse to flaunt it. (7) The compulsively passive alienated person who focuses on social objects becomes independent: he distrusts others, but he prefers to go his own way rather than pick a fight. (8) And finally, the compulsively passive alienated person who focuses on norms does not flaunt the rules but breaks them through various strategies of evasion. [1976 : 194]

In addition to commenting on the issue of the "direction" or form deviance takes through his typology of deviant tendencies, Parsons endeavored to address this problem in a second and more concrete fashion. As Smelser and Warner have noted, Parsons's typology was an attempt to differentiate "analytically 'pure' tendencies" toward deviant behavior (1976 : 195). Later, however, Parsons went on to examine how the variables he specified actually structure deviant behavior in the "real world," or in Parsons's words, to examine "the principal ways in which the factors in deviant behavior which have been reviewed tend to 'structure out' in types of concrete pattern forms in the social system" (1951 : 283). Towards this end, Parsons set forth several empirical propositions. For example, he observed that the "actively oriented person is predisposed toward individualized crime," while "the passively oriented anti-conformist may be predisposed to such a pattern as 'hoboism' " (1951 : 284). In a like manner, he suggested that an alienative orientation, if focused on norms, elicits "crime against 'law and order' or objects that symbolize normative rules" (1951 : 288).

THE LIMITS OF PARSONS'S STRUCTURING ANALYSIS

Structuring ideas thus reach the core of Parsons's major statements on deviant behavior. At the same time, the concept of structuring variables is not always applied in a consistent fashion throughout his writings. Consequently, though Parsons addressed the question of the way in which deviant outcomes are structured at many junctions in his writings, in other places his theorizing is marked by the deterministic assumption that stress leads ineluctably to one form of deviance.

One example of such straightforwardly deterministic thinking is evident in Parsons's assertion that insecurity manifests itself in "the form of neurotic behavior" (1954a : 98). Of course, it is necessary to ask why neurotic behavior and not another mode of deviance transpires. Indeed, it is somewhat ironic yet theoretically important that in another essay Parsons hypothesized that insecurity fosters an alternative deviant form, aggression (1947). Similarly, Parsons maintained that the strain engendered by " 'mother fixation' is involved in all types of neurotic and psychic disorders of Western men" (1947 : 170). This observation notwithstanding, Parsons did not pursue the question of when one or another "psychological disorder" results, or, for that matter, when an antisocial, aggressive adaptation—a response Parsons also linked to "mother fixation"—emerges.

Perhaps the clearest instance of Parsons's deterministic theorizing is his analysis of student protest, a form of behavior Parsons considered deviant.[12] Along with his collaborator Gerald Platt, Parsons located the cause and character of student protest in the stresses engendered by the socialization experiences that students endure. For Parsons, the college years are turbulent times. Not only are youths subject to the strains arising from "the real tensions in the wider society" and from "displaced personal problems," but, more significantly, they must also confront the intense "affective frustration resulting from college socialization" (with Platt, 1973 : 218). Specifically, as Smelser has observed, Parsons argued that the purpose of college socialization is to give students "a more differentiated personality" which permits the youths "to cope more effectively with the complexities of role demands and social involvements that adult life brings" (1973 : 410).

This goal is not easily attained, however. Higher educational institutions often are not adequately equipped to be effective socializers. More importantly, the process of differentiation runs counter to the "loyalty values" of youth culture, which "stress an undifferentiated and egalitarian peer-group organization" (with Platt, 1973 : 219). Socialization thus engenders much strain. As Parsons and Platt noted, students seek to reduce this strain by asserting an

> undifferentiated value-orientation linking value-commitments to affective components at an equivalent level of differentiatedness and to further connect these to an ideological cause, such as justice or self-liberation. Linking value-commitments to affective components implies a dedifferentiation of cognitive, affective, and moral orientations as well as the social and cultural systems involved. The manifestations of dedifferentiation are moral absolutism and diffuse solidarity which exludes all others from belonging to the significant "we"—thus negating pluralism—and cognitively fosters what Erikson calls "totalistic logic." [1973 : 219]

On a concrete level, "dedifferentiation" is manifested both in the students' casting of university faculty and administrators (who, ironically, hold values quite similar to those of the students) in an adversary position and in the students' inability to attend to the complexities or "gray areas" surrounding most social issues. Consequently, student protest is marked, as Smelser has summarized Parsons's thoughts, by "the condemnation of university faculty and administration for complicity in the sins of society; the charge that the academic community is competitive and divisive; the charge that students are powerless and that the system is undemocratic; and the charge that the system is repressive in various ways" (1973 : 410).[13]

In short, Parsons set forth the thesis that student protest is a direct response to the strains, particularly those emanating from college socialization, that youths endure. The difficulty with this assertion, however, should not be overlooked. The strains arising from the competing role pressures which Parsons (and Platt) describe are constant; if the analysis is correct, such strains continually affect university students. But political protest by students is rare. In other words, a constant source of strain is being employed to explain a rare and episodic mode of deviance. Further, it has been far more typical of students to respond to such pressures by dropping out of school, by using drugs and alcohol, or even by committing suicide. Nothing in the analysis offered explains why these more typical adaptations were precipitously superseded or supplemented by the extraordinary collective protests which swept the campuses in the 1960s. On a more general level, by assuming a one-to-one deterministic relationship between stress and protest, Parsons neglected the question of why students experiencing strain will pursue certain adaptations and not others and how the structuring of such adaptations might vary across different historical eras.[14]

Deterministic thinking about stress and deviance is thus far from absent in Parsons's writings. Nevertheless, it is still the case that Parsons addressed the question of the way people deviate more often and more systematically than Merton and many other deviance theorists. It is equally clear, however, that Parsons's insights on the structuring of deviance have not always gained the notice of theorists in the field; the same can be said of Merton's thoughts in this direction. Instead, students of Parsons and Merton have often focused exclusively on those portions of their paradigms that illuminate the origins of a master stress. As a consequence, these analysts tend to proceed on the assumption that stress leads directly to particular deviant outcomes, and thus their work often fails to account for the way in which deviant behavior is socially structured.

Notes

1. Merton has presented several revisions of "Social Structure and Anomie" (1948a, b; [1957] 1968b) as well as three works that extended his deviance paradigm (1955, [1957] 1968c, 1964). For the most part, the 1968b reprint of Merton's 1957 version of "Social Structure and Anomie" will be cited in the discussion that follows. Similarly, I will cite the 1968c reprint of Merton's 1957 version of "Continuities in the Theory of Social Structure and Anomie."

2. While the two theorists converge on the means-goal disjunction idea, it is difficult to discern whether Merton consciously borrowed the idea from Durkheim. Merton did not reference Durkheim in this regard. Further, as Rothman's work indicates, the means-goal gap/deviance notion has a long tradition in America (1971 : 115). It is also possible that Merton may have drawn this formulation from Parsons's scheme of action (1937).

3. As will be seen later in this review, Merton did consider the causal relationship between anomie and deviant behavior. The causal impact attributed to anomie in his paradigm, however, is subsidiary to that attributed to suffering a means-goal disjunction and the pressure it generates.

4. In response to a critique leveled by Albert Cohen, Merton admitted that his theory ''does not purport to account for all forms of deviant behavior'' (1968c : 231). Yet, while accepting this limitation, Merton did so only grudgingly. Once he admitted that Cohen was correct in suggesting that his theory was not all-inclusive, Merton then refuted Cohen's claim that his theory could not account for irrational or non-utilitarian modes of deviance. Further, Merton made no attempt to delineate those forms of deviant behavior that his theory could not explain. Equally significant, Merton did not delineate any forms of deviant behavior that he believed could not be covered by or fit into his typology of adaptations. In sum, despite his disclaimer, the major thrust of Merton's work was to construct a general theory of deviance, including a typology that was logically exhaustive (i.e., that would cover all forms of deviance). At the very least, this was true of all of his versions of ''Social Structure and Anomie.''

5. Some of the blame for the misuse of the term anomie by scholars must be shouldered by Merton who was not always consistent in his own usage of the concept. (Compare 1964 : 218 with 1964 : 226.) Nevertheless, the distinct way in which Merton links the factor of anomie (as opposed to that of stress) to deviance can be discerned through a careful reading of his work.

6. Smelser and Warner's analysis of Merton's stress theory leaves the impression that Merton dealt rather extensively with the question of why people deviate in a certain way (Smelser and Warner 1976 : 182). Merton's own admission that he had addressed this question in only a restricted fashion undercuts their argument, however. Further, other authors have concurred ''that although Merton has a good deal to say on the sources of strain and on the variety of possible responses, he has relatively little to say about the determinants of this or that response'' (Cohen 1966 : 108; cf. Cloward 1959, Cloward and Ohlin 1960, and Lindesmith and Gagnon 1964). On the other extreme, Thio has asserted that Merton's ''theory is plainly meant to explain the causation of one type of deviance only . . . 'innovation' '' (1975 : 140). Again, Merton's own remarks contradict this contention. In his 1959 comment on Cloward, Merton admitted the importance of explaining when a particular kind of adaptation—and not just innovation—will occur and maintained that his earlier work had made a ''bare beginning'' in this direction. Finally, though Merton did neglect to systematically analyze the structuring of adaptations, he did nevertheless present a strong proposition regarding overall rates of deviance: they were hypothesized to be higher among the lower class.

7. Parsons offered two definitions of deviant behavior. From the perspective of the individual actor, he proposed that deviance is the ''motivated tendency for an actor to behave in contravention of one or more institutionalized normative patterns.'' The idea that violation of a norm constitutes deviance is, of course, the definition of deviance that sociologists have employed with greatest frequency. In addition, Parsons held that, from the perspective of the system, deviance could best be conceived of as the ''tendency on the part of one or more of the component actors to behave in such a way as to disturb the equilibrium of the interactive process'' (1951 : 250). Parsons, as well as Smelser and Warner (1976 : 187), have suggested that these two definitions are consistent with one another. This would not appear to be the case, however. As analysts of the ''functions'' of deviance have made evident, behavior that contravenes institutionalized normative patterns can, at times, contribute to rather than disturb a system's equilibrium (cf. Dentler and Erikson 1959; Coser 1962, 1966; Matza 1969 : 53–62). Utilizing Parsons's definitions, it is quite unclear how such behavior should be classified; since it transgresses norms, it is ''deviant,'' but, since it sustains equilibrium, it is not deviant. Of course, the same difficulty in classification is encountered when the converse situation occurs, that is, when behavior conforms to institutionalized expectations yet at the same time, perhaps through an unanticipated consequence, upsets the system's equilibrium.

8. The influence of Freud on Parsons is manifest here: youths have special difficulties negotiating the oedipal stage and often adapt by means of a reaction formation. Throughout his writings on the origins of deviance, Parsons largely embraced a Freudian interpretation of personality. At the same time, it must be emphasized that he constantly sought to place personality development within a broader structural context. Thus, with regard to the etiology of aggressive impulses, the novelty of Parsons's theory is that it reveals how transformations of the social structure of Western societies fundamentally alter family socialization experiences and hence exacerbate the difficulties youths have in resolving the stages of personality development.

9. Parsons maintained that, by cross-tabulating the dimensions of dominance and activity/

passivity, it is possible to construct a typology of deviant adaptations that converges with that of Merton's 1938 model (1951 : 257–58). The matched pairs yielded, with Merton's adaptations stated first, are: innovation and activity/conformative dominance; ritualism and passivity/ conformative dominance; rebellion and activity/alienative dominance; retreatism and passivity/ alienative dominance. Parsons also contended that the generality of his concepts, as well as the further differentiation of his scheme into eight types, allowed his paradigm to subsume that of Merton (1951 : 258).

10. Though he did not state it explicitly in *The Social System*, Parsons (with Bales et al. 1955 : 145–46) later proposed that each of these personality dimensions emerged, at least at its "deepest level," during distinct stages of personality development. Thus, he held that conformity/ alienation arises during the oral stage, activity/passivity during the anal stage, and a focus on social objects/norms during the oedipal stage.

11. It is not totally clear whether Parsons's typology of deviant "tendencies" was meant to be a classification of different forms of deviant behavior or of different types of deviant motivation. While Parsons does in fact at times utilize the terms "tendency" and "motivation" interchangeably in the section in which he formulated his typology, the fact that Parsons believed his scheme to subsume Merton's behavioral typology of adaptations as well as the very substance of Parsons's analysis (see especially 1951 : 259–60) indicate that his interest was in delineating a classification of behavior. Smelser and Warner would appear to concur with this interpretation.

12. It would appear that Parsons believed most social movements to be, at least to a substantial degree, deviant or pathological. Thus, he wrote that

> it is, conversely, clear that the psychology of most movements which tend to a drastic break with this same institutional heritage, especially perhaps those of the fascist type, is one which exploits precisely the opposite elements of character structure, those most closely bound up with "neurotic" types of reaction patterns, ideological distortion and affective overreaction. [1954e : 173]

Supportive of my appraisal of Parsons, Lopreato suggested that

> Parsons now is preoccupied beyond justification with the normative and integrative aspects of the widest spectrum of institutions. In the process, he paints a picture in which the discontented, the deviates, the rebellious have no role except a pathologically devisive one. [1971 : 321]

Coser apparently also reached a similar conclusion:

> Focusing on normative structures, which maintain and guarantee social order, Parsons was led to view conflict as having primarily disruptive, dissociating and dysfunctional consequences. Parsons considers conflict primarily a "disease." He feels with Shakespeare that "when degree is shaked . . . the enterprise is sicked." [1956 : 21]

13. The ideas that ineffective socialization can result in an inappropriate level of cognitive or affective "differentiation," and that inadequate differentiation can foster an "oversimplification of the 'definition of the situation' " are not recent additions to Parsons's theorizing (cf. Parsons and Bales et al. 1955 : 180–81, 183).

14. For a fairly recent example of Parsons's work that contains both structuring ideas and deterministic theorizing, see Parsons and Gerstein (1977).

chapter 6

The Chicago School of Criminology: Thrasher, Shaw and McKay, and Sutherland

Although stress theorizing has achieved considerable popularity, not all observers have located the origin of deviant behavior in stressful social conditions. At times, nonstress theorists have argued that due to their upbringing or some other social experience, people are not sufficiently tied to the conventional world that they need endure special or unusual strains in order to violate society's standards. Similarly, on other occasions, these theorists have asserted that pressures toward deviance are so pervasive in everyday life that simply explaining their presence does not allow us to distinguish conformists from nonconformists. Other conditions, such as the weakening of social bonds or the strength of a person's self-concept, are seen to determine who in the society is unable to resist these deviant impulses and thus likely to transgress prevailing moral boundaries.

The most dominant nonstress theoretical tradition has long been the Chicago School of criminology. While those within this approach differ in many respects, they all substantially embrace the proposition that illegal behavior results from a person's contact with and socialization into values of a criminal nature. In this regard, early members of the Chicago School, such as Thrasher and Shaw and McKay, were especially interested in exploring the relationship between slum life and lawlessness among juveniles. Writing in a period of growing concern over the consequences of urbanization, they began with the notion that slum areas are marked by "social disorganization" or a breakdown of conventional institutions and social controls. Such a weakening of conventional controls frees people to engage in behaviors disapproved of by the dominant social order and eventually sets the stage for the emergence of cultural values encouraging criminal involvement. Moreover, once criminal values come into existence, they constitute a "tradition" or "subculture" that is passed down from generation to generation and from population group to population group in the same neighborhood. Given the dilution of controls and the existence of this tradition, slum youths are bound to be socialized to possess a criminal orientation just as they might otherwise have been socialized to hold a conformist orientation in neighborhoods exhibiting stronger conventional institutions.

In this light, Kornhauser has commented that the early Chicago School theorists, most notably Shaw and McKay, "were responsible for the first efforts to combine social disorganization and cultural deviance theories in a model of delinquent subculture" (1978 : 21). Kornhauser has thus characterized Shaw and McKay's theory as a "mixed model" because "they vacillated between developing a pure control (social disorganization) model and incorporating elements of a cultural deviance model into their theory, eventually joining the two" (1978 : 27). She has further described its components in the following fashion:

> Initially a dependent variable fully explained by social disorganization, the delinquent subculture is transformed into a partially autonomous cause of delinquency by virtue of its stability over time, its regulation of an alternative structure of status and opportunity, the numbers of its constituents, and the strength of their commitment to delinquent subcultural values. As an independent variable, it explains additional variance in delinquency, over and above whatever aspects of social disorganization contribute to its origin and persistence. The delinquent structure and culture also feed back into and become components of social disorganization. [1978 : 26]

The image of the criminal portrayed by the early Chicago School theorists is thus decidedly different than the image set forth in the stress literature. Criminals are not pictured as individuals driven to violate the law—indeed, to violate standards they may strongly endorse—by unbearable pressures. Instead, criminal involvement, in a context of a breakdown of controls due to conditions of social disorganization, is a natural, nonstressful expression of values encouraging such behavior, just as church-going or playing baseball is an expression of values encouraging these activities.

This is not to say that notions of stress did not find their way into the writings of theorists like Thrasher and Shaw and McKay. As close observers of urban slum life, they were well aware of the deplorable conditions and concomitant life-stresses that slum residents endure. Nevertheless, they did not consider stressful social conditions to be a major source of criminal motivation. If anything, the criminogenic effects of such conditions were indirect: they help give rise to the criminal cultural values which, once in existence, are transmitted and generate the motivation to commit crime. In this regard, both Thrasher and Shaw and McKay touched upon the idea that the origin of criminal traditions can be traced to the inability of slum residents to participate in and have their needs met by conventional institutions.

It remained for Sutherland to formalize and generalize the insights of the early members of the Chicago School. Similar to his predecessors, Sutherland did not introduce the concept of stress to account for criminal motivation. Yet it might be added that he did not embrace as fully as Thrasher or Shaw and McKay the notion that social disorganization and an accompanying attenuation of social controls were major causal factors of crime and delinquency. Instead, he concentrated his efforts on the development of a set of nine propositions that clarified the principle that the etiology of criminal motivation rests in a person's association with an excess of criminal as opposed to conventional values or "definitions." He called this the "principle of differential association." As Kornhauser has noted, Sutherland thus "elaborated the first pure cultural deviance model" (1978 : 21). Sutherland also rejected the notion implicit in his predecessors' writings that only the crime of slum residents results from contact with criminal values. For one thing, criminal traditions exist elsewhere in society, such as in the business world. For another, regardless of their social location, those who encounter an excess of definitions favoring violation of the law are likely to manifest criminal behavior. Sutherland held, then, that the principle of differential association applies to all; the principle was also seen to explain all criminality.

Thus, it is clear that the Chicago School differs markedly from stress theory in its explanation of crime. Less apparent but of greater significance, however, is the fact that theorists of the Chicago and stress paradigms have often been concerned with the *same* question: what motivates people to engage in the single deviant form of crime? Moreover, while the substance of their response to this question varies, the logic of the answers offered by those within these competing paradigms is identical: a specific social condition—whether it is frustrated ambitions or exposure to criminal values—is held to determine or cause criminal involvement.

Given this deterministic approach, one might expect that members of the Chicago School did not explore why actors engage in one form of crime and not another or, more generally, why crime is chosen and not some alternative deviant path. However, such an expectation would be less than accurate. To be sure, no theorist within the Chicago School saw the structuring of deviant behavior as a problem deserving systematic attention. Yet despite this apparent oversight, much of their writing, especially the life-histories of criminals and delinquents they compiled, is permeated with structuring ideas. Indeed, much of their writing vividly illustrates that people not only acquire the predisposition to deviate by exposure to a criminal tradition, but also become particular kinds of criminals through their association with others who are already engaged in specific criminal patterns.

Let us now consider the contributions of Thrasher, Shaw and McKay, and Sutherland in greater detail, with special emphasis on the way various portions of their work highlight the very idea which they did not always fully comprehend, namely, that deviant behavior is socially structured.

Thrasher on Crime and Deliquency

THRASHER'S THEORY

In 1927, Frederic Thrasher published his seminal book *The Gang*, a volume that anticipated many of the themes which informed research on juvenile delinquency over the next half-century. Like others in the Chicago theoretical tradition, Thrasher started by portraying the America of his day as experiencing a vast transformation wrought by the social forces of immigration, urbanization, rationalization, mobility, and industrialization. This transformation had its bright side in the "prosperity and progress" it engendered (Thrasher [1927] 1963 : 338). But it had its darker side as well. While most sectors of society could "progressively reorganize" in the face of a changing social world, some could not. Particularly burdened was the city, itself an evolving and burgeoning social phenomenon, for not all parts of the urban area were blessed with adaptive capabilities. Indeed, the crisis precipitated by massive social change was felt most deeply in the "zone of transition," a circular belt that surrounded the core of the city (i.e., the "central business district"). Thrasher held that the zone of transition was plagued by "social disorganization." Moreover, he believed the gang to be a product or "symptom" of disorganization and thus to be especially prominent in this area (pp. 337–38).

In Thrasher's view, institutional breakdown constitutes the essence of social disorganization. In turn, by institutional breakdown, Thrasher implied the onset of two conditions. First, social institutions become so weakened that actors are no longer structurally or normatively integrated into the conventional social fabric. As a result, institutions lack the power to regulate or control behavior.[1] Second, the conventional institutions are no longer able to satisfy the needs or "wishes" of the populace. Thrasher held that institutional breakdown in general and these two conditions in particular set a favorable context for the emergence of the gang and delinquent activity.

To be more specific, Thrasher believed that the origin of the gang can be traced to the "play group." These play groups develop in a spontaneous and natural fashion out of the everyday life experiences of youths. Even though play groups are more prevalent in slum neighborhoods, they are present in all communities. However, the play groups in organized and disorganized (slum) areas differ qualitatively. In organized settings, institutions are sufficiently strong to direct and supervise the youths' activities and thus to insure that the play groups remain "innocent and wholesome" (p. 29). By contrast, institutions in disorganized areas possess little regulatory power. Institutions are particularly weak in controlling the behavior of the most frequent participants in play groups, adolescents. For it is at adolescence that slum youths escape the control inherent in the dependent nature of childhood. As such, adolescent play groups are not constrained to engage exclusively in "wholesome" endeavors. Instead, they are free to pursue unconventional activities, ranging from bad personal habits (e.g., smoking) to crime.

According to Thrasher, social disorganization involves not only an increasing impotence of controls but also an inability of conventional institutions to satisfy an actor's needs. This is particularly true with respect to slum youths. As offspring of immigrants, they encounter an array of customs and experiences unfamiliar to their families, and hence they possess "needs of which their parents never heard" (p. 179). Moreover, compensatory measures from the established social order (e.g., the school) are not forthcoming. Rather, between the slum youths "and the conventional American community exists this barrier of unsympathetic social blindness" (p. 180).

In an effort to satiate unfulfilled needs, the slum youths form or join a "nonconformist" play group which eventually evolves into a gang. The absence of institutional control frees juveniles from the social order and creates the possibility of a deviant response. The actual motivation to evolve and participate in the nonconforming play group (gang), however, is supplied by a different factor: the lure of unconventional as opposed to conventional behavior. Simply put, conforming behavior neither fulfills wishes nor promises to be much fun. In contrast, an unconventional play group offers "the thrill and zest of participation in common interests, more especially corporate action, in hunting, capture, conflict, flight, and escape" (pp. 32–33). Such a lifestyle is so exciting that "it would be a marvel indeed if any healthy [regulated] boy could hold himself aloof from it" (p. 23; cf. p. 266).[2] In sum, the unconventional play group (gang) can perhaps best be conceived of as an attractive functional alternative to conventional activity. As Thrasher observed, "gangs represent the spontaneous effort of boys to create a society for themselves where none adequate to their needs exists" by offering "a substitute for what society fails to give" (pp. 32–33).

It is interesting that Thrasher distinguished between the slum play groups and gangs. For him, play groups are "gangs in embryo" (p. 23). The primary distinguishing feature of gangs is their degree of organizational development. Unlike the loosely arranged play groups, gangs are marked by "tradition, unreflective internal structure, esprit de corps, solidarity, morale, group awareness, and attachment to local territory" (p. 48).[3] As the phrase "gangs in embryo" suggests, Thrasher believed that there was a continuity between play groups and gangs. The conditions which give rise to unconventional play groups in disorganized areas—a breakdown of controls and the inability of institutions to fulfill needs—are integrally involved in nurturing the evolution of these play groups into gangs (they also contribute to the persistence of the gang once in existence). The emergence of a gang, however, depends upon one other crucial factor: conflict. Anticipating Coser's idea of the "functions of conflict" (1956), Thrasher maintained that conflict facilitates the development of a gang by promoting a group consciousness (p. 26). Two types of conflict were singled out as particularly important. First, converging with the labeling theory stance that social control can increase deviance, Thrasher held that "opposition on the part of the conventional social order" to the play groups could help create gangs (p. 23, cf. Tannenbaum 1938). And, second, he predicted a similar outcome as a result of the conflict of a group "with groups of its own class" over the control of turf within a neighborhood (p. 23).

From his observation of "1,313 gangs in Chicago," Thrasher surmised that not all gangs are alike. In a very real sense a forerunner of later research on the different kinds of delinquent subcultures (cf. Cohen and Short 1966 : 115–19), Thrasher argued that it is possible to categorize gangs using the state of their organizational development as his primary criterion. Thrasher was able to distinguish such "types of gangs" as diffuse, solidified, conventionalized, criminal, and secret society.

In conclusion, Thrasher proposed that gangs are a by-product of the social disorganization engendered by vast societal transformation. In disorganized communities, conventional institutions are so ineffective that they lack the capacity to regulate behavior or meet personal needs. The absence of controls sets the slum youth in "drift," permitting the youth to pursue either conforming or deviant behavior. Since conventional institutions are unable to fulfill their wishes, the spontaneous play groups that youths form and/or join to satisfy their needs take an unconventional path. The most attractive aspect of this functional alternative is that it provides a setting for ready excitement and fun. While institutional breakdown nurtures the evolution of the unconventional play groups into a gang, the play group does not become a gang until it develops a group consciousness. This occurs when the play group experiences social conflict—either with agents of conventional society attempting to suppress their deviant activity or with other groups with whom they are competing for scarce resources. Once in existence, the gang is an important factor in fostering crime. As an organized setting for instruction in crime, it contributes to the criminal involvement of its members. Moreover, the gang's criminal tradition may lead contemporary or future slum youth to select a deviant lifestyle.

THRASHER AND THE STRUCTURING OF DEVIANT BEHAVIOR

While Thrasher never explicitly stated the concept of structuring variables, observations of the way in which deliquent involvement is socially patterned are scattered throughout *The Gang.* One place where such notions entered Thrasher's work was in his discussion of "types of gangs." Here, he argued that it is possible to categorize gangs according to their stage of organizational development. But similar to many theorists who create typologies of deviant behavior (cf. Merton 1938, Dubin 1959, Simon and Gagnon 1976), Thrasher had little to say about the conditions leading to one or another sub-type in his classificatory scheme. As Short has noted, Thrasher confined his attention to cataloging and describing the varieties of delinquent gangs, thus making his comments on "the forms of collectivity which the gang may take . . . taxonomic rather than hypothetical-deductive or explanatory" (1963 : xxi). Nevertheless, by searching through Thrasher's many discussions, it is possible to find several variables which he in effect argued structure or pattern the type of gang that evolves.

In Thrasher's view, the length of time the gang has been in existence and the degree of conflict it has experienced are two variables which regulate the development of a solidified gang out of a diffuse gang (p. 50). He argued as well that a gang will become conventionalized into a conformist grouping "if it is encouraged to do so by a politician, a saloon keeper, or welfare agency" (p. 52). Conversely, the absence of such external guidance or supervision contributes to the emergence of a criminal gang (pp. 54–55).[4] Further, a "secret society" with the capacity to carry out varied "delinquent enterprises" will evolve if a criminal gang is subjected to a harsh and well-organized crusade to break it apart (p. 225).

But whatever the state of its development, the youth gang does not entirely invent the activity in which it engages. The forms of criminal behavior which emerge are controlled by various features of the slum environment. This generalization is nowhere more apparent than in Thrasher's discussion of "junking" (stealing materials and selling them to junk dealers). Thrasher observed that participation in the criminal form of junking is not possible unless three factors occur. One is the "opportunity to sell junk" (p. 110). This is usually readily available to slum youth, because there are "numerous junk dealers of whom many are anxious to buy from boys" (p. 109). Equally important is the "opportunity to procure junk" (p. 110). Railroad tracks and yards, common features of disorganized areas, provide an ideal setting for gathering junk. Indeed, their presence helps to "direct" or structure the gang's behavior: "the mere accessibility of railroad tracks indicates the importance of the technic environment in determining the direction of the gang's activities" (pp. 111–12). A final factor facilitating junking is the ability to "acquire a special technique for securing and disposing of loot without interference of the law'' (p. 113). Of further significance is Thrasher's realization that slum characteristics not only structure participation in junking but in other criminal behaviors as well. Junking is not an isolated empirical instance, but merely an illustration of ''how elements in the situation complex turn the gang's activities in a particular direction'' (p. 118).

Structuring notions are also present in Thrasher's observation that the gang, by serving as a learning environment, provides access to criminal behaviors which would not be available to the solitary juvenile delinquent. Membership in a delinquent subculture is thus seen to be an important factor that structures the forms of criminality in which a juvenile can engage. In particular, gang membership makes new kinds of crime possible by giving juveniles the opportunity to study the activity of older delinquents who function as criminal ''role-models.'' Through these associations, novices learn the ''techniques of crime'' and acquire partners who will shepherd their initial ventures into the criminal world (pp. 268–69). A range of illegal enterprises previously beyond reach are now readily within their grasp. Among other things, the criminally connected youth learns how to procure junk, how to shoplift, how to burglarize without being detected, and how and where to fence stolen merchandise (pp. 269–70).

As indicated above, Thrasher was able to describe how membership in a gang and subsequent contact with a criminal subculture structures the kind of offender a person may become. Yet, while Thrasher was aware that slum neighborhoods have an impact on the type of criminality pursued, he may not have envisaged the more general implications of these observations. For instance, he made no attempt to explore how gang membership may not only channel youths into certain types of crime but also may preclude or permit involvement in other deviant adaptations (e.g., alcohol abuse, suicide). Neither did he see the possibility that all deviant gangs and subcultures, and not simply those of a criminal variety, structure the kind of deviant path a person follows. If he had, he might have been able to broaden his perception that characteristics of slum neighborhoods pattern criminal activity (e.g., type of gang that develops). In particular, he might have investigated such issues as how these characteristics structure involvement in other forms of deviance, and how features of all (and not just slum) neighborhoods exert a structuring effect on criminal and deviant behavior.

Shaw and McKay on Crime and Delinquency

SHAW AND MCKAY'S THEORY

Thrasher's emphasis on the way in which delinquent and criminal values in particular kinds of neighborhoods are transmitted from one age level to another found even fuller expression in the work of Shaw and McKay. Their research led to the conclusion that certain neighborhoods exhibit a criminal tradition that is so clearly defined that it could be treated as a "culture" which is inherited like any other culture. Their thoughts on the structural distribution and effects of this criminogenic process have come to be known as the theory of "cultural transmission."

Similar to Thrasher and the other Chicago School theorists, Shaw and McKay rooted their analysis of delinquency and crime in the Park-Burgess model of the city. Existing within the context of a general transformation of American society, emerging urban areas were seen as places where the tenacity of the traditional social fabric was being severely challenged. The "zone of transition" was one section of the city where this challenge was not successfully met. Subject to the continual overflow of business and industry, as well as the constant influx and succession of immigrant groups, this zone inevitably experienced physical and social decay (1929 : 204–6, 1972 : 18–22). The most important aspect of this social decay was the breakdown of the zone's conventional institutions, that is, the onset of social disorganization.

Shaw and McKay believed that delinquency emanated primarily from the condition of social disorganization, and hence was an endemic feature of the disorganized zone of transition. In contrast, violations of the law were seen to be less prevalent in other sectors of the city. Specifically, Shaw and McKay proposed that crime, while concentrated in inner slum neighborhoods, decreased as one moved away from the center of the city and toward the "outlying residential communities" (1929 : 204). To substantiate this claim, Shaw and McKay presented extensive ecological data on the distribution of offenses, as measured by official statistics, throughout Chicago and other urban areas (1929, 1972).[5]

It is noteworthy, however, that Shaw and McKay were not simply interested in the epidemiology of delinquency. Instead, they wanted to know why and how conditions of social disorganization produce youthful misconduct. To flesh out their understanding of this problem, they supplemented their statistical studies with criminal "life-histories"—autobiographical accounts describing how a person became involved in a life of crime (Shaw 1930, Shaw and Moore 1931, Shaw et al. 1938). From these various sources, they concluded that the essence of social disorganization was the absence of institutional control. The conventional institutions of organized areas were seen to exercise a singular effect by directing youths along conformist paths and by "insulating" them "from direct contact with deviant forms of adult behavior" (1972 : 171). In contrast, Shaw and McKay argued that the regulatory power of institutions in disorganized areas had become weakened. No longer could they effectively channel juveniles into acceptable behavior. With the abrogation of social bonds, youths were free to pursue any course of action.

Shaw and McKay did not contend that juveniles would become delinquent simply because they experienced a dearth of control over their behavior. Delinquent involvement would occur only if a second factor was also present: exposure to a "delinquent tradition"—"a coherent system of values supporting delinquent acts" (1972 : 173). According to Shaw and McKay, such a tradition was not present in organized communities. This fact, coupled with the strong controls that institutions exercised, accounted for the low rates of delinquency in organized areas. Shaw and McKay observed, however, that in disorganized communities a criminal tradition existed side by side with a conventional tradition (1972 : 170–83). The presence of this criminal tradition created the possibility, indeed the likelihood, that uncontrolled slum youths would participate in criminal activities. More generally, the existence of delinquent values, when taken together with the ineffectiveness of institutional controls, largely accounted for the high rate of crime in disorganized communities.

Shaw and McKay went on to specify a third factor contributing to the differential prevalence of delinquency in slum areas: the presence of criminal forms of organization. These organizational forms are significant because they serve as the mechanism through which criminal values and techniques are transmitted. Important in this regard are the linkages between juveniles and adult criminals, such as fences, professional thieves, and racketeers. Even more crucial in transmitting a criminal heritage are play groups and gangs. Building on Thrasher, Shaw and McKay documented the influence of these youth gangs throughout their work:

> As was pointed out in the preceding chapter, delinquency and crime have been for many years part of the social tradition of the community in which the Martin brothers resided. For the most part, play groups, street crowds, and gangs are the bearers of this tradition. Its perpetuation is dependent upon these natural social groupings and upon a community milieu in which there is low resistance to delinquency and in which the residents in various ways give sanction and encouragement to the child in his delinquent activities. The process of transmitting traditions of delinquency from group to group is illustrated by the play groups and gangs to which the brothers belonged. [Shaw et al. 1938 : 109; cf. Shaw 1930 : 10]

One of the most persistent criticisms leveled at the early Chicago School theorists is that they took the existence of a criminal tradition (culture conflict) in disorganized communities for granted, a charge that can be leveled at Shaw and McKay. In *Juvenile Delinquency and Urban Areas*, however, they recognized that "it is important to ask what are the forces which give rise to these significant differences in the organized values in different communities" (1972 : 317). In addressing this problem, they touched upon two factors. First, they held that criminal values will arise and persist only so long as "traditional conventional control is either weak or nonexistent'' (1972 : 188). Particularly conducive to this slippage of control is the urban (slum) setting ''where traditional means of social control, effective in primitive and in isolated rural communities, have been . . . rendered especially ineffective'' (1972 : 188). Second, they argued that criminal values and, by implication, structure, will arise and persist when conventional institutions are unable to meet a populace's needs or wishes. Here, Shaw and McKay converged with Thrasher's view of the gang as a functional alternative to unsatisfying conventional institutions. However, in proposing that it is the poor who are differentially blocked from attaining their desired ends, and that it is the disjunction between the cultural and social structure which progressively weakens the power of conventional standards in slum neighborhoods in favor of a criminal tradition, Shaw and McKay achieved an even greater congruence with the anomie tradition (1972 : 319; cf. Merton 1968c, 1964).[6]

Finally, attention must be given to one of Shaw and McKay's most classic propositions: the crime rate of an ethnic (or racial) group will change according to the community (zone) in which it is located; or a bit differently, it is the nature of the community and not the nature of the ethnic group which determines involvement in crime. Taken historically and in light of the concept of ethnic succession, this proposition adds a sense of optimism to their work. To be more specific, Shaw and McKay held that the new ethnic groups arriving in urban areas were destined to reside in the zone of transition and thereby be subject to a range of social problems (including a high crime rate). Yet this did not have to be a permanent affliction. Since no people were inherently disorganized, a social group could alleviate its plight by moving out of the zone of transition and into a conventional community. Significantly, this is what Shaw and McKay observed. They noted that ethnic groups are eventually able to reorganize sufficiently to leave a disorganized area for an organized one, where, by implication, the construction of conventional institutions would be completed. Succeeding them are new ethnic groups which in turn are subject to the ongoing processes of social disorganization and reorganization (cf. Finestone 1976 : 27–28).[7] The flavor of their thinking about crime is captured below:

> In short, with the process of growth of the city, the invasion of residential communities by business and industry causes a disintegration of the community as a unit of social control. This disorganization is intensified by the influx of foreign, national and racial groups whose old cultural and social controls break down in the new cultural and racial situation of the city. In this state of social disorganization, community resistance is low. Delinquent and criminal patterns arise and are transmitted socially just as any other cultural and social pattern is transmitted. In time these delinquent patterns may become dominant and shape the attitudes and behavior of persons living in the area. Thus the section becomes an area of delinquency [1929 : 205–6].

SHAW AND MCKAY: THE STRUCTURING OF DEVIANT BEHAVIOR

Shaw and McKay's influence was wide and significant. Sutherland drew heavily from them, as did Cloward at a later date. Indeed, in developing his thesis on the structuring effects of access to illegitimate means, Cloward relied greatly on their discussion of the transmission of a criminal culture and on the rich descriptive materials they presented in their criminal life-histories (1959 : 169–70). Cloward believed that Shaw and McKay's work could be interpreted as an analysis of the way in which juveniles gain access to some criminal roles but not others. In this regard, he noted the special attention that Shaw and McKay had given to the integration of different age-levels of offenders. The materials they collected revealed that it is through association with older criminals (such as in gangs) that juveniles acquire the resources needed to commit sophisticated types of offenses. Moreover, Cloward concluded that the ecological work of Shaw and McKay suggested that access to a "criminal tradition" and hence the means to engage in particular kinds of crimes are differentially distributed throughout the social structure. Thus, Shaw and McKay had observed that

> certain types of delinquency have tended to characterize certain city areas. The execution of each type involves techniques which must be learned from others who have participated in the same activity. Each involves specialization of function, and each has its own terminology and standards of behavior. Jack-rolling, shoplifting, stealing from junkmen, and stealing automobiles are examples of offenses with well-developed techniques, passed on by one generation to the next. [1972 : 174–5]

In passages such as these, Shaw and McKay attributed differences in forms of criminal behavior to variations in neighborhood social structure. Yet they might have generalized their insight to include features of social organization generally—not just features of neighborhood social organization specifically. Shaw and McKay had clearly focused on structuring variables, but they had seen them only in terms of neighborhood social organization and mainly in terms of the way they produce one kind of deviant behavior, namely, lower-class property crime.

Nevertheless, the structuring perspective is indebted to Shaw and McKay for a wealth of information about the nature of collective forms of crime and delinquency. Particularly noteworthy is their observation that these collective patterns can become institutionalized, persisting from one generation to another, and that the existence of these stable collective forms can both transmit the motivation to deviate and structure the resulting deviations. In other words, "deviant traditions" can be a powerful force both in creating deviance and in shaping its direction.

Sutherland on Crime and Delinquency

It is often stated that theories of deviance may operate on two distinct levels of explanation, structural or social-psychological. As Akers has noted, this leads to a consideration of two issues: "(a) accounting for the group and structural variations in rates of deviancy, and (b) describing and explaining the process by which individuals come to commit acts labelled deviant" (1968 : 456; cf. Cressey 1960). Most analyses, however, tend to focus on one problem or the other; they rarely consider both simultaneously. A notable exception is Edwin A. Sutherland's work on the etiology of criminal behavior. Sutherland attempted to confront both of these theoretical problems (though the latter in far more depth than the former) through the principles of "differential social organization" and "differential association."

Clearly the more well-known portion of Sutherland's model is his statement of the "theory of differential association," which he formulated to explain why individuals become criminal. Briefly, two ideas constitute the essence of this theory. The first is that people will commit crimes when they come into contact with a higher ratio of "definitions favorable to violation of law" than "definitions unfavorable to violation of law." This, Sutherland termed the "principle of differential association." It should be recognized that this principle assumes that society is marked by "culture conflict" (cf. Sellin 1938). Quite plainly, for *differential* association with definitions relative to the law to be possible, there must be two conflicting cultures: one which prescribes behaviors precluded by the law, and one which prescribes behaviors protected by the law.

The second idea central to the theory of differential association is that criminal behavior is learned in the same fashion as any other behavior. In setting forth this proposition, Sutherland was attempting to refute the popularly held notion of his day that criminal predilections are psychopathological (or inborn). Implicit in the idea that illegal behavior is learned like any other is that it is the social environment and not an aberrant psyche which moves people to engage in crime. In short, criminals are not special "kinds of people" (Cohen 1966 : 42), but rather are much like the rest of us.

To a degree, Sutherland's rejection of the image of the offender as mentally ill is a manifestation of his sociological orientation. It can be remembered that Merton also felt the need to debate prevailing Freudian notions that the origins of deviant motivations rest most firmly within the inner reaches of the psyche and not in the character of the social structure (1938). Further, the tradition of the Chicago School from which Sutherland emerged had always had a deep suspicion of intrapersonal explanations. As Matza has observed, these theorists only "begrudgingly admitted the existence of personality and its disorders. But since the admission was begrudging, personal pathologies had no secure place in the conceptual system'' (1969 : 47). Yet despite these influences, Sutherland's attack on the mental illness-crime link was not merely ideological but also fundamentally empirical. He thus took care to reveal the absence of data confirming a relationship between psychopathology and criminal behavior. Particularly important in this respect was the class-biased nature of psychological research. Typically, the samples employed did ''not include vast areas of criminal behavior of persons not in the lower-class,'' and thus wrongly assumed that characteristics associated with the lower class (such as psychopathology) cause crime (1940 : 2).

Drawing on his experiences and associations at the University of Chicago and Indiana University, Sutherland evolved his principle of differential association during the mid-1930s. In 1939, he first published a formal theoretical statement composed of seven hypotheses. Later, in 1947, Sutherland expanded his theory of differential association to nine propositions. These are set forth below:

1. Criminal behavior is learned.
2. Criminal behavior is learned in interaction with other persons in a process of communication.
3. The principal part of the learning of criminal behavior occurs within intimate personal groups.
4. When criminal behavior is learned, the learning includes (a) techniques of committing the crime, which are sometimes very complicated, sometimes very simple; (b) the specific direction of motives, drives, rationalizations, and attitudes.
5. The specific direction of motives and drives is learned from definitions of legal codes as favorable and unfavorable.
6. A person becomes delinquent because of an excess of definitions favorable to violation of law over definitions unfavorable to violation of law. This is the principle of differential association.
7. Differential associations may vary in frequency, duration, priority, and intensity.
8. The process of learning criminal behavior by association with criminal and anticriminal patterns involves all of the mechanisms that are involved in any other learning.
9. While criminal behavior is an expression of general needs and values, it is not explained by those general needs and values since noncriminal behavior is an expression of the same needs and values. [Sutherland, and Cressey 1970 : 75–76]

As suggested, Sutherland's theory of differential association has exercised a persistent, if controversial influence on the field of deviance since its appearance. On the one hand, it has been the focus of considerable criticism, and has even been categorically rejected as trivial (Radzinowicz 1966 : 82, Nettler 1978 : 266–74; cf. Sutherland and Cressey 1970 : 78–87). On the other, it has spawned important theoretical reformulations (Glaser 1956, Burgess and Akers 1966, Akers et al. 1979), and few would contemplate writing a criminology text that ignored Sutherland's thoughts on differential association. In marked contrast, Sutherland's work on differential social (or group) organization—which he set forth to explain group rates of crime—has received little attention. Thus, summaries of Sutherland's model often fail to discuss this concept altogether. Much of the blame for this state of affairs must be shouldered by Sutherland, for he never constructed a systematic theory of differential social organization similar to his theory of differential association. Instead, his discussions of the principle invariably were limited to a few pages tacked onto a more detailed treatment of differential association and were not fully consistent from one article to another.

Despite Sutherland's failure to systematically set forth the principle of differential social organization, it is possible to discern the basic thrust of this idea, and to see in turn that his perspective is not exclusively a social psychological theory devoid of any structural aspects. Paralleling his idea that a person could associate with two different types of definitions—those favorable and those unfavorable to violation of the law—Sutherland maintained that there are two different types of social or group organization: organization for criminal behavior and organization against criminal behavior. A careful reading of Sutherland's writings indicates that he believed "organized for crime" to involve two primary elements (see especially 1973d : 25). The first is that conventional institutions are weakened. There is a notable breakdown of the mechanisms required to transmit traditional values, and a weakening of the social factors (e.g., stable community) that commonly insure the vitality of conventional culture. Second, however, organization for crime does not simply entail the absence of supports for conventional culture. It involves as well the presence of supports for a criminal way of life. This would include the existence of a criminal culture or "definitions favorable to violation of the law," the structural mechanisms to transmit this culture, and the opportunities to perform criminal roles. Of course, "organization against criminal behavior" implies the converse of organization for criminal behavior: the absence of criminal institutions and the presence of sturdy conventional institutions and effective social control procedures.

Sutherland argued that a group's crime rate was determined by the degree to which a group was organized for or against crime. In those groups in which organization for crime is predominant, members would stand a greater chance of associating with definitions favorable to violation of law, and thus the crime rate of that group would be high. The converse would be true of groups organized primarily in a conventional direction, whose members are likely to come into contact with a higher ratio of definitions unfavorable to violation of law. Importantly, by arguing that differential group organization regulates differential association and hence criminal participation, Sutherland succeeded in integrating his two levels of analysis. He remarked that "differential group organization, therefore, should explain the crime rate, while differential association should explain the criminal behavior of a person. The two explanations must be consistent with each other" (1973a : 21).

Of further note is that Sutherland derived the essence of the principle of differential social or group organization from Shaw and McKay's concept of social disorganization. In his early work, Sutherland actually employed the latter concept, but discarded it as he and the sociological community came to recognize its inadequacies (Mills 1942, Whyte 1943a,b).[8] It is thus of little surprise that Sutherland shared Shaw and McKay's view that the differentially organized/disorganized urban slum areas were fertile ground for the breeding of crime.

A major criticism leveled at Chicago School theorists is that they had a near exclusive concern for lower-class criminality. Sutherland, however, attempted to avoid such class-biased research by embarking on his now classic study of white-collar crime (1940, 1949). While he agreed with Shaw and McKay and other Chicago theorists that slums are quite conducive to crime, he recognized that crime was prevalent, perhaps equally so, in the more affluent sectors of society. Significantly, he went on to argue that crimes of the rich and poor could be explained by the same theoretical principles. Thus, he observed that, similar to slum areas, the white-collar business world "has a rather tight organization for violations of business regulations" (1949 : 255). Invoking the concept of anomie, Sutherland noted that the occupational sphere lacks the conventional standards which will dictate ethical behavior (1949 : 254). Moreover, a culture prescribing violation of the law as well as the mechanisms to transmit this culture within and among businesses have emerged. On the other hand, neither the public nor the government has successfully organized against this violation of the law. Consequently, those within the business world are almost invariably exposed to a high ratio of definitions favorable to violation of law. As such, novices in business soon come to participate in white-collar offenses, while old-timers continue to persist in their criminal way of life. Needless to say, on a group level, these conditions eventuate in a high crime rate (1949 : 234–56).

Sutherland has also been criticized for attending solely to the persistence and transmission of a criminal culture, while ignoring the problem of the culture's origin. He did, however, address this issue, albeit in a very restricted fashion. Converging with Sellin (1938) and anticipating the stances taken by later conflict theorists and politically sensitized labeling theorists, Sutherland argued that a culture becomes criminal when a powerful group defines it as such. It can thus be said that "crime is conflict" and that "the law is a device of one party in conflict with another party" (1973c : 103; cf. 1973a : 24). However, while this reasoning may explain how the criminal label is ascribed to a subculture, it does not address the issue of why two conflicting cultures arose in the first place. Then again, Sutherland was aware of the limitations or, as some would prefer, the incompleteness of his model in this respect: "the hypotheses point to and describe the conflicts of standards but provide no satisfactory explanation of the genesis of conflicts" (1949 : 256).

Sutherland's overriding goal throughout his career was to formulate a general theory of crime—whether it be the crime of the rich or that of the poor. In this light, his major contribution was in formalizing two of the major crime-causation themes expressed by his predecessors, namely, (1) that contact with criminal values predisposes people to violate the law, and (2) that groups differ in the degree to which they are criminogenic. As we have seen, Sutherland attempted to systematize these insights by developing his principles of differential association and differential group organization.[9]

Sutherland and the Structuring of Deviant Behavior

Like earlier theorists of the Chicago School, Sutherland was preoccupied with the problem of why people commit crimes and, to a lesser degree, why certain groups have a higher overall crime rate. Yet his overriding concern with the etiology of crime per se led him to pay far less attention to the question of why people engage in certain forms of crime (or to why social groups have a higher or lower rate of any given offense). Because he was predominantly interested in demonstrating that exposure to an excess of definitions favoring violation of the law would result in criminal behavior, explaining the content of such behavior was simply not elevated to an issue of equal theoretical concern. Thus, his purpose in exploring white-collar crime was not to illustrate how class position structures the kind of crime that is pursued but rather to show that, regardless of the nature of the offense, people of all classes commit crimes for the same reason—differential association with criminal values (cf. Geis and Goff 1982 : 15).

It is clear, then, that Sutherland devoted less effort to specifying the conditions under which differential association with illegal definitions produces one criminal response over another. However, though he was essentially unconcerned with this issue, it would be wrong to conclude that his writings are devoid of clues about what factors might structure criminal behavior. For example, from the life-history material presented by Chic Conwell—the offender studied in Sutherland's earliest major publication, *The Professional Thief*—Sutherland came to the realization that because "everyone has an inclination to steal," such an "inclination is not a sufficient explanation of the genesis of the professional thief" (1937 : 212–13). Instead, to engage in the particular criminal form of professional theft, it is necessary to have acquired a "complex of abilities and skills, just as do physicians, lawyers, or bricklayers'' (1937 : 197). Further, similar to the intricate, technical knowledge bases of other professions, the knowledge base of professional thievery cannot be self-taught. Indeed, building on Conwell's assertion that criminal education is needed for involvement in this enterprise, Sutherland observed that the prerequisite skills and techniques can only be gained through association with and tutelage by professional thieves. "The thief who has not been taught these skills cannot," in short, "become a professional" (1937 : 43). What is more, access to such tutelage is not universally available; like other professional education, it is "given only to a few persons selected from the total population." (1937 : 212).

Sutherland thus realized that simply being predisposed to violate the law or having "an inclination to steal" does not determine the type of criminal career a person may pursue. Independent of criminal motivation (which for Sutherland would be a product of differential association), people can only become professional thieves if they have access to a criminal learning environment where the skills and accomplices needed to engage in professional theft can be acquired. In making this insight, Sutherland converged with Thrasher and Shaw and McKay who also were aware that criminal learning environments have an impact on the types of offenses juveniles commit. But, like his predecessors, Sutherland might have broadened his perspective here and *systematically* investigated how the availability of different kinds of learning environments structures involvement in various kinds of criminal or deviant behaviors. Hence, building on his knowledge that not everyone has access to the learning environment needed for professional theft, he could have examined how access to such environments and thus participation in this form of theft is distributed throughout the social structure. Interestingly, Sutherland ignored this latter possibility even though his informant, Chic Conwell, did not. Thus, Sutherland did not follow up on Conwell's observation that access to professional theft in general as well as to particular modes of professional theft varies according to such statuses as class, age, ethnicity, and sex. In this regard, Conwell maintained that "few professional thieves come from the amateur thieves who are reared in the slums, for these youngsters seldom have the social abilities or front to become professional thieves" (Sutherland 1937 : 21). Similarly, Conwell remarked that "the very young and the very old are eliminated. Color places certain limitations. . . . Jews perhaps specialize a little more on the cannon than any other racket. Chinese pickpockets are rare. . . .Women are found in many rackets, where they aid the male members of the troupe as steerers or stalls" (1937 : 24).

Another anticipation of structuring ideas appeared in a 1944 paper in which Sutherland assessed the limitations of his model of crime. In response to criticisms, Sutherland admitted that exposure to an excess of definitions favorable to violating the law and the criminal motivation this creates does not necessarily result in criminal behavior. Instead, he reasoned that criminal behavior in general, as well as specific types of offenses, cannot ensue unless people "have the opportunity to commit the crime" ([1942] 1973b : 32). Further, he went on to propose that opportunities to engage in certain forms of crime are distributed throughout the social structure, thus influencing the way in which people located in various statuses deviate. To illustrate, Sutherland observed that "Negroes are seldom convicted of embezzlement because they are seldom in positions of financial trust, in which alone embezzlement is possible" (1973b : 32). He likewise noted in *White Collar Crime* that "unskilled laborers do not violate antitrust law or commit fraud in advertising, because they are not in a position appropriate for such crimes" (1949 : 263).

Finally, Sutherland also touched upon the idea that some variables (differential association) generate a general criminal inclination or motivation while other variables regulate the actual form of criminal behavior that occurs. In other words, he anticipated the concept of structuring variables. Hence, in his discussion of traditional views on the origin of crime, Sutherland asserted that the conditions commonly thought to cause illegal behavior are not criminogenic in nature. He went on to observe, however, that such factors may have an impact on the type of offense committed:

> The conventional theories do not explain lower-class criminality. The sociopathic and psychopathic factors which have been emphasized doubtless have something to do with crime causation, but these factors have not been related to a general process that is found both in white-collar criminality and lower-class criminality; therefore, they do not explain the criminality of either class. They may *explain the manner or method of crime*—why lower-class criminals commit burglary or robbery rather than false pretenses. [1940 : 10, emphasis mine]

But again, Sutherland chose to concentrate on the conditions that generate the predisposition to violate the law and not on the factors which determine the particular way in which this general criminal predisposition is manifested. As a result, this insight on the structuring of criminal behavior remained largely undeveloped.

The Chicago School: Concluding Remarks

For the most part, members of the Chicago School were not concerned with the question of why people engage in a particular form of crime. Instead, their dominant interest lay with the issue of why people would be moved to violate the law in the first place. Like many stress theorists, they often proceeded as though understanding the source of criminal motivations was the most important task of the criminological enterprise. And in this regard, it must be emphasized that they made important and lasting contributions to the field.

Yet even though theorists like Thrasher, Shaw and McKay, and Sutherland did not always seek to enrich their explanations by consistently integrating structuring variables into their thinking about crime causation, their writings nevertheless contain numerous and often vivid examples of the way in which social conditions shape the direction a person's criminality takes. In this regard, perhaps the most valuable contribution of their work was their illustration that contact with subcultural traditions not only creates the motivation to violate the law but also structures the kind of criminal a person may become.

This insight assumes particular significance when one considers the more general question it suggests: what role does the deviant subculture play in the transmission of other forms of deviance? Thus, existing theories regarding the intergenerational transmission of crime—or of alcoholism or mental ill-ness—may prove to be more than theories of motivation; they may also contain insights on the way in which people are led to adopt specific forms of deviance through subcultural participation. The problem for research is to examine various deviant adaptations in order to determine the degree to which, if at all, exposure to deviant subcultures constitutes a force by which individuals are recruited and socialized for these same deviant roles. It is hoped that such research will make possible generalizations regarding the way in which deviant subcultures of one kind or another influence people to adopt one form of deviance or another. If so, we will have arrived at new and potentially im-portant propositions regarding the social structuring of deviant behavior (cf. Cloward and Piven et al. 1977).

Notes

1. In linking "deregulation" to both normative and structural conditions, Thrasher converged with Durkheim's analysis of "anomie" (attenuation of normative control) and "egoism" (de-regulation growing out of structural non-integration).

2. Thrasher's portrayal of the gang delinquent as having fun and enjoyment differs significantly from the more serious, burdened, and intense images of the delinquent that have been fostered in more recent theoretical works. See Bordua (1961) and Finestone (1976).

3. While Thrasher characterized slum neighborhoods as being disorganized, he also devoted much of *The Gang* to a description of the organization of juvenile and adult gangs. As Cloward has noted, the inconsistency of referring to criminal organization as being disorganized was a common feature of the work of the early Chicago theorists (1959 : 170). See also Whyte (1943a,b) and Mills (1942).

4. Matza has maintained that "most theories of deliquency take no account of maturational reform," that is, of the fact that most juveniles "do not apparently become adult violators" (1964 : 22). Thrasher, however, was not guilty of ignoring the issue of maturational reform. As should be apparent, his discussion of the "conventionalization" of the gang is relevant to this problem. In addition, he argued that marriage could terminate involvement in gang delinquency by integrating a youth into conventional society, thereby subjecting the youth to proper social control (1963 : 170).

5. Shaw and McKay's empirical findings regarding the ecological distribution of delinquency have been questioned on two accounts. First, they employed ecological data yet made theoretical statements about individual behavior. As a result, they may have committed an ecological fallacy (cf. Robinson 1950). Second, they utilized official crime statistics as measures of the true prevalence of crime—a practice which was criticized long before the emergence of labeling theory (cf. Kitsuse and Cicourel 1972). As regards the latter point, Shaw and McKay were aware of the problems surrounding the use of official statistics (1972 : 43–46). See also Shaw et al. (1938 : 353–54) for a critique of psychiatric labels that approaches that voiced today by labeling theorists (cf. Szasz 1970).

6. In arguing that crime is generated by a combination of the lack of institutional regulation and the existence of criminal "temptations" in slum neighborhoods, Shaw and McKay assumed a stance quite similar to that held by nineteenth-century European theorists such as Mayhew as well as by American crime theorists of that same era (Shaw and McKay 1972 : 8–9, Platt 1969, Rothman 1971, cf. Lindesmith and Levin 1937).

7. Shaw and McKay later agreed that certain groups (e.g., blacks) have been able to reorganize to such an extent that they have experienced a declining crime rate without moving to an outer zone (1972 : 385).

8. As Sutherland noted in 1942, he "borrowed" the concept of social disorganization from Shaw and McKay without fully weighing the wisdom of doing so ([1942] 1973a : 21). In particular, he did not consider that the notion of "disorganization" was more a reflection of the Chicago School's negative appraisal of the "pathology" prevailing in the slum neighborhoods than an accurate assessment of criminal behavior, much of which is complex and intricate in its organization. At the urgings of Albert Cohen, Sutherland thus decided to cast aside the concept of disorganization and to replace it with "differential social organization." That is, he now concluded that groups were not organized or disorganized, but rather either organized for crime or organized against it.

9. On the surface, it might seem plausible to argue that the central etiological condition set forth by the Chicago School—exposure to criminal values—would result only in criminal behavior. It is possible, however, that other factors might prevent the direct expression of the criminal motivations produced by this condition in illegal behavior by precluding the performance of criminal roles (e.g., via institutionalization or expulsion from a gang). When criminal drives are blocked in this manner, it is conceivable that an actor will seek out an alternative deviant adaptation—perhaps as a way of dealing with the pressure such as experience can generate (cf. Cloward 1959, Taylor et al. 1973 : 271–72).

chapter 7

Revisionist Explanations of Crime and Deviance: Labeling, Control, and Conflict Theories

It appears accurate to assert that the two orientations reviewed thus far—the Chicago School and the Durkeim-Merton stress perspective—have been the dominant theoretical paradigms for the greatest part of this century (Cole 1975, Wolfgang 1980). For a long time, the influence of these traditions was overwhelming, as the bulk of the work in the field was directed toward assessing their empirical adequacy (cf. Clinard 1964) or toward exploring how the two perspectives might be combined to furnish a more complete understanding of deviant involvement (Cloward and Ohlin 1960, Cohen 1955; cf. Kornhauser 1978). Recently, however, the capacity of these traditions to capture the full attention of scholars has been noticeably diminished. Indeed, as will be discussed in this chapter, the past two decades have witnessed the vibrant emergence, in Gibbons's words, of "new directions in criminological theory" (1979). Nevertheless, it must be understood that much of the popularity of each of these "new" perspectives is due to the very fact that they have endeavored to revise the causal propositions advanced by the Chicago and stress-anomie schools of thought. In this light, it is clear that the works of theorists like Merton and Sutherland have not been reduced to the status of mere theoretical artifacts to be read out of historical fancy. Instead, these writings are of such continuing salience that "revisionist" theorists invariably feel compelled to discuss them in full before departing on a new criminological enterprise (cf. Schur 1973, Hirschi 1969, Taylor et al. 1973).

Three revisionist explanations are reviewed below. The first, often called *labeling or societal reaction theory*, begins with a rejection of the idea that people become committed to deviant or criminal roles because they are unable to negotiate the rigors of everyday life or because they grow up in deviant social surroundings. By contrast, labeling theorists have contended that transitory deviant episodes evolve into a stabilized pattern or "career" because of the efforts of other people—most notably governmental agents like police and correctional officials—to suppress the behavior in question. A second group of authors, known as *control or social bond theorists*, has similarly questioned whether exposure to stressful circumstances and contact with nonconformist cultures can account for wayward conduct. While admitting that such conditions may give rise to deviant motivations, they have maintained that this observation is of little theoretical consequence. For in modern society, impulses to deviate are so pervasive that explaining their existence is not equivalent to explaining when such feelings will be acted upon. Rather, it is by understanding when social bonds weaken and society loses its power to regulate deviant desires that we will learn the real origins of socially disapproved behavior. Finally, scholars embracing *conflict, radical, or critical theory* have called attention to the virtual neglect of power relationships in competing perspectives. As such, they have argued that other paradigms have failed to see how the character of the political economy intimately conditions the nature of deviant activity. In particular, radical theorists have alerted us to the overriding role the capitalist social order plays in fostering demoralizing behavior both among the rich and among the poor.

As with our "rethinking" of other perspectives, the discussion of these three revisionist theories will follow the format of initially reviewing the central tenets of the theory and then of exploring how structuring insights are manifest within each tradition of scholarship. One caveat, however, should be mentioned at this point. Unlike the theories of the Chicago School and the stress tradition, the revisionist explanations are not clearly dominated by a few select figures—such as a Sutherland or a Merton. To be sure, each camp can readily point to a cadre of theorists who have been particularly influential in the evolution of their paradigm; however, the numbers within these theoretical elites are not small. For instance, labeling theorists are able to find their roots in the work of authors ranging from Tannenbaum to Lemert, Becker, Goffman, Kitsuse, Cicourel, Erikson, Scheff, and Schur, among others; those partial to control theory will look not only to Reckless but also to Sykes, Matza, Nye, Reiss, Toby, Hirschi, Briar, and Piliavin; while those more radically disposed can ponder the writings of Marx, Bonger, Vold, Quinney, Chambliss, Greenberg, Platt, and Taylor et al. In light of this, no attempt will be made here to fully embellish the finer distinctions among the varied offerings that fall within each broad orientation. Those seeking such information are encouraged to consult other sources (cf. Empey 1982, Gibbons 1979, Liska 1981, Davis 1975, Taylor et al. 1973). Instead, the primary goal here will be to set forth the central thrust of the three revisionist models. Further, in each case, the general relationship of the theory to the structuring perspective developed in this book will be articulated in some detail.

Labeling Theory

THE THEORY

"Labeling" or "societal reaction" theory emerged as an important paradigm during the 1960s and early 1970s (Cole 1975, Schervish 1973, Thio 1973). Much of the perspective's popularity stemmed from its revisionist nature. Since the rise of positivist orientations, most deviance theorists had focused exclusively on the characteristics of the deviant person in an attempt to discern the etiology of deviant behavior (Jeffrey 1972, 1977). In contrast, labeling theorists endeavored to shift the focus away from the "deviants" and their behavior and toward the behavior of those who label or react to others as deviant. "Societal reaction" thus became the object of analysis, and its origin and effects were now viewed as problems of major theoretical significance.

Those within the labeling paradigm thus devoted their attention to four central issues (Cullen and Cullen 1978a,b). First, they were concerned with the origin of "deviant labels" or categories of deviant behavior. They asserted that the deviant status of a behavior should not be taken for granted, as had traditionally been the case. Instead, it is essential to explain why a particular behavior is defined as "deviant" at one time but perhaps not at another. Moreover, it is also necessary to explain why a behavior receives a particular deviant label and how this might vary from one era to the next—for instance, why "hearing voices" might be characterized as "witchcraft" during one historical period and as "mental illness" during another (Szasz, 1970).

Second, once deviant labels are established, it is likely that they will be applied when social control procedures are enacted. Thus, being publicly designated and subsequently treated as a deviant is of no small consequence; both the social meaning of a person's act as well as the status of the person who is labeled are fundamentally altered.[1] Not unexpectedly, then, labeling theorists were very concerned with the issue of who gets labeled and why. In the past, it had largely been assumed that the reason people are labeled is because their behavior violated a normative standard. Labeling authors, however, contended that it was not this simple: some actors break norms and are not labeled, while others are labeled even when they have done no wrong (Becker 1963). An actor's behavior thus could not be the only determinant of societal reaction. Consistent with their revisionist orientation, labeling theorists suggested that we must also analyze how characteristics apart from the nature of a person's behavior (e.g., minority-group status, self-interest of police or psychiatrists) influence the labeling process.

In these first two central issues of the perspective—the origin of deviant labels and the contingencies of labeling—societal reaction is treated as a *dependent* variable. Alternatively, the third and fourth chief concerns of labeling theorists involve two different ways in which societal reaction operates as an *independent* variable (Orcutt 1972). First, analysts have examined the consequences that labeling and treating actors as deviant can have for a social system. Following a long tradition which posits the functionality of rule-breaking and builds more directly on a theme present in the work of several noted theorists (Durkheim 1961 : 165–67, Mead 1918, Waller 1932 : 200–201), some labeling theorists have proposed that societal reaction can be functional for a system (Erikson 1964, 1966, Sampson et al. 1964, Schur 1971, Szasz 1970). The equilibrating consequences of reaction most frequently cited in the labeling literature are those of normative boundary maintenance and increased social solidarity.

Second, labeling theorists sought to provide an answer different from that usually given by deviance theorists to the question, why do people violate social norms? In contrast to traditional perspectives, labeling theorists proposed that the origins of deviance do not rest in the characteristics of the deviant person. Instead, these theorists set forth the controversial view that societal reaction—when a person is defined and treated by others as a deviant—is the major cause of nonconformity. To be more precise, labeling authors held that initial excursions into deviant behavior are typically ephemeral and episodic; and if left alone, a person will eventually drift back into a conventional life-style. If these otherwise transitory behaviors are subject to social control, however, it is likely that they will be stabilized into a persisting deviant pattern. Hence, labeling and treating an actor as deviant will cause that person to accept a deviant identity and to reject a conventional self-image. This identity transformation in turn fosters commitment to a deviant career as individuals strive to act in a manner consistent with their self-concept. Similarly, if state intervention results in institutionalization, the actor will be exposed to environments where the encouragement and skills needed to perform wayward roles may be acquired. Futhermore, the stigma of being publicly designated a deviant may exclude an individual from legitimate social and economic roles, and thus increase the attractiveness of illegitimate activities. After all, who feels comfortable with or wants to hire a parolee or former mental patient? In these ways, then, societal reaction has the unanticipated and ironic consequence of heightening the very behavior it was invoked to control.

Interestingly, these latter insights reveal points of convergence between the societal reaction perspective and the works of both the Chicago School and the Mertonian tradition. Specifically, it appears that labeling theorists embraced the notions that differential association with deviant subcultures (most notably when institutionalized) and denial of access to conventional avenues of advancement will motivate people to intensify socially disapproved conduct. Unlike their predecessors, however, labeling authors implicitly suggested that a person's structural location—whether it is in a disorganized neighborhood as Shaw and Mckay highlighted or in the lower-class setting Merton discussed—is largely unimportant in precipitating commitment to a deviant way of life. Instead, labeling theorists contended that the circumstance which engenders the persistent desire to continue deviant conduct is ultimately rooted in something that at least initially is external to the social situation in which a person lives, namely, in societal reaction.

Numerous authors over the years have proposed that the exercise of social control mechanisms such as institutionalization can deepen an actor's criminality or deviant behavior. Current labeling theorists, however, have typically traced the beginnings of this vision of the origins of nonconformity to the writings of Tannenbaum, who offered the observation that "the process of making the criminal . . . is a process of tagging, defining, segregating, describing, emphasizing, making conscious and self-conscious; it becomes a way of stimulating, suggesting, emphasizing, and evoking the very traits complained of. . . . The person becomes the thing he is described as being" (1938 : 19–20). In the early 1950s, this thesis was advanced further when Lemert initially distinguished between "primary" and "secondary" deviance (1951). According to Lemert, the first category subsumes deviant acts caused by a range of sociocultural factors which do not force a person to engage in a major reinterpretation of identity or a readjustment of life-style. In contrast, the latter category includes those deviant and related actions that occur as a result of being labeled and reacted to as a deviant and which cause people to organize their "life and identity . . . around the facts of deviance" (1972 : 63). In Lemert's words:

> Primary deviation is assumed to arise in a wide variety of social, cultural, and psychological contexts, and at best has only marginal implications for the psychic structure of the individual; it does not lead to symbolic reorganization at the level of self-regarding attitudes and social roles. Secondary deviation is deviant behavior, or social roles based upon it, which becomes means of defense, attack, or adaptation to the overt and covert problems created by the societal reaction to primary deviation. In effect, the original "causes" of the deviation recede and give way to the central importance of the disapproving, degradational, and isolating reactions of society. [1972 : 48]

It was not until the 1960s, however, that the theme underlying these earlier insights was generalized sufficiently to constitute a separate, and quite popular theory of the origins of deviant behavior. Although the labeling theory literature which emerged at this time was substantial, it is perhaps fair to say that Becker's *Outsiders* (1963) was the most influential in focusing attention on the consequences of societal reaction. Like his predecessors Tannenbaum and Lemert, Becker was "not so much interested in the person who commits a deviant act once as in the person who sustains a pattern of deviance over a long period of time, who makes of deviance a way of life, who organizes his identity around a pattern of deviant behavior" (1963 : 30). He then went on to highlight the importance of societal reaction in fostering a continuing "commitment to a deviant career": "One of the most crucial steps in the process of building a stable pattern of deviant behavior is likely to be the experience of being caught and publicly labeled as a deviant. Whether a person takes this step or not depends not so much on what he does as on what other people do, on whether or not they enforce the rule he has violated" (1963 : 31).

LABELING THEORY AND THE STRUCTURING OF DEVIANT BEHAVIOR

Of the four concerns of labeling theory—the origin of deviant labels, the contingencies of societal reaction, the consequences of reaction for a social system, and the effects that being labeled have for an actor—it is the final one which is of primary interest to us here. It is this aspect of the labeling paradigm that addresses the question that has long dominated the attention of more traditional deviance theorists: why do people deviate? In contrast to stress and nonstress theorists, labeling authors have located the cause of rule-breaking, at least of a stable variety, in societal reactions and not in the characteristics of the deviant. Yet, if this has made labeling theory a revisionist perspective, it has not always prevented those within the labeling paradigm from employing the same kind of deterministic thinking that has at times informed the writings of authors falling within more traditional perspectives.

Thus, just as others within the field of deviance have tended to neglect the problem of indeterminacy, so too has the importance of this issue escaped many labeling theorists. We can again be reminded that these authors have asserted that societal reaction will deepen or increase a person's involvement in a deviant career. In setting forth this innovative proposition, however, they have typically assumed that labeling determines or is etiologically specific to a particular form of deviance. As Robins has noted, "labeling theory argues that labels encourage the very behavior specified by the label. That is, one steals because one is labeled a thief; one acts 'crazy' because one is designated psychotic" (1975 : 23). Of course, this reasoning obscures the possibility that the experience of being defined and treated as a particular kind of deviant might inadvertently trigger other forms of nonconformity as well.[2] For instance, the stresses generated by the experience of being stigmatized as a thief and being exposed to the rigors of prison life could lead not exclusively to heightened involvement in crime but also to such adaptations as suicide, drug use, and mental illness. If so, the next logical step—one not usually undertaken by labeling scholars—would be to explain the social circumstances that condition the ways in which people respond to the potentially traumatic event of state intervention into their lives.

In short, as Tittle has cautioned, it is important to be sensitive to how "sanctioning for a given type of deviant act spills over to the other kinds of deviance" (1975 : 407). Notably, however, this possibility has been largely ignored not only by labeling theorists but by the perspective's critics as well. Thus, similar to the evaluations of Merton's paradigm, those weighing the impact of societal reaction invariably ask a series of essentially deterministic questions: Does labeling increase crime? Delinquency? Mental illness? Sexual deviance? Drug abuse? This orientation is apparent in the widely read volume edited by Gove (1975, 1980). Here, a number of influential deviance scholars each selected a form of deviance in which they had special expertise, and then proceeded to assess the extent to which societal reaction caused this one deviation.

It is also instructive that in evaluations such as these, researchers typically marshall much evidence which disputes the labeling theory claim that societal reaction increases deviant behavior. Summarizing the thrust of the essays contained in his book, Gove thus concluded that "the evidence reviewed consistently indicates that labeling is not the major cause of the development of stabilized deviant behavior" (1975 : 295; cf. Hepburn 1977, Wellford 1975). Such findings are often taken to imply that societal reaction is of little or no etiological significance. Thus, Hirschi's literature review enabled him to state that "labeling . . . has no effect" (1975 : 197), while Nettler has proclaimed that the perspective "does not answer the perennial questions about crime . . . that are asked by most people . . . 'What causes crime?' 'What accounts for increases and decreases in crime rates?' " (1978 : 305). And more recently, Gove again succinctly stated his position that reaction processes "exist but their overall impact is small" (1980 : 286).

What is more, it appears that labeling theorists have largely accepted this declaration that it would be best to partake in a requiem for their perspective as an explanation of the origins of crime and deviance—despite, I might add, evidence to the contrary (cf. Ageton and Elliot 1974, Jensen 1972, Klemke 1978, O'Connor 1970, Shannon 1982, Wheeler 1978, McCord 1978, 1981, Gersten et al. 1977). They have thus retreated from the stance that the perspective can furnish meaningful insights into the question of causation. For example, in reconsidering his earlier work *Outsiders* and the interpretation it has received since its publication in 1963, Becker asserted that "the original proponents" of labeling theory "did not propose solutions to the etiological question'' (1974 : 42). Similarly, Kitsuse has disclaimed any notion that this revisionist orientation was ever meant to address the problem of why people deviate. Instead, the real value of labeling theory in his eyes is quite the opposite, in that it "explicitly proposed a shift of focus from questions about the etiology of 'deviant behavior' to the processes by which behaviors and persons come to be perceived, defined, and treated as deviant'' (1975 : 279).[3]

A structuring perspective would immediately suggest, however, that such conclusions may prove premature and misplaced. To begin with, it must be remembered that the prevailing empirical research, informed by deterministic logic, examines only how societal reaction is related to a single form of deviance at a time. As a result of this restricted methodology, the degree to which a given intervention "spills over," to use Tittle's terminology, and precipitates deviations other than the form being studied is simply not measured. Notably, new research by Palamara et al. has indicated that this possibility may be worth pursuing. In a five-year, longitudinal study of the impact of the intervention of police and mental health officials in the lives of New York City youths, Palamara and her associates discovered that societal reaction not only deepens deviant involvement, but that it can also give rise to more than one form of juvenile deviance (1983).

Yet we can push beyond the question of whether the experience of being designated a nonconformist moves people to become deviant. Indeed, even if the evaluation research conducted by critics were to be proven correct, it would still be erroneous to conclude that the labeling perspective contains no etiological worth whatsoever. For what such researchers have not considered is that societal reaction may also function as a variable which shapes the deviant choices people make by closing off certain options while creating others. That is, quite apart from whether labeling heightens deviant involvement per se, it may have large effects in accounting for the *type* of deviance that occurs. In this light then, the potential structuring influences of societal reaction will be illustrated below by reexamining the literature on the consequences of being imprisoned.

PRISONS AND THE STRUCTURING OF DEVIANT BEHAVIOR

In their classic study of the American prison system, Gustave de Beaumont and Alexis de Toqueville commented that "it is customary, in order to know what influence the penitentiary system has upon society, to meet the question thus: Has the number of crimes augmented or diminished since the penitentiary system has been established?" ([1833] 1964 : 92). Over the years, this question has elicited different responses. There have been those, for instance, who believe that incarceration decreases criminality by functioning either as a source of punishment that deters future offenses by scaring the wicked straight or as a therapeutic context in which an offender can be rehabilitated.

Yet, consistent with the labeling perspective, it has more frequently been suggested that prisons serve as "schools of crime" and hence deepen a person's commitment to a life of crime. Such a view was prevalent among early students of crime, even though they otherwise pledged allegiance to divergent theoretical positions. Thus, the classical-utilitarian theorist, Jeremy Bentham, cautioned that "an ordinary prison is a school in which wickedness is taught by surer means than can ever be employed for the inculcation of virtue. Weariness, revenge, and want preside over these academies of crime" (quoted in Hawkins 1976 : 57). Similarly, the positivist Lombroso was of the opinion that "the degrading influences of prison life and contact with vulgar criminals . . . cause criminaloids who have committed their initial offences with repugnance and hesitation, to develop later into habitual criminals" ([1911] 1972 : 110–11). This theme appears as well in the Marxist work of Bonger who reasoned that by incarcerating "young people who have committed merely misdemeanors of minor importance . . . we are bringing up professional criminals" (1969 : 118).

In America, nineteenth-century prison reformers were equally troubled by the criminogenic effects of prisons (Platt 1969, Rothman 1971). One may point to Major R.W. McGlaughry, Warden of Joliet State Penitentiary, who in 1891 remarked that "you can not take a boy of tender years and lock him up with thieves, drunkards and half-crazy men without teaching him lessons in crime" (quoted in Platt 1969 : 132). Moreover, this notion retains some appeal among current-day criminologists. Thus, Jeffrey has maintained:

> We are using prisons to combat the crime rate, whereas in fact prisons create more crime than they eliminate. At the end of the criminal justice process operates a correctional system that neither deters nor rehabilitates. . . . We are supporting a correctional system today that does not prevent new crimes or recidivism, and it acts as a criminogenic force in creating hardened criminals among those who enter into the system. [1977 : 80]

However, despite the persistence of the idea that prisons are schools of crime, an alternative perspective has emerged that is now accorded considerable credence: incarceration has no effect on the level of criminal involvement. That is, prisons not only fail to rehabilitate or deter, but they also do not make an offender more criminal:

> The available research on the impact of various treatment strategies both in and out of prison seems to indicate that, after controlling for initial selection differences, there are generally no statistically significant differences between the subsequent recidivism of offenders, regardless of the form of "treatment." This suggests that neither rehabilitative nor criminogenic effects operate very strongly.

> Therefore, at an aggregate level, these confounding effects are probably safely
> ignored. [Blumstein et al. 1978 : 66]

Instead, commentators assert that violations of the law are a product of the
traits an offender possesses prior to imprisonment and not of prison experiences (Irwin and Cressey 1962). Hence, after a comprehensive review of
research on prisons, Hawkins commented:

> One concludes with doubt about the criminogenic effects of imprisonment on
> grounds which imply not merely that inmates are not being corrupted but rather
> that neither their attitudes nor their behavior are being affected in any significant
> fashion by the experience of imprisonment. . . . Moreover it must clearly have
> policy implications of a fundamental character, for it suggests that the question,
> to use Barry Schwartz's words, "whether people-changing organizations really
> socialize or merely serve as arenas wherein predispositions earlier acquired are
> acted out," must be answered in favor of the latter alternative. [1976 : 72–73]

All this is usually taken to mean that imprisonment has no impact on
criminal behavior whatsoever. Yet saying that incarceration does not result
in a firmer commitment to a criminal career is not the same as saying that it
does not influence the type or form of crime that an offender pursues upon
release from prison. In this regard, we have seen that prisons have frequently
been characterized as "schools of crime." It may well be true that prison
"education" does not make an inmate more criminal; after all, it must be
admitted that it is primarily habitual criminals that our legal system sends to
prison in the first place. Nevertheless, the prison literature is sprinkled with
examples of how such education provides inmates with skills that will enable
them to assume new kinds of criminal roles.

For instance, while in a "house of corruption," Shaw's jack-roller Stanley
learned how to pursue a more profitable form of crime, the rackets:

> "Kid you're in here for a year for jack-rolling. This ought to teach you a lesson.
> Leave me tell you, the next time you pull anything off, pick out a racket where
> there's dough, so if you get caught it's worth doing time for, and if you get
> away, you're all set for the rest of your life. Now compare us here. We both
> got the same rap, one year in this hell-hole, but I pulled a ten-thousand-dollar
> deal, and you got less than a hundred dollars. Don't you get me? Besides, get
> into a respectable racket, so you can dress well and mingle in society. A jack-
> roller hain't got any chances anywhere. Take it from me, kid, when I get out
> of here I'm going to pull off one big haul and then retire for the rest of my
> life. . . ." I felt humiliated inwardly, and made up my mind to get a racket
> that would bring me good returns. Halfpint promised to help me in working
> out my plans, and I had a whole year to do it in. [1930 : 153–54]

Modern-day criminals furnish similar accounts:

> In the shop that I was working at, that is, in the reformatory, I got to talking
> to one guy about laying notes. And he showed me a couple of ways of laying

notes, and explained to me how lucrative it could be. . . . And I learned safecracking from A to Z in here, in theory, in that shoe shop. [Letkemann 1973 : 121, 126]

Further, for some time academics have made comparable observations. Thus, Lombroso stated early in this century:

In fact, in prison, criminals have an opportunity of becoming acquainted with each other, of instructing those less skilled in infamy, and of banding together for evil purposes. . . . Moreover, in prison, mere children of seven or eight, imprisoned for stealing a bunch of grapes or a fowl, come into close contact with adults and become initiated into evil practices, of which these poor little victims of stupid laws were previously quite ignorant. [1972 : 148]

More currently, Inciardi proposed that

the prison setting represents one of the more active centers in recruitment and training of professional criminals. Both amateurs and veteran offenders often gain entrance into the underworld of more skilled criminal practitioners through institutionalized tutelage. [1974 : 332]

And, based on interviews with prison inmates, Letkemann has concluded:

None of my respondents suggested any degree of specialization before their first prison sentence—*it was during prison that the illegitimate career took on form and structure.* . . . Through association with experienced criminals, the offender is introduced to, and has some basis to assess, alternative modes of crime. He realizes that not all criminal modes are viable alternatives. An assessment of his own abilities, qualified by his prison experience, provides direction quite different from earlier, impulsive, peer-group pressures. He learns that some skills cannot be developed simply through the process of trial and error; he will need the help and confidence of those more experienced. Prison provides the opportunity for such association. [1973 : 129–30, emphasis mine]

Apart from the criminal skills that are acquired, prisons also may enable offenders to establish friendships that will allow them to engage in new forms of crime when they are returned to society. This has been vividly portrayed by Ianni in the *Black Mafia* (1974). Ianni observed that prison policies lead blacks to group together into small cliques. The experience of continuous primary-group interaction, which membership in these cliques provides, allows these inmates to develop close social bonds. In turn, by serving as functional alternatives to the ethnic-familial bonds that link Italians together, the friendships formed in prison permit blacks upon release to engage in organized criminal enterprises which as individuals they would have been unable to pursue. Incarceration is thus an important factor in regulating whether individualistic or organized forms of crime will be committed. According to Ianni:

Throughout the various networks that we observed, we found that prisons and the prison experience are the most important locus for establishing the social relationships that form the basis for partnerships in organized crime, both among blacks and among Puerto Ricans. The Italians do not form their criminal partnerships in prison, both because they do not go to jail as often as blacks and Puerto Ricans do now and because they form their organized crime networks on the Mafia-oriented basis of kinship. . . . But we have not been aware of the great extent to which criminal partnerships are formed in prison. . . . In our study we found that the common practice in prisons of segregating prisoners informally by race produces a number of closely knit social groups—"prison courts"—in which organized crime partnerships are first created and which then structure similar relationships outside the prison. [1974 : 142]

Now, while imprisonment makes new and sophisticated forms of crime available to some, this is not true for all inmates. Like the criminal world outside the prison walls (Sutherland 1937), only certain inmates (such as those who demonstrate intelligence and solidarity with the inmate culture) are selected for tutelage in "professional" crime (Letkemann 1973). Moreover, incarceration may at times channel offenders into less sophisticated types of crimes than they had previously committed. For example, Sutherland noted that a professional thief who serves a lengthy prison sentence "knows that his connections will be lost, a new bunch will be grifting, and he will not be able to build up gradually as things develop. He becomes absolutely dissociated from his outfit and its ideas" (1937 : 186). Consequently, when former thieves finally leave prison, they are often unable to participate in professional crimes and are instead limited to the pursuit of more readily available, nonprofessional options (e.g., passing bad checks or robbery).

Finally, it should be recognized that prisons may serve as a learning environment not only for new forms of crime but for other kinds of deviant behavior as well. In this regard, Halleck has asserted that the establishment of mental health programs in a prison may structure an inmate's behavior by fostering a milieu conducive to the manifestation of psychiatric symptomatology as opposed to other antisocial conduct. Thus, the presence of treatment personnel can create the opportunity for offenders to "behave neurotically" because a "sick role is available" and can be learned, if unconsciously at times, in this therapeutic context. Somewhat "paradoxically," then, rehabilitation programs may "increase rather than decrease the incidence of mental illness" (1967 : 75).[4]

In sum, both critics and exponents of labeling theory have focused almost exclusively on the issue of whether societal reaction increases or decreases deviant involvement. In doing so, they have been reluctant to explore the way in which societal reaction might structure the form an actor's deviance takes. This oversight might prove to be a large one. We have already seen how one mode of labeling, imprisonment, may structure the type of crime and deviance an actor selects. Yet, this is only the beginning. To arrive at a clearer understanding of the structuring effects of societal reaction, it would be necessary to undertake a comprehensive analysis of how other kinds of labeling processes permit actors to follow certain deviant paths and not others. In concluding our discussion of labeling theory, it might prove useful to illustrate this latter point further.

THE STRUCTURING EFFECTS OF SOCIETAL REACTION: FURTHER EXAMPLES

Apart from formal methods of control such as the institutionalization of deviant populations, it can be anticipated that informal patterns of societal reaction would also operate to structure deviant choices. Instructive in this regard is that the informal reactions of men restrict the capacity of most females to engage in the deviant activity of begging. Now as Rosenblum has suggested, one factor that deters women from undertaking this activity is the "internal limits which make begging unattractive to women" (1976 : 180). Of greater import, however, may be "the unwillingness of others to accept women in the sociopathic role" of a beggar (1976 : 180). Particularly for the young, a "woman without a physical handicap is seldom a professional beggar chiefly because most men who encounter her in such a role would treat her as a prostitute" (1976 : 180). Thus, in addition to the "internal limits" women commonly possess, females encounter societal reaction which serves to exclude all but a few from engaging in this form of deviance.

Similarly, the ability of elites and other interest-groups to label certain deviant behaviors as criminal through the passage of laws and empower state agents to control such activity can structure participation in these behaviors. Again, using female offense patterns as an example, it is notable that prior to the criminalization of drug-related activities early in this century, "female drug addicts outnumbered male addicts by a ratio of two to one" (Adler 1975 : 114, Cuskey et al. 1972 : 9–12, Lindesmith and Gagnon 1964 : 164, Waldorf 1973 : 176). Before the Harrison Act in 1914, "opiates were generally available to anyone who wished to buy them, without a doctor's prescription" (Lindesmith and Gagnon 1964 : 165). Since female alcohol use was culturally proscribed, women often employed opiates as a legitimate "social lubricant and personal pacifier" (Adler 1975 : 115). Further, during the nineteenth century, opiates were "liberally and carelessly used in medical practice, and countless patent medicines which contained them were widely advertised and sold as cures for most of the ills of the flesh." "A large proportion of the addicts became addicted through self-medication or by using drugs prescribed for them by physicians" (Lindesmith and Gagnon 1964 : 165–66). Since women were prone to use drugs for medicinal purposes, their rates of addiction reflected this fact. Once drug activities were outlawed, however, the proportion of female addicts "had shrunk to 25 percent by the early 1930s. Today it stands at about 20 percent" (Adler 1975 : 122). As Adler has pointed out, the illegal status of drugs precluded their usage by effectively socialized women. "Even more conformist than men, respectable women generally did not take their habit underground, into the clandestine world of the black marketeer and drug pusher, as many men did when opium became illegal and disreputable. Consequently, after 1920, opium addiction declined sharply among women, gradually among men" (1975 : 116). Succinctly stated, "women were deterred by the criminalization of addiction; men were not and became the majority of addicts" (Waldorf 1973 : 177).

Apart from normative considerations, the criminalization of drugs served to restrict female drug use and addiction in other ways as well. First, prior to the Harrison Act, drugs were inexpensive. With the passage of this act, access to legitimate sources of drugs were closed. To meet the existing demand for narcotics, illicit sources began to develop. The pressing demand for drugs and the monopolistic control of the illicit drug supply combined to escalate the cost of narcotics (Lindesmith and Gagnon 1964 : 166–68). Since women are generally in a disadvantaged economic position, they are less likely than men to possess the resources either to buy drugs for experimentation or, in particular, to support an expensive drug habit. Second, in addition to increasing the price of narcotics, the criminalization of drugs and the subsequent closure of legitimate sources made the procurement of drugs problematic. Following passage of the Harrison Act, alternative sources of narcotics had to be found. Significantly, in both the conventional and unconventional spheres, women were and are less likely to be in a position to secure drugs. Thus, fewer females work in occupations such as medical doctor, pharmacist, and jazz musician, which afford ready access to narcotics (Clausen 1966, Clinard 1974, Winick 1959–60, 1961). Similarly, women usually do not have the chance to join deviant subcultures in which the continuous supply of narcotics is available (cf. Clinard 1974 : 414–15).

A final instance of the structuring effects of societal reaction is present in Gary Marx's innovative essay on the "ironies of social control" (1981). Of particular interest here are his observations on the role "authorities" play in creating fresh opportunities for criminal activity. From Marx's viewpoint, law enforcement strategies ranging from intense surveillance to the "covert facilitation" or encouragement of unlawful behavior can have the unanticipated consequence of amplifying deviant conduct. Marx was particularly aware of the fact that social control efforts often pattern the character of criminality by increasing the attractiveness of some options (e.g., through nonenforcement) while avidly discouraging others. Further, control measures may in certain circumstances enable people to engage in "new varieties" of illegality. This is particularly likely when police employ such practices as the use of "decoys, false fronts, and 'buy' money for narcotics." On a broad theoretical level, then, it is perhaps not surprising that Marx perceived the link between his insights on societal reaction and the "theory of illegitimate means":

> The perspective suggested here has implications for approaches to deviance beyond that of labeling. . . . Cloward and Ohin (1960) have stressed the importance of illegitimate opportunity structures as provided by adult criminals for the behavior of juveniles. . . . The ideas and evidence considered in this paper suggest the need to broaden the conceptions of opportunity structure . . . to the role that control agents themselves (rather than adult criminals) . . . may play in generating illegitimate opportunities and contexts for victimization and in then encouraging would-be offenders to take advantage of them. [1981 : 240]

Control Theory

THE THEORY

In their attempt to explain the causes of deviant behavior, theorists have traditionally asked, what moves people to violate social norms? It has thus been a shared belief among theorists that delineating the source of the *motivation or predisposition to deviate* provides a complete explanation of the source of *deviant behavior*. We have seen that many authors have located the origins of deviant motivation in the stresses that people endure, while others have pointed to such social conditions as exposure to a nonconformist value system or the internalization of a deviant identity.

Those belonging to the "control" or "social bond" perspective have challenged the prevailing idea that knowing why people are predisposed to deviate tells us why they will actually transgress a norm. Much like the Freudian-Hobbesian tradition which views human nature as a bundle of deviant impulses ready to erupt when restraints weaken, control theorists have proceeded on the assumption that all people would deviate if given the chance. Deviant motivation is not regarded as problematic and its origin therefore requires no special explanation. Cohen and Short have observed that "the implied model of motivation" of control theories of delinquency "assume that the impulse to delinquency is an inherent characteristic of young people and does not itself need to be explained" (1961 : 112). In a like manner, Hirschi has stated:

> In the end, then, control theory remains what it has always been: a theory in which deviation is not problematic. The question "Why did they do it?" is simply not the question the theory is designed to answer. The question is, "Why don't we do it?" There is much evidence that we would if we dared. [1969 : 34]

Now, if everyone is motivated to deviate, then it is clear that understanding the etiology of such motivation will not reveal who will or will not conform. Instead, to distinguish between conformists and deviants, it is necessary to learn the conditions which either permit or preclude deviant motivations from being actualized in deviant behavior. In this regard, those within the control paradigm have proposed that deviant acts result only "when an individual's bond to society is weak or broken" (Hirschi 1969 : 16). Otherwise, controls remain firm, deviant motives are constrained, and conformity is enforced.[5]

The idea that a breakdown in controls or social bonds frees people to act on their nonconformist impulses has frequently appeared over the years (Kornhauser 1978). Psychodynamic explanations, for instance, have long traced the origins of aberrant conduct to weak ego or superego controls that permit antisocial urges to boil over and drive a person to deviate (Empey 1982 : 162–84). One can point as well to Durkheim who felt that normative deregulation of needs would allow deviant motivations to flourish, and to Merton who on occasion observed that anomic social conditons, even in the absence of status frustration, would encourage waywardness. This theme also found its way, indeed more fully, into the writings of the Chicago School. It might be remembered that theorists such as Thrasher and Shaw and McKay believed that the weakening of institutional controls in disorganized neighborhoods first generates a criminal tradition and then allows youths to be cast out unprotected into slum areas where this tradition will be internalized.

Other scholars continued to work in the control theory tradition. Thus, Reiss maintained that delinquency emerges from the "failure of personal and social controls to produce behavior in conformity with the norms of the social system to which penalties are attached" (1951 : 196). For Briar and Piliavin, a youth's "commitment to or stake in conformity" regulates deliquent involvement. Hence, "a youth with strong commitments to conformity is less likely to engage in deviant acts than is one for whom these commitments are minimal, given that both experience motives to deviate in the same degree" (1965 : 39). Similarly, Nye posited that "delinquent behavior occurs in the absence of controls or if controls are ineffective"(1957 : 3). He placed special emphasis on the causal significance of familial controls in contributing to or limiting delinquent activity. Toby, however, has sought to broaden Nye's perspective by demonstrating that apart from the family, "there are many social-system contexts in which deviant personality tendencies can be extirpated or reinforced, . . . the peer group, the educational-occupational system, and the formal control system of the larger society" (1974 : 91).

Another variety of control theory is found in Reckless's "containment theory," developed in conjunction with his associates during the 1950s. Trained at the University of Chicago, Reckless was initially fascinated by the issue of why some boys remain "good" even though they grow up surrounded by "bad boys" in disorganized, criminogenic neighborhoods. To explain this perplexing occurrence, he proposed that the evolution of a self-concept of a "good boy" insulates youths from the deviant influences prevailing within their environment. He thus commented:

A good self-concept is assumed to represent a favorable internalization of presumably favorable life experiences, including an acceptance or incorporation of the proper concern which significant others have had for the person. It acts selectively on experiences and holds the line against adversities (pressure), the subculture of delinquency, wrongdoing and crime (pull), as well as discontent and frustrations (pushes). . . . The poor self-concept represents a "normal" lack of inner containment against the ordinary pressures, pulls, and pushes. [1961 : 351–52][6]

Reckless went on to observe, however, that delinquency will not always result if a youth's self-concept is weak. It is still possible that those around the youth will compensate for the lack of inner control by keeping the youth in line. As such, as long as "outer containment" stays firm, an individual may still be prevented from acting out deviant impulses:

The self-concept, as good or poor inner containment, operates in a framework of outer containment in the individual's milieu. Effective outer containment is achieved through effective family life and an effective supporting structure in the neighborhood and in the larger society. If family life and the surrounding social organization are adequate to contain practically every individual living within the system, the self-concept does not need to be as favorable as it does when an individual is confronted with adversities and disorganization in his milieu. In the latter instance, the inner controls or containment must be strong enough to hold the line. [1961 : 352]

In light of the many works of Reckless and others which extend from the early days of the field to more present times, it might seem somewhat anomalous to claim that social control theory is a "revisionist explanation." Nevertheless, pure social control models have long been overshadowed by the more dominant understandings that deviance is a manifestation of either the transmission of deviant cultural values (Chicago School) or exposure to intense, stressful experiences (Durkeim-Merton tradition). Indeed, it was not until the writings of such leading figures as Sutherland and Merton waned in popularity that control theory achieved sufficient power to capture the attention of large numbers of students of crime and deviance. More specifically, it was not until the publication of Matza's *Delinquency and Drift* (1964) and, in particular, of Hirschi's *Causes of Delinquency* (1969) that control theory emerged as a truly distinct perspective which both widely challenged more familiar explanations of deviant behavior and became the object of continuing empirical research.

The groundwork for Matza's work in 1964 was initially set forth in an essay coauthored with Gresham Sykes seven years earlier (cf. Sykes and Matza 1957). Building on Cressey's discussion of "violators' vocabularies of adjustment" (1953 : 95–138) and Redl and Wineman's investigation of "the delinquent ego and its techniques" (1951 : 172–84), Sykes and Matza started with the hypothesis that the commission of a crime is dependent on a person's possessing "techniques of neutralization." This notion is based on the premise that conventional institutions exercise considerable influence on almost everyone and hence all but a few people are bonded to society. Moreover, these bonds are so potent that the simple contemplation of an illegal act is enough to evoke a sufficient amount of guilt to deter any wrongdoing. Consequently, it is only when one can justify or rationalize an offense prior to its commission that the social bond and concomitant guilt will be neutralized and the execution of the offense made possible. According to Sykes and Matza:

> These justifications are commonly described as rationalizations. They are viewed as following deviant behavior and as protecting the individual from self-blame and the blame of others after the act. But there is also reason to believe that they precede deviant behavior and make deviant behavior possible . . . Disapproval flowing from internalized norms and conforming others in the social environment is neutralized, turned back, or deflected in advance. Social controls that serve to check or inhibit deviant motivational patterns are rendered inoperative, and the individual is freed to engage in delinquency. [1957 : 666–67]

In Sykes and Matza's terminology, the different kinds of justifications used to abrogate society's control are best thought of as "techniques of neutralization." Further, it is possible to illustrate the process which they had in mind by briefly focusing on one such technique, "denial of the victim." (The other techniques were called denial of responsibility, denial of injury, condemnation of the condemners, and appeal to higher loyalties.) Here, Sykes and Matza alerted us to the possibility that youths could step outside the law if they could convince themselves that the potential "victim" deserved to be set upon. Thus, should someone cheat on a bet, put the "moves" on a date, or perhaps be of the "wrong" racial group, the usual constraints proscribing a physical attack on another can be "neutralized by an insistence that the injury is not wrong in light of the circumstances...it is a form of rightful retaliation or punishment" (1957 : 668).

These points were later elaborated by Matza in his popular treatise *Delinquency and Drift* (1964). Here, Matza began by criticizing previous theories for embracing the logic of the positivist school of criminology, which suggests that deviants are fundamentally different from the rest of us. If such imagery were correct and delinquents were indeed constantly under the sway of deviant forces—whether these be intense strains or learned criminal values—then we would anticipate, Matza reasoned, that such youths would embark on unlawful ventures all of the time. The vast majority of wayward youths, however, have not been made into sociopaths. Instead, all but the most hardened and unusual offenders are only transiently delinquent; further, as they mature, nearly all reform and give up their flirtations with the law. As such, Matza asserted that traditional theories suffer an "embarrassment of riches" because they "account for too much delinquency. Taken at their terms, delinquency theories seem to predict far too much delinquency than actually occurs" (1964:21).

As an alternative, Matza reasserted the notion expressed previously in conjunction with Sykes that youths generally subscribe to the moral mandates of the dominant social order. To escape normative control, it is thus necessary for juveniles to possess the "techniques" required to "neutralize" society's hold over them. It is here that Matza introduced new thinking by answering the question, what happens when a youth is freed from social restraint? His response was that unregulated juveniles experience a state of "drift," in which they "exist in a limbo between convention and crime" (p. 28). As Matza made clear, to be in drift does not lead inexorably to a delinquent rampage. Instead, "drift makes delinquency possible or permissible by temporarily removing the restraints that ordinarily control members of society, but of itself supplies no irreversible commitment or compulsion that would suffice to thrust the person into the act" (p. 181).

What, then, does propel potential delinquents in drift to move outside the law? To solve this problem, Matza borrowed from the imagery of the classical school and proposed that "the missing element which provides the thrust of impetus by which the deliquent act is realized is will" (p. 181). At the same time, Matza realized that having the "will" to deviate is not equivalent to exercising total freedom over one's destiny. For the capacity to "activate" such a will is itself shaped by past and present circumstance. In this regard, Matza illuminated two conditions that make the activation of will possible. One of these, "preparation," involves both the possession of the behavioral proficiency needed to accomplish a wayward act and the development of sufficient confidence or unconcern that one is not too apprehensive to leap into a delinquent adventure. The other, "desperation," is more applicable in unusual circumstances in which youths are overwhelmed by the forces enveloping them. To overcome this sense of "fatalism," the juvenile in drift actively chooses delinquency as a means of "dramatic reassurance that he can still make things happen" (p. 189).

It remained for Hirschi to present what has perhaps become the most influential statement of the control perspective (Hirschi 1969; cf. Empey 1982, Gibbons 1979:121). From the preface onward, Hirschi sought to distinguish his orientation from both stress theory and the ideas of the Chicago School and to launch a strong empirical challenge to the adequacy of these long-standing criminological traditions:

The theory I advocate sees in the delinquent a person relatively free of the intimate attachments, the aspirations, and the moral beliefs that bind most people to a life within the law. In prominent alternative theories, the delinquent appears either as a frustrated striver forced into delinquency by his acceptance of the goals common to us all, or as an innocent foreigner attempting to obey the rules of a society that is not in position to make the law or to define conduct as good or evil. Throughout the book, I stress the incompatibility of these images and the contrasting predicitions to which they lead us. [1969, in preface]

Now unlike Sykes and Matza, yet similar to traditional control theorists, Hirschi questioned the view that most people, including those who deviate, are bonded to society. For Hirschi, the ability of a person to formulate links to society and therefore to resist deviant motivations is variable; some people do, some people do not, and some people do in part. As such, it is not the neutralization of social bonds that makes delinquency possible but rather the failure to possess sufficiently firm bonds in the first place. That is, "delinquent acts result when an individual's bond to society is weak or broken" (p. 16). Further, Hirschi embellished his general proposition on the relationship of social ties to delinquency by specifying four "elements of the bond": affective *attachment* to others, most notably parents; a *commitment* to or stake in conventional goals such as academic achievement; *involvement* in wholesome activities like youth groups or athletic teams; and *belief* in the legitimacy and salience of the law. Again, the more of each of these bonds an adolescent has, the more insulated against the attractions of deviance the youth becomes. Thus, in relation to the belief component of the social bond, Hirschi reasoned that "there is *variation* in the extent to which people believe they should obey the rules of society, and, furthermore, that the less a person believes he should obey the rules, the more likely he is to violate them" (p. 26).

CONTROL THEORY AND THE STRUCTURING OF DEVIANT BEHAVIOR

Control theorists have taken a distinct approach to the study of deviance. In contrast to traditional stress and nonstress theorists, they have rejected the notion that aberrant predispositions lead ineluctably to deviant behavior. Instead, they have asserted that variables intervene between deviant motivation and behavior, and regulate when deviance as opposed to conformity will occur. Yet, if their distinct approach has allowed control theorists to demarcate an important set of intervening variables, it has not always kept them from operating on the assumption that the absence or weakening of controls results in a *single form* of deviance. It is particularly common, as we have seen, for authors to hypothesize that a lack of control leads specifically to crime/delinquency.

However, such a stance is not easy to defend. To begin with, it leaves open the question of why the absence of control or bond to society produces one form of criminality and not another. Thus, while Matza has furnished us with valuable insights on how ties to the social order are set aside, a reading of his work tells us little of why a youth in "drift" shoplifts rather than robs, or seeks to escape by getting high rather than running away. What is more, the deterministic bent to control theory risks obscuring the likely possibility that a breakdown in control may generate other varieties of deviant involvement. It is significant that certain deviance theorists have argued as much. Thus, a review of literature on political protest has led Cloward and Piven et al. to conclude that "a substantial and enduring body of work exists that attributes eruptions of civil disorder not to the stress generated by socioeconomic change, and not even to the stress which intervenes when institutionalized social controls weaken, but simply to the breakdown of these controls" (1977 : 256). Glancing back once again to Durkheim, we see a theorist who believed that the attenuation of normative guidelines set in motion conditions that eventually result in suicide. Moreover, nearly every major form of nonconformity has been traced to the breakdown in social control engendered by the "disorganized" black family:

> Nonetheless, at the center of the tangle of pathology is the weakness of the family structure. Once or twice removed, it will be found to be the principal source of most of the aberrant, inadequate, or antisocial behavior that did not establish, but now serves to perpetuate the cycle of poverty and deprivation. [Office of Policy Planning and Research, 1965 : 30][7]

The remarks of Schuessler are also instructive in this regard:

> A weakening of institutional controls need not be accompanied by an increase in crime, if there are countervailing circumstances. . . . *Crime is only one of several possible reactions to a slackening of institutional ties*, and its relative ascendancy will depend on the predominance of social arrangements and cultural perspectives *that direct attention to crime and correspondingly divert it from other solutions*. [1962 : 321, emphasis mine]

In short, there is much reason to hold that an indeterminate relationship exists between the general absence of control and any particular form of deviance. Yet even if control theorists can be criticized for not attending to this issue, it would be unfortunate if the rich theoretical possibilities within their work were not resurrected and developed. Thus, it should be recognized that control theory and the structuring perspective share the common understanding that detailing the origins of deviant impulses does not fully account for the emergence of deviant *behavior*. Instead, each embraces the position that this explanatory task is performed by variables which intervene between motivations and potential deviant outcomes. But again, control theorists have been preoccupied with the question of why deviance and not conformity occurs, and consequently they have paid less attention to why a particular type of waywardness becomes possible. Hence, Sykes and Matza developed the concept of techniques of neutralization mainly to explain why delinquency as such occurs (1957). Indeed, as Hirschi observed, Sykes and Matza assumed "that neutralization occurs in order to make many delinquent acts possible" (1969 : 25).

Yet, might it not be the case that Sykes and Matza's insights here can be used to furnish us with novel ideas on how people's deviant choices are structured? In this light, one fruitful line of inquiry might be to explore how different kinds of neutralization techniques permit participation in different kinds of deviant activities. Indeed, Sykes and Matza alerted their readers to this very possibility. Near the end of their essay, they urged future researchers to consider the relationship of the justifications used to break controls to "various types of delinquent behavior. Certain techniques would appear to be better adapted to particular deviant acts" (1957 : 670). Such an observation, even if made only in passing, is not surprising because much of Sykes and Matza's discussion clearly reveals how the *content of neutralizations* very much shapes the *content of the delinquent act* which emerges. For instance, the technique of "the denial of the victim" might allow juveniles to beat-up "homosexuals or suspected homosexuals" or to launch "attacks on members of minority groups who are said to have gotten 'out of place'" (1957 : 668). But while this neutralization might permit certain assaults, it does not justify other sorts of predatory behavior (e.g., assaults on in-group members, robbery for economic gain). As such, by learning more about the nature of techniques of neutralization and how these are patterned throughout the social structure, it seems quite likely that we will enrich our understanding of why certain deviant avenues are open to people while others remain beyond thought and reach.

Further illustrations of the structuring thesis suggested by Sykes and Matza are prevalent in the literature dealing with crime in the workplace. Students of occupationally related crime have long been confronted with the perplexing problem of how it is that workers who ostensibly are committed to a conventional line of work and have a "stake in conformity" can nevertheless engage in unlawful behavior. In other words, how can these people deviate when they are bonded to the dominant economic order? Of course, a plausible answer, indeed one which has gained many adherents, is that workers neutralize controls by situationally invoking justifications that temporarily allow them to step outside the law.

It is instructive, however, that observers of workplace criminality have not asserted that all types of lawlessness can be equally rationalized. Rather, it is common for them to find that workers are quite likely to pilfer company

materials and merchandise, because they can, in Sykes and Matza's terminology, "deny injury"; after all, the company is large, profitable, and has
its losses covered by insurance. By contrast, stealing from a co-worker, a
case in which the victimization is personalized and the injury obvious, is not
so readily justified and hence occurs much less frequently. In the same vein,
the proclivity of corporate executives to ignore the constraints of prevailing
laws is well documented (Sutherland 1949, Clinard and Yeager 1980). Their
lawlessness is not indiscriminate, however. While morally upright in most
aspects of their lives, corporate executives might at the same time engage in
business practices that involve the enormous loss of money (e.g., price-fixing)
and danger to lives (e.g., environmental pollution, defective products). What
makes corporate but not personal crime possible is, again, the availability of
neutralization mechanisms. Unlike traditional street crimes that are defined
as reprehensible, acts on behalf of the corporation can be justified as being
"illegal but not really criminal" (cf. Conkin 1977) or perhaps as the result
of "only following orders" or of being a "team player." In short, the character of workplace crime is very much structured by the nature of the techniques of neutralization that are available within this social context. Significantly,
in summarizing the literature on employee pilfering, Barlow captured this
very point when he noted that existing "verbalized motives or justificatory
rationalizations" provide "workers with a normative framework with which
to shape their own subsequent conduct . . . the discrimination in the choice
of theft items suggests action *guided by* these rationalizations (1978 : 235, cf.
Horning, 1970).

The logic informing both the study of workplace neutralizations and Sykes
and Matza's theory of delinquency can be traced most fully back to Cressey's
classic analysis of embezzlement, *Other People's Money* (1953, cf. 1950).
Yet apart from appreciating the impact Cressey had on future thinking about
crime, it is essential to realize that Cressey has relayed a vivid account of
how criminal behavior is socially structured. To be specific, Cressey began
with the premise that many who end up embezzling "other people's money"
are initially faced with a "nonshareable problem," such as worries over
unpaid gambling debts or excessive family expenses. Cressey was quite aware,
however, that not everyone could resolve this problem by embezzling company funds. Instead, committing this particular form of crime is ultimately
contingent on the material and social psychological resources at a person's
disposal. Hence, Cressey observed that embezzlement could only occur if an
employee occupied a position of financial trust; otherwise, the structural
opportunity to abscond with monies simply is not present. Yet Cressey also
knew that merely possessing the occupational position to embezzle is not
enough to allow a violation of financial trust. Having developed loyalty to a
company after many years of service or having been socialized to have a

strong moral fiber, most people are simply too bound to the social order to succumb to temptation. In order to take the money, Cressey thus realized that employees had to have some way to neutralize the guilt that otherwise would keep them in tow: one must also be equipped with a set of social-psychological rationalizations or justifications that allow the violation of financial trust to be defined as a way of "making up for all the years I have been underpaid" or as "only a temporary loan." Indeed, unless society's hold is broken prior to the criminal act, the person simply is not free to go through with the theft. In short, then, Cressey has furnished us with an explanation of why it is that troubled people respond to their difficulties by embezzling funds rather than by robbing a stranger on the street, finding relief in a bottle, suffering a mental collapse, or seeking a more permanent escape through self-destruction. That is, he has shown us how the choice of embezzlement is socially structured.

It should also be noted that thoughts which might advance the structuring perspective are contained as well in Matza's later work, *Delinquency and Drift*. It might be recalled that Matza proposed that once a juvenile was set free from controls into a state of drift, delinquency would occur if the youth had sufficient "preparation" to activate the will to misbehave. Yet this observation can easily be extended to explore the extent to which such preparation not only conditions *if* delinquency transpires but also *what kind* of transgression is "willed." Indeed, it is just this possibility that much of the writing of the Chicago School illustrated. To be sure, it must be admitted that these theorists were most concerned with institutionalized learning structures (e.g., gangs, age-graded integration between adult felons and juveniles) which made the performance of stable criminal roles possible, while Matza's interests were in the more regular features of youth culture which make those in drift feel as though they can, on occasion, embark upon a delinquent adventure. And it can also be agreed that Matza's imagery perhaps fits the average delinquent better than that set forth by his predecessors. Nevertheless, to say that the preparation needed to encourage the will to deviate is not brought about in a systematically planned way through criminal associations is not to say that it is a totally random phenomenon. Thus, it can be anticipated that the preparation Matza speaks of varies quite clearly by sex roles and that this in turn differentially shapes the kinds of delinquencies that boys and girls manifest. More concretely, males in drift might sense that they can jump-start a car and take it on a joy ride, or maybe that they can climb up to a second story window to explore what is inside a building. In contrast, young women may see such activities as a bit beyond reach but, alternatively, may think that they can shoplift some cosmetics from a department store without detection.

Finally, the implications of Hirschi's control theory for the structuring of deviant behavior deserve attention. Again, Hirschi offered us a parsimonious explanatory equation: delinquency and the strength of social bonds are inversely related. This proposition has proven persuasive to many in the field, and has generally been supported by empirical research (Hirschi 1969, Empey 1982 : 277, Gibbons 1979 : 121). Yet it seems equally true that this thesis could benefit from further elaboration. In this vein, throughout his theoretical pronouncements, Hirschi treated delinquency as one category. Similarly, all of the empirical tests presented in his *Causes of Delinquency* measure only whether social bonds increase or decrease delinquency as such. While this orientation and methodology reaped theoretical rewards, it also limited the issues that Hirschi could address. For by choosing not to address the reality that "delinquency" encompasses many diverse varieties of deviance—ranging, for instance, from petty theft and underage drinking to murder and robbery—Hirschi left us guessing as to how the strength and character of social bonds influence involvement in particular *kinds* of delinquency.

Thus, we would have learned much about how social controls shape the content of a juvenile's deviance had Hirschi explored how the "elements of the social bond" (attachment, commitment, involvement, belief) might interact to differentially close off or permit access to alternative delinquent options. Further, what happens when social controls are sufficiently powerful to preclude all delinquent behavior? Does this mean that youths, regardless of how severe their life-stresses, will not turn to other deviant responses, such as acting "crazy" or ending their life? Or might it be that the controls which make it impossible for juveniles to break the law do not lead strictly to conformity but rather channel youths in a different deviant direction where resistance is less pronounced? In this regard, it is significant that scholars have observed that while the controls inherent in the female gender-role push women away from a life in crime (cf. Hagan et al. 1979; Wolfe et al. 1982), such firm social bonds do not insulate them from all deviant involvement. In particular, women appear to display especially high rates of depressive psychiatric symptomatology, an adaptation which at once is consistent with their socialization and, as "sickness behavior," is likely to precipitate social sanctions which are more subtle and perhaps less harsh than those reserved for illegal conduct (cf. Dohrenwend and Dohrenwend 1976, Cloward and Piven 1979).

Conflict Theory: The Rise of the New Criminology

THE THEORY

The notions that crime is a reflection of the capitalist order and that true criminal justice awaits the arrival of true social justice are not new discoveries (cf. Jenkins 1982). Willem Bonger, as seen in Chapter 2, went to great lengths in 1916 to demonstrate that "criminality" is ultimately bound up in "economic conditions.'' Moreover, Bonger endeavored to convince his readers that only when the capitalist system is refashioned into an equitable order will crime fade away. He claimed that a socialist ''society will not only remove the causes which now make men egoistic, but will awaken, on the contrary, a strong feeling of altruism. . . . In such a society there can be no question of crime'' ([1916] 1969 : 200). Similarly, George Bernard Shaw observed some years ago ''that governments use the criminal law to suppress and exterminate their opponents'' and that while a poor person ''snatches a loaf from the baker's counter and is promptly run into gaol,'' the businessman ''snatches bread from the tables of hundreds of widows and orphans and simple credulous souls who do not know the ways of company promoters; and, as likely as not, he is run into Parliament'' (1946 : 61, 69–70). And in our own nation, we can see thoughts of this genre in the writings of Clarence Darrow. In *Resist Not Evil*, first published in 1902, Darrow called upon others to see that ''in the penal institutions of the world are confined . . . the propertyless class'' ([1902] 1972 : 132–33). This was the case, Darrow claimed, because the ''ruling class'' has ''made certain rules and regulations to keep possession of the treasures of the world, and when the disinherited have reached out to obtain the means of life, they have been met with these arbitrary rules and lodged in jail'' (p. 134).

Yet if such radical understandings of crime and criminal justice are not new creations, it was not until a decade ago that thinking in this vein became sufficiently widespread to coalesce into a recognized school of deviance theory. It was at that time, particularly within the field of criminology, that the boundaries of the radical paradigm crystallized and students of crime and deviance began to take sides. Indeed, the consciousness of leftist scholars allowed them to speak of their perspective as introducing a ''new criminology'' (Taylor et al. 1973) and to weigh the ''prospects for a radical criminology in the United States'' (Platt 1975). Faced with a flow of essays commenting on the ''crimes of the powerful'' (Pearce 1976) and on ''crime and privilege'' (Krisberg 1975), it was also an occasion for the more traditional in the field to take stock of what was happening and to assess what the ''rise of critical criminology'' was all about (Sykes 1974, 1978, Meier 1977, Gibbons 1979).

These emerging works were revisionist insofar as they revealed how existing theories had virtually ignored the fundamental role that social conflict and power relationships play in shaping both the nature of deviance and subsequent state reactions to it. Again, while this thesis was stated with much sophistication and increasing vigor, it was not, strictly speaking, new. Indeed, it is perhaps more accurate to say that much of what we witnessed was an intellectual revival (cf. Jenkins, 1982). This observation sensitizes us to the fact that the renewed popularity of radical ideas on crime and deviance was based only in part on their logical force; otherwise, their appeal would not have fluctuated across different historical periods. Instead, it seems that the "rise of the new criminology" was more fully a manifestation of the emergence of a social context which suddenly made radical explanations seem eminently plausible to more than a few isolated scholars (Gouldner 1970).

Of course, the rise and fall of all deviance paradigms can be understood in these terms (cf. Rothman 1971, 1980, Szasz 1970). In this light, it is both interesting and instructive that Merton's model of social structure and anomie did not truly come to dominate deviance theorizing until more than two decades after its initial publication in 1938 (Cole 1975). For it was not until the 1960s that political elites spoke clearly of the pressing need to create a "great society" and that the civil rights movement revealed how pernicious patterns of racism and discrimination excluded many from having a fair chance at the American dream. In this social climate, the proposition that denial of opportunity could drive many into deviance assumed much salience.

Later in the 1960s, the appeal of "status frustration" theory waned in favor of labeling theory. Now some of the decline of Merton's stress perspective was due to the fact that attempts to confirm his propositions achieved only occasional success; some more was undoubtedly due to the fact that the labeling perspective offered a fresh array of intellectual puzzles to be researched and thus new avenues for advancement in the field (Cole 1975, Hagan 1973; cf. Kuhn 1962). But this is not the whole story. Earlier in the decade, many believed that the state would be a partner in change, that it would provide the disadvantaged with job programs and young children with a "head start." As time passed, however, it became clear that the grand promise of an equitable order held out a few years before would not be fulfilled. For one thing, optimism dimmed as the limits of the welfare state became known (Bayer 1981). For another, events transpired which suggested that not only did the state not have the capacity to paternalistically elevate the disadvantaged, but also that it lacked the will to do so. In the face of Vietnam, Kent State, and Attica—all of which showed the capacity of the state to use coercion to protect its interests and suppress dissent—it became increasingly difficult to sustain an image of the state as an instrument of benevolence (Cullen and Gilbert 1982, Cullen and Wozniak 1982).

With the bad motives of the state now transparent, it is understandable that labeling theory won so much support at this time. For as the very legitimacy of the state was being called into question, it became quite tempting to believe in a perspective which argued that governmental agents distort official statistics to serve bureaucratic interests, that police and correctional personnel label according to discriminatory criteria, that societal reaction causes more harm than good, and that the best policy agenda is to limit the ability of the state to intervene in the lives of people (Schur 1973, Kittrie 1971, Rothman 1978; cf. Palamara et al. 1983).[8]

Radical theory was also a child of these times (Sykes 1974, Empey 1982 : 423–

24, Greenberg 1981 : 5). It may very well be that those who chose to move further to the left than labeling theorists were touched more deeply by the events of the day, or at least in a different way. As they witnessed riots in the slums and killings in Vietnam, participated in campus protests, and had inter-generational disputes with parents, one conclusion became eminently clear: conflict is a ubiquitous feature of social life and is typically settled in favor of those who exercise the most power. This view, combined with a reading of Marx, brought the realization that protecting deviants and other vulnerable dependent populations from state repression could not be accomplished simply by extending due process rights or by preaching the merits of non-intervention (cf. Kittrie 1971, Fogel 1975). Such liberal remedies would at best allow for cosmetic changes. Rather, it was manifest that the struggle for justice must penetrate much deeper to the very power structures underlying the social order which both produce and suppress deviant conduct. In particular, this meant revising the reigning political economy to insure a more equitable distribution of material and hence political resources.

Thus, as Alvin Gouldner had predicted, the social turmoil of the times sensitized many sociologists, including deviance theorists, to the influences of conflict and power (1970). In Peter Berger's (1979) terminology, scholars were now equipped with "plausibility structures" that furnished such interpretations with much legitimacy, with a feeling that "of course" wealth and power matter. Yet while conditions were now conducive for the "rise of critical criminology" and for new radical theoretical enterprises, the maturing of a paradigm does not always happen quickly. As such, it is perhaps not surprising that the initial concerns of conflict theorists were substantially borrowed from labeling theorists. In fact, much of the early writing done by the "new criminologists" is best viewed as an effort to politicize the insights illuminated by those in the societal reaction school (Meier 1977).

To be specific, radical commentators were at first much more preoccupied with the origins and operations of state social control than they were with questions on the etiology of deviant behavior. This choice of issues could have been due to the continuing salience of concerns surrounding the use of state power (one only has to remember Watergate here) or to the fact that theorists do not easily escape the influence of a paradigm that has captured so much attention in the field. No matter what the reasons, a number of theorists took special pains to show that the accounts of labeling authors paid insufficient attention to how inequalities in power influence the exercise of social control. While it was admitted that members of the labeling perspective were aware that the poor and black are differentially arrested and sentenced to prison, the radicals asserted that this was only a shallow understanding of the politics of punishment. For such an exclusive focus on the processing of offenders misses the more general, structural issue of how social conflict manifests itself in the laws and deviant categories that are created.

Thus, it became common for radical analysts to resurrect the writings of George Vold, who saw clearly that "the whole political process of law making, law breaking, and law enforcement becomes a direct reflection of deep-seated and fundamental conflicts between interest groups and their more general struggles for control of the police power of the state. Those who produce legislative majorities win control over the police power and dominate the policies that decide who is likely to be involved of the law" (1958 : 208–9). Of similar interest was Chambliss's analysis of the emergence of vagrancy laws which, at least in rough terms, signaled the beginnings of the rise of the new criminology (1964). Here, Chambliss revealed that law, rather than being a reflection of general social consensus, could be manipulated to serve economic interests. In particular, he showed that vagrancy statutes were initially used by landed aristocrats to maintain a cheap labor supply by prohibiting the travel of serfs to towns, and then later invoked by the commercial class of the sixteenth century to rid the countryside of the unencumbered poor who might prey on those who had set out on a trading venture. This sort of thinking on the relationship of "conflict and criminality" received further elaboration by Turk when he set forth his "theory of criminalization" (1966). Again, the concern here was not with etiological questions but instead with how differentials in power intimately affect both the values represented in prevailing legal standards and the likelihood that a person will be designated a criminal—that is, will be "criminalized"—by state authorities. The same line of reasoning is apparent as well in Quinney's *The Social Reality of Crime*, where it is common to find such statements as "criminal definitions are applied by the segments of society that have the power to shape the enforcement and administration of criminal laws" (1970 : 18). Finally, Platt exposed that even "child saving" is not immune from political considerations (1969). Hence, he suggested that the very founding of the juvenile justice system was conditioned by the values and interests of middle-class women who saw themselves as rescuing youths from the evils inherent in "disorganized" slum life.

Given the social context, these varied works were found to be quite persuasive and earned increasing acclaim. However, as the new criminology and the scholars within it matured, these early insights came to be seen as less than fully adequate (compare Platt 1969 with 1974, and Quinney 1970 with 1977). Thus, there was a growing push to reject analyses that saw law and the application of sanctions merely as a manifestation of group conflict. Instead, it was argued that radical theorists must take up the larger question of how state control is enmeshed in the capitalist system and how the mode of societal reaction varies as the mode of production is altered (cf. Rusche and Kirchheimer 1939, Sellin 1976). Now more completely informed by Marxian constructs, radical authors set about the task of discovering the political economy of punishment.

This posture led, for instance, to revised interpretations of the founding of the penitentiary. No longer was it seen as a great effort at liberal reform whose good intentions had been tragically corrupted. Rather, the prison and, more broadly, the institutionalization of deviant populations were held to have evolved as a means of protecting class interests and of disciplining those of the proletariat who did not fit easily into the work force (Foucault 1977, Ignatieff 1978, Takagi 1975, Miller 1980, 1982). Similarly, it was argued that rates of imprisonment are more fully explained by rates of unemployment and the corresponding need to preserve the socioeconomic order in times of crisis than by levels of crime (Jankovic 1977). Alternatively, Scull contended that the decarceration movement of the 1960s and beyond was not motivated out of kindness of heart but rather was precipitated by the need to reduce the financial strains inherent in advanced capitalism that were being exacerbated by the enormous costs of institutionalization. The ultimate consequence of decarceration, in his view, was to increase state control by bringing unprecedented numbers under the surveillance of community "treatment" personnel. Further, as "criminal justice" emerged as an area of much academic concern, efforts were made to unmask the criminal justice system's role as an instrument of oppression. Quinney, more radical by this point, commented that "crime control in capitalist society is accomplished through a variety of institutions and agencies established and administered by a governmental elite, representing ruling class interests, for the purpose of establishing domestic order" (1973 : 94). A few years later he added that "criminal justice, as the euphemism for controlling class struggle and administering legal repression, becomes a major type of social policy in the advanced stages of capitalism" (1977 : 107–8). The issue was put even more succinctly by Reiman when he proclaimed that "the rich get richer and the poor get prison" (1979).

While such analyses proved provocative and challenged many traditional understandings, this preoccupation with matters of state control had the unfortunate consequence of retarding theory development within the paradigm on the etiology of deviant and criminal behavior. Indeed, as Greenberg observed, "the refusal to address the question of causes left radicals ill-equipped to participate in the political debates that arose over the increase in common forms of crime that took place in the 1960s" (1981 : 59, cf. Platt 1982). Rather, it seemed that discussions did not go much beyond, or at times measure up to, Bonger's thesis voiced many years before that capitalism causes crime.

To be sure, exceptions to this tendency, particularly in recent years, have emerged. Taylor, Walton, and Young, authors of *The New Criminology*, did spell out what the "requirements" of a radical theory would be (1973 : 269–78). Because their main purpose was to offer a critique of existing paradigms, however, they did not go on to flesh out their outline of the questions that theorists should address. Further, Quinney has offered an extended discussion of "crime and the development of capitalism" (1977 : 31–62), while others have provided insights into the etiology of delinquency (Schwendinger and Schwendinger 1976, 1982, Greenberg 1977), organized crime (Pearce 1976), corporate crime (Barnett 1981), street crime (Gordon 1973, Humphries and Wallace 1980), and sex offenses (cf. Balkan et al. 1980, Thio 1978). It might be added that radicals have also called attention to such violations of human rights as "war, racism, sexism, and poverty," and in turn have argued that these acts should be labeled as "crime" and their origins investigated (Schwendinger and Schwendinger 1975). Despite these contributions, the potential for the new criminology to yield significant insights into the causes of wayward conduct—whether in the upper world or (especially) in our streets—remains largely undeveloped.

CONFLICT THEORY AND THE STRUCTURING OF DEVIANT BEHAVIOR

While conflict-oriented theorists have only recently swung their attention more fully toward questions of deviance causation, they have nevertheless been especially aware that social circumstances very much structure the kinds of adaptations available to people at different levels of the social hierarchy. The early Marxist scholar Willem Bonger not only argued that crime was ultimately rooted in the strains inherent in capitalist arrangements, but also that factors like occupational status determine how egoistic impulses might be expressed. Notably, similar thoughts are found in the writings of those who would feel comfortable in claiming Bonger as their intellectual forefather. Thus, current radical criminologists have taken pains to point out that class membership intimately shapes the forms of unlawful behavior which people manifest. Braithwaite, for instance, has noted the need for "class-based theories which explain why certain types of crime are perpetrated disproportionately by the powerless, while other forms of crime are almost exclusively the prerogative of the powerful" (1981 : 49). Much the same thinking is evident in the following comment by Chambliss:

> In actual practice, however, class differences in rates of criminal activity are probably negligible. What difference there is would be a difference in the type of criminal act, not in the prevalence of criminality. . . . The data also support the hypothesis that criminal activity is a direct reflection of class position. Thus, the criminality of the lawyers, prosecuting attorneys, politicians, judges and policemen is uniquely suited to their own class position in society. It grows out of the opportunities and strains that inhere in those positions just as surely as the drinking of the skidrow derelict, the violence of the ghetto resident, the drug use of the middle-class adolescent and the white collar crimes of corporation executives reflect different socializing experiences. [1975 : 166–67]

And on a broader level, radical British criminologists Taylor, Walton, and Young have contended that individuals may respond in a myriad of ways to a given "problem of adjustment." A "formal requirement" of any paradigm of crime and deviance, in their view, is thus to explain why a particular deviant solution is chosen from the range of potential alternatives.

> Men may choose to engage in particular solutions to their problems without being able to carry them out. An adequate social theory of deviance would need to explain the relationship between beliefs and action, between the optimum "rationality" that men have chosen and the behaviors they actually carry through. A working-class adolescent, for example, confronted with blockage of opportunity, with problems of status frustration, alienated from the kind of existence offered out to him in contemporary society, may want to engage in hedonistic activities (e.g., finding immediate pleasure through the use of alcohol, drugs, or in extensive sexual activities) or he may choose to kick back at a rejecting society (e.g., through acts of vandalism). . . . The formal requirement at this level then is for an explanation of the ways in which the actual acts of men are explicable in terms of the rationality of choice or the constraints on choice at the point of precipitation into action. [1973 : 271–72]

Perhaps the most elaborate discussion of the structuring of criminal behavior has been presented by Quinney (1977). Like other Marxist theorists, Quinney was convinced that "crime is inevitable under capitalist conditions" (p. 58) and that "to understand crime we must understand the development of the political economy of capitalistic society" (p. 32). It is significant, however, that Quinney was careful to note that the ways in which people are related to the means of production regulate not merely overall rates of participation in illegal activities but also the "nature" or content of the criminality that emerges. To be specific, Quinney observed that class position leads people to engage either in crimes of "domination and repression" or in crimes of "accommodation and resistance." Of course, the former are committed by capitalist elites who seek to sustain their advantage by suppressing dissent and incipient insurgent movements and by maximizing profit through practices that insure the continued availability of a large surplus labor force. And in this regard, Quinney was able to distinguish three sorts of offenses that are either carried out or sanctioned by elites. These include "crimes of control" such as police brutality and the violation of civil liberties, "crimes of government" like corruption and the assassination of foreign officials, and "crimes of economic domination" ranging from price-fixing to environmental pollution (pp. 50–52).

Alternatively, Quinney proposed that working people may make either of two general responses to their dehumanizing and demoralizing existence under capitalism: accommodation or resistance. While both constitute "means of survival," their content is much different. The category of accommodation encompasses traditional varieties of street-crime such as "predatory" or property crimes and "personal" or violent crimes. In contrast, "crimes of resistance" involve attempts by working people to attack existing social arrangements that perpetuate their exploitation. Notably, Quinney also endeavored to explain the conditions under which resistance as opposed to accommodation is most likely to occur. In this regard, he argued that the crucial factor structuring working class adaptations to the pains endured under capitalism is the character of the "consciousness" that people have developed. Thus, Quinney contended that crimes of accommodation, which often involve extensive intra-class victimization, are predominately "an expression of false consciousness, an apolitical expression, an individualistic reaction to the forces of capitalist production" (p. 54). However, illegal resistance to exploitation, manifested in behaviors extending from the destruction of factory machinery by workers to "acts of rebellion" (p. 59), is also possible if the right circumstances prevail. According to Quinney, the most important precondition for this adaptation is the realization of class interests. For "with the emerging consciousness that the state represses those who attempt to tip the scales in favor of the working class, working-class people engage in actions against the state and the capitalist class. This is crime that is politically conscious" (p. 59). It should be added that this logic suggested to Quinney that "the task of a Marxist criminology is to develop a political consciousness among all people who are oppressed by the capitalist system" (pp. 104–5). Indeed, only in this way will criminologists help to channel the conduct of working people away from accommodations that persist in dividing the proletariat and toward paths that more directly resist exploitation and quicken the advance toward a more equitable social order.

Of interest as well is socialist criminologist David Greenberg's study of the social structuring of juvenile delinquency (1977). Writing in the radical tradition, Greenberg argued that patterns of delinquency are a function of the "structural position of juveniles in an advanced capitalist economy" (p. 213). On the one hand, the social location of youths is seen to expose them to strong motivations to violate or rebel against the normative standards of the dominant order. Such drives range from the desire to obtain funds required to participate in social activities with peers, to the need to exert autonomy in the face of repressive school controls, to the strains generated by attempts to resolve masculine status anxiety. The sources of these deviant motivations are largely an outgrowth of the historically changing relationship of youths to the means of production, namely, their progressive exclusion from the work force.

Greenberg understood, however, that explaining the origins of delinquent motivations would not, in and of itself, enable analysts to predict which behavioral outcomes were likely to emerge. Greenberg maintained instead that the potential costs of apprehension and punishment by state agents of social control operate to structure which delinquent options are rejected or embraced. In his words, "so far some possible sources of variation with age in motivation to participate in common forms of criminal activity have been identified, but this is only half the story, for one may wish to engage in some form of behavior but nevertheless decide not to do so because the potential costs of participation are deemed unacceptably high" (pp. 208–9). Greenberg went on to observe that access to "illegal opportunity structures" not only permits continued involvement in a stable criminal role but also alters the forms of crime that may be pursued. Thus, "those few delinquents who are recruited into organized crime or professional theft face larger rewards and less risk of serious penalty than those not so recruited. . . . They should be less likely to desist from crime, but their offense patterns can be expected to change" (p. 211). More broadly, Greenberg asserted that the largely apolitical character of delinquency is "predicated on the low level of . . . consciousness present among most American teenagers" (p. 216). While prospects for an alteration in the thinking of youths do "not appear especially bright," should circumstances precipitate a raising of consciousness then we could anticipate that the form of American delinquency would be fundamentally transformed. Echoing themes voiced by Quinney, Greenberg thus commented that "responses to objective conditions—including criminal responses—are contingent on the level of group awareness of the origins of oppressive objective conditions in class dynamics and of the possibilities for engaging in collective action to change these conditions" (p. 216). In short, the way in which people adapt to the strains induced by their material situation is structured by a consciousness that either lends legitimacy to hedonistic if not predatory acts or, alternatively, reveals the possibility of collective protest to revise damaging social relations.

Finally, radical scholars have been sensitive to how the nature of the political economy creates opportunity structures for some forms of criminality but not for others. That is, in O'Malley's terms, they have investigated "the conditions of existence" that account for the "appearance, maintenance, or disappearance" of a specific type of socially proscribed behavior (1979). One example of this orientation is Brill's illuminating study of auto theft (1982). Again, the focus here is not on why people are motivated to steal cars, but rather on why the very opportunity for this form of theft is so readily available. Following this line of reasoning, Brill has located the source of the nation's flourishing rate of auto theft in the economic interests of "big business." In particular, he has revealed that both the automobile and insurance industries have balked at attempts to mandate the installation of an anti-theft device— whose "cost to the consumer could be as low as $17"—because lower rates of stealing would threaten to diminish their profits. This thesis takes on meaning when one realizes that at least 50,000 new sales each year are made to people who have had their cars stolen. The insurers have been equally resistant to attempts to curtail the theft rate even though this would ostensibly bolster profits by allowing premiums to be scaled downward. As Brill has noted, however, "reducing premiums, even if somewhat advantageous to the insurance end of the business, would not appeal to the investment-minded insurance industry. . . . The more cars stolen, the higher the insurance premiums climb, and the more money the insurance companies accumulate to invest" (p. 66). Taking these considerations together, it thus becomes clear that the critical condition underlying the existence of a healthy opportunity structure for auto theft is "the routine, lawful, profit-making operations of the auto and insurance industries . . . the widespread persistence of auto theft and the ineffectiveness of the police in controlling it are structurally determined conditions which are institutionally generated by big business in its legal practice" (p. 68).

Conclusion

Over the past two decades or so, the three perspectives reviewed in this chapter have offered challenging and creative insights into the origins of criminal and deviant conduct. While these paradigms are not without their own intellectual predecessors, they nevertheless deserve the label "revisionist." Indeed, it is not too much to assert that they have fundamentally changed how the past generation of students of crime and deviance has come to think about their subject matter. For our purposes, however, it is equally important to see that each of these revisionist explanations might also contain fresh ideas concerning the structuring of deviant choices. It would be difficult to imagine that such factors as the nature of societal reaction, the way in which people establish or loosen bonds to the conventional order, and the material conditions people find themselves in would not intimately shape the wayward paths individuals are able to follow. It is not, then, too optimistic to expect that a closer examination of the many contributions of labeling, control, and conflict theorists would reveal much about the social structuring of deviant behavior.

Notes

1. For this reason, labeling theorists departed from the traditional usage of the term "deviance" by proposing that deviance was not a behavior that transgressed a norm—this they preferred to call rule-breaking behavior. Instead, independent of whether a rule of conduct was violated, "the deviant is one to whom that label has successfully been applied; deviant behavior is behavior that people so label" (Becker 1963 : 9; cf. Erikson 1964 : 11, Kitsuse 1964).

2. Indeed, as Robins continued on to observe, "labels for one kind of deviance frequently prognosticate different types of deviance as well or better than they do the continuation of the same type" (1973 : 23). However, Robins voiced these comments in the context of a general critique of labeling theory informed largely by deterministic logic, and hence did not pursue

fully the very point these comments suggest: that the effects of societal reaction may in fact be indeterminate and not determinate, and that this possibility should not be casually dismissed prior to careful empirical consideration.

3. Although some would concur that labeling theory was set forth more as an approach or orientation to thinking about the phenomenon of deviance than as a theory of the etiology of wayward behavior (cf. Sagarin 1975 : 121–22), the work of Becker and Lemert, among others, clearly argued that societal reaction influenced whether "rule-breaking" conduct would be transitory or permanent. Further, subsequent scholars have agreed that, like other prevailing paradigms, labeling "theory" did in fact advance an answer as to why deviance transpired— people are designated and treated as outsiders (Gove 1975 : 12–13, 296). Thus, while nearly all explanatory models in the field fall short of a rigorous standard for a scientific theory, it appears that the labeling perspective, though sensitizing scholars to a range of definitional or labeling issues, is as much an etiological theory as other existing approaches.

4. While some research exists that suggests that treatment interventions in correctional settings may have the salutary effect of suppressing the seriousness of future criminality (Halleck and Witte 1977 : 375–76, Sechrest et al. 1979 : 32), evaluation studies have not generally examined whether imprisonment induces switching of crime patterns; instead, they have looked exclusively at the phenomenom of recidivism. As a consequence, empirical evidence is not available to access in any systematic way whether incarceration structures criminal choices in general or to allow us to identify which populations import stable criminal patterns into prison (such as the gang members described by Jacobs in *Stateville*) and which are susceptible to learning new forms of crime or deviance. The value of a structuring perspective, however, is that it sensitizes us to a new research puzzle and thus opens up the possibility of a reinterpretation of the full effects of imprisionment.

5. Some control theorists have admitted that a complete theory of deviance would entail an explanation of both the absence of control and the origin of the motivation to deviate (Briar and Piliavin 1965, Matza 1964, Toby 1974). Even here, though, delineating the source of deviant motivation is either simply mentioned as an issue that should be addressed or is treated in a secondary way. In contrast, Eve's empirical analysis of high school rebellion is an example of a work which argues that a complete understanding of the origins of deviant behavior must assess both the independent and interactive effects of motivational (strain, culture conflict, deviant identity) and control variables (1978).

Control theorists differ in another respect as well. Most frequently, control authors have held that the motivation to deviate exists prior to the breakdown of control, and hence that deviance will automatically occur when controls are abrogated. Others, however, have viewed deviant motivation as arising after control weakens; once freed from control or once in a state of "drift" (Matza 1964), an actor becomes a candidate to choose or to be pushed into deviant activity. And still others have envisaged the breakdown of control itself to be very much a part of the source of deviant motivation (Durkheim 1951, Shaw and McKay 1942).

6. See also Reckless and Dinitz 1967, Reckless, Dinitz, and Murray 1956, 1957, Reckless, Dinitz, and Kay 1957, Dinitz et al. 1962, Scarpitti et al. 1960.

7. It should be noted that this conclusion has been questioned on the basis of its empirical adequacy as well as for its implicit "blaming the victim" ideology which focuses attention on "family problems" as opposed to the larger structural injustices that strain social institutions and diminish the quality of life among the disadvantaged (Ryan 1971).

8. When the prevailing social context is taken into account, one more easily understands why labeling theory appealed to those embracing an "underdog ideology," in which deviants were viewed more as victims than as victimizers of society (Sagarin 1975 : 132–34). Sagarin has aptly captured this point:

> It is interesting to consider why labeling arose and took hold at the time that it did. It was an expression of the rejection of the small-town middle-America view, tenaciously held by early American sociologists, that assumed the propriety of the existing rules of behavior and hence the evil of those who violated them. It went further than Freudianism, cultural transmission, and anomie in turning the world of respectability upside down and demonstrating sympathy for the rule-breakers by questioning the norms and their upholders. It was a period of intense social change, the 1960s, when labeling had its heyday, and during this decade it proved useful to see deviants more as victims than as victimizers. [1975 : 144]

chapter 8

Concluding Remarks

Although the themes underlying the structuring perspective have been elucidated above, it might prove useful to conclude by restating the central theoretical assumptions and the methodological implications of the perspective. Further, an effort will be made to outline the potential significance of a structuring perspective and to present a beginning discussion of the kinds of social conditions that future structuring investigations might find fruitful to consider.

Theoretical Assumptions

The structuring perspective starts with the assumption that an adequate theory of the origins of deviant behavior must address two distinct questions: (1) What conditions motivate or predispose people to violate social and legal norms? and (2) What conditions account for the specific form that a deviant response takes? In turn, this means that identifying the factors that explain the etiology of deviant motivations does not allow us to account fully for the particular deviant adaptation that might emerge. This is true because there is an indeterminate relationship between the circumstances that give rise to deviant motivations on the one hand and the actual behavioral outcome on the other. That is, deviant motivational conditions—whether they be stressful life-events or exposure to deviant values—do not have a direct one-to-one relationship with any single form of deviance; instead, they may precipitate several or many possible responses. Consequently, to understand when any particular form of deviance will occur, it is necessary to specify additional variables which structure deviant choices and thus regulate why one deviant path is followed and not another. As distinct from motivational variables, these additional factors are called "structuring variables."

Methodological Implications

As has been suggested, there is a tendency to assume the existence of a determinate rather than indeterminate relationship between motivational conditions and particular deviant outcomes. Now it might be argued that theorists who link a specific condition like status frustration to a single deviant form such as mental illness do not actually embrace the notion that this is the only response engendered by this motivational state. As such, if questioned, these authors undoubtedly would concur that "of course" other outcomes are possible. Yet this is less important than the logic that ultimately prevails in their work. While perhaps recognizing the possibility of indeterminacy, these theorists have proceeded as though there were a direct relationship between a motivational condition and a given form of deviance. In turn, this has often hindered them from perceiving how incorporating structuring variables into their research designs might enrich their subsequent theoretical formulations.

The assumption of determinacy is also reflected in the research strategy that students of crime and deviance frequently employ. Two procedural rules guide their methodological approach: (1) select a single form of deviance to examine, and (2) then attempt to delineate the motivational condition that determines or is etiologically specific to this particular deviant form. Implicit in this strategy are the notions that involvement in only one mode of deviance is to be explained and that a specification of a motivational condition is sufficient to fulfill this theoretical task. As a consequence, the possibility that the hypothesized motivational state can produce deviant forms other than the one of initial interest is not considered and in turn the need to demarcate the variables that structure when any one of these potential responses will occur remains obscured. In contrast, an approach to the study of deviance that is sensitive to the indeterminate relationship of motivational states to deviance would follow a vastly different set of procedural rules. These would include: (1) setting forth conditions that are thought to generate deviant motivations, (2) uncovering the different adaptations that can arise from these conditions, and (3) specifying the structuring variables that regulate when any particular adaptation will occur.[1]

The Significance of the Structuring Perspective

Perhaps the most promising feature of the structuring perspective is the potential it has for making our theories more adequate. Indeed, it is only with considerable risk that scholars can afford to reject the idea of indeterminacy, hold onto deterministic conceptions of deviance causation, and hesitate to introduce structuring variables systematically into their paradigms. For at the very least, their explanations would appear to remain less than complete. That is, by specifying only motivational and not relevant structuring conditions, analysts are unlikely to account for as much variance in their dependent variable—the origins of a particular mode of deviance—than might otherwise be the case. At worst, however, their models may be misconceived.

One illustration of these possibilities is found in the work of Gove and Tudor (1973). This is a particularly poignant example because the authors are well-known for their thoughtful and thought-provoking analyses and because this work has received much attention from subsequent researchers. As might be remembered from Chapter 4, Gove and Tudor began with the assumption that role stress produces mental illness; the more role stress there is, the more mental illness is manifested. They went on to note that women evidence greater rates of psychiatric symptomatology, and thus they were led to the inevitable conclusion that women must experience more role stress than their male counterparts. Yet a stress theorist of the deviant form of alcohol abuse, or perhaps of crime, would reach the *opposite* conclusion: since men have a higher incidence of alcohol abuse and crime, they must endure more stress than females. Admittedly, the amount of stress experienced by the sexes remains an empirical question. Nevertheless, we can anticipate that sex differentials in rates of various forms of deviance are less a function of differences in exposure to stressful circumstances and more a function of those aspects of the sex status which open up some deviant alternatives for men and others for women.[2]

It can be noted further that, without the benefit of a structuring perspective, the full etiological effects of some variables may be left unknown. Again, as discussed in the last chapter, numerous authors have investigated the impact of incarceration on rates of recidivism. An emerging view, voiced by Hawkins among others, is that imprisonment has "no effect," that is, does not substantially deepen or lessen criminality (1976). Yet through the lens of a structuring perspective, we can see that a very different question can be asked: does imprisonment lead inmates to switch their offense patterns, to engage in new forms of crime upon release? Or stated a bit differently, although this mode of societal reaction may not contribute to the overall amount of crime, may it not still have the important effect of structuring deviant choices? Similarly, in recent times there has been considerable debate over the relationship of crime rates to social class. One popular view is that class variations in crime are minimal and hence that it is a myth to assume that social class has a significant impact on criminal involvement (Tittle et al. 1978; cf. Braithwaite 1981). However, as both white-collar and radical crime theorists have understood, it may be less important to concentrate—as has been the tradition in sociology—on whether the rich or the poor commit more crimes and of greater importance to examine how social class structures the types of criminality that people situated in different strata may pursue. If it does indeed become apparent that class exerts little influence on one's overall inclination to violate the law or other social standards, it would nevertheless remain true that this variable could still have major effects in accounting for the form of the criminal and deviant choices actors make.[3]

A structuring perspective might also permit us to reinterpret the effects of motivational conditions. When researchers find a negligible association between a particular motivational condition and a form of deviance being studied, they typically conclude that this factor has no etiological impact whatsoever. Some caution, however, should be exercised before such a conclusion is accepted. To the extent that the assumption of indeterminacy is viable and thus that motivational conditions may give rise to a variety of possible responses, a general low correlation between a given condition (e.g., status frustration) and any *one* adaptation would not be surprising. However, while such a factor may not "determine" or be closely associated with any particular type of nonconformity, it may be an important determinant of a person's *overall* propensity to violate social norms. That is, while a motivational variable may not regulate the form or content that a person's adaptation takes, it may nevertheless increase the likelihood that an actor will be moved to deviate in some undetermined way.

Finally, a structuring perspective has implications for the evaluation of intervention strategies. For instance, a social control program that successfuly reduces the rate of one form of deviance may not be a success: it may simply have had the effect of closing off one deviant option and channeling actors into other, more destructive, forms of deviance. Alternatively, an evaluation study that finds a control strategy to be ineffective in suppressing, for example, the overall amount of crime may be misleading if it does not assess the impact of this intervention on the kinds of offenses that are now being committed— might they have become less serious? (cf. Short 1975 : 200, Sechrest et al. 1979, Hakim and Rengert 1981 : 11). Without a structuring perspective, then, potentially important consequences of social control policies will inevitably remain latent.

Kinds of Structuring Variables

This book has predominantly been a theoretical enterprise aimed at introducing readers to the logic and concepts of a structuring perspective. To be sure, the works reviewed throughout the previous pages furnish us with numerous empirical instances of the social structuring of deviant behavior. However, because these examples have been discussed over the course of several chapters and in differing contexts, the indications they offer as to how one might begin a "structuring analysis" may not be readily apparent. It would therefore seem useful to delineate some of the common threads that might be of value in directing further inquiry. In this light, it appears that it is possible to distinguish at least four broad categories of variables that have been shown to help account for the structuring of deviant behavior.

1. *Macro-level Conditions.* This rubric encompasses the broad struc-

tural features and historical transformations that determine the kinds of illegitimate opportunity structures which prevail at any one time. The focus thus is on the "conditons of existence" underlying specific forms of deviance (O'Malley 1979). To illustrate, one could examine how the emergence of technological innovations such as the automobile and computers have contributed to the rise of car theft and computer crimes, or perhaps how the capacity to manufacture large amounts of alcohol and drugs permits the widespread abuse of these substances. Similarly, it is possible to see that the advance of capitalism creates new opportunities for a range of criminal acts stemming from corporate illegality and the embezzlement of large sums by executives to pilfering in the workplace and shoplifting in department stores (cf. Ross 1907 : 4). Another example can be found in the burgeoning of the welfare state which now provides chances for fraudulent activities not only to recipients but also to the providers of services (e.g., medicaid fraud by physicians and pharmacists). In a similar vein, Cohen and Felson's (1979) "routine activities approach" sensitizes us to how changes in the patterns of everyday life during a particular social era may enable the opportunity structure for certain forms of criminality to flourish. One ready instance is that the increased participation of married women in the work force may encourage daytime household burglaries and place females in settings where rape is more likely to occur. Finally, as pointed out by theorists in the Chicago School, such social forces as urbanism and the mobility of ethnic and racial groups may shape neighborhood organization, and in turn influence the very nature of the deviant roles that appear and persist in a social area.[4]

2. *Social Psychological Factors.* Assuming that a given range of deviant adaptations are available during a particular historical period, why does a person turn in one of these directions rather than in another? Part of the answer to this question can be found in the internalization of what might be called "selection mechanisms." One of these would be the values and norms people come to embrace, which have long been shown in the sociological literature to influence the choices people make. This notion can be illuminated by considering again how deeply rooted features of Jewish and Irish culture attach distinct meanings to intoxication, and thus help to account for ethnic variations in rates of alcohol abuse. This line of reasoning is found as well in discussions of how the acquisition of passive or aggressive value orientations might determine whether one manifests depressive symptomatology or "acts out," takes one's own life or another's, or perhaps robs rather than shoplifts (cf. Dohrenwend and Dohrenwend 1976, Parsons 1951).

Cultural stereotypes, or "type-scripts" as Harris (1977) called them, also function as internalized selection mechanisms. These are the impressions people have acquired during socialization experiences about which forms of deviance are "appropriate" for those occupying specific social statuses. Thus, just as it is "common knowledge" that men become doctors and lawyers while women become nurses and secretaries, it is well known that men rob and burglarize while women shoplift and pass bad checks. Whether in the conventional or deviant world, the social realities that have been constructed can be expected to affect the occupational and deviant paths people see open to them (Cullen and Link 1980; cf. Berger and Luckman 1966). Of course, these insights regarding the structuring effects of type-scripts can be applied more generally to see what forms of deviance are defined as "normal" for people in certain statuses but not in other. As such, apart from structural constraints, the research problem here would be to examine how the selection of adaptations is conditioned by stereotypes of what is a socially expected deviation for someone who might be male or female, black or white, rich or poor, or old or young (Rahav 1979).

Other kinds of selection mechanisms can be found in the revisionist explanations reviewed in the previous chapter. Thus, it seems likely that the content of Sykes and Matza's techniques of neutralization will allow people to justify some adaptations but not others. It may also prove to be true that the bonds to the conventional order which Hirschi enumerated may close off criminal options and unwittingly push troubled youths into alternative deviations such as a psychiatric "sick role" (something that can be more easily rationalized within the framework of a legitimate belief system). From labeling theory and Reckless's work on "inner containment," one can see that the self-conceptions people come to believe in might condition the particular deviant paths that "someone of their sort" should follow. The insights of more radical commentators are relevant here as well. In particular, their work on ideology and consciousness indicates that the ability of the working class to realize its true interests will affect whether workers continue to victimize one another or rise up in protest against the more dominant class. Notably, the extent to which people no longer blame themselves for failing but rather question the legitimacy of arrangements and blame the system for their plight has often been viewed as a precondition for collective forms of deviance.

3. *Status-specific Opportunities.* This category would include much of what Cloward meant when he used the concept of illegitimate means to encompass both "learning and performance structures" (1959). Simply stated, his message is that in order to participate in any given form of deviance, people must both have acquired the talents required to accomplish the act and be in a position to actually discharge the role for which they have been prepared. Further, he asserted that access to learning environments and the opportunity to carry out a disapproved behavior is regulated by one's location in the social structure. In short, then, Cloward argued that the chance to learn and perform deviant roles is status-specific.

These principles are not difficult to illustrate. For instance, regardless of someone's deviant motivations, embezzlement is not possible without an occupational position involving financial trust; rising into the upper echelons of organized crime is all but unheard of without the necessary ethnic and familial ties; joining a delinquent gang is a distinct option for youths living in the inner city of Chicago and Philadelphia but an unlikely occurrence for those residing on a farm in Illinois or among the Pennsylvania Dutch; becoming a professional thief or fence is difficult, as Sutherland (1937) and Klockars (1974) suggest, without the right tutelage and personal talents; and it is clear that the aging process diminishes an individual's ability to take to the streets and commit a predatory assault.

Some final matters deserve mention here. Because Cloward drew much of his insight about the structuring of deviance from the Chicago School, he focused largely on how people get access to stable criminal roles like a professional thief or a gang delinquent. However, the more general conclusion is that learning environments are equally important for the performance of other deviant roles. In this regard, we only have to consider Becker's observations on becoming a marijuana user (1963), Glassner and Berg's thoughts on problem drinking (1980), and Goffman's understanding of how institutional life teaches mental patients to play a sick role (1961). Beyond this, it is important to realize, as Matza (1964) did, that much of the preparation needed to engage in different varieties of nonconformity is not specifically deviant in its content. Thus, in contrast to the image of a youth being schooled in the ways of professional thievery, the prerequisite talents to commit many wayward acts are acquired in the course of the *legitimate* socialization that people in different statuses receive. To illuminate this point further, it is typical for boys to learn how to tinker with cars and lift weights, while it is often the case that girls will enjoy shopping with their mothers and will be subtly instructed that flirtations and sexual favors can be exchanged for attention from the opposite sex. It is thus not surprising to discover that such "normal" preparation makes it more likely for males to steal automobiles and physically assault others, and for females to shoplift or perhaps become prostitutes. In short, we can see that status-specific access not only to explicitly illegitimate learning environments but to legitimate or socially accepted ones as well structures the adaptations people make.

4. *Societal Reaction.* Finally, it would seem that societal reaction or state social control may operate to structure deviant involvement in at least two ways. First, the actual experience of being labeled and treated as an outsider may condition not only the degree of a person's waywardness, but also the nature of the specific deviation that is manifested. Again, the concern here is with how exposure to labeling processes ranging from institutional-

ization to the more informal reactions endured during the course of everyday life shape the direction of a person's deviant career. Second, on a broader level, it is also possible to examine how governmental control policies either close off or help to sustain illegitimate opportunity structures (cf. Marx 1981). For instance, a police campaign against prostitution may, if only temporarily, make this deviation an excessively costly one. Thus, aware of the crackdown, a man may hesitate to approach a prostitute for fear that she may be a police decoy, and may instead visit a massage parlor or drink too much at a local bar. At the same time, a streetwalker may choose to travel to another community, or to switch to other criminal means like shoplifting in order to secure needed funds. Alternatively, while a complicated matter (cf. Stone, 1975), the reluctance of the state to criminally prosecute corporate lawlessness must also in part be held responsible for permitting the violation of certain kinds of existing statutes by executives (Reiman 1979, Cullen et al. 1983). Similarly, scholars have argued that the criminalization of drug use (and other victimless crimes) in the face of continuing consumer demand makes selling drugs a highly lucrative undertaking (cf. Schur 1965). At the same time, the risk of legal penalties requires that narcotic entrepreneurs be able to avoid detection and prosecution. Notably, this situation is ideal for the flourishing of the "Mafia," because the syndicate has the capital needed to buy large quantities of drugs and the organizational capacity to deflect most enforcement attempts. Seen in this light, it may very well be that one condition of existence of the deviant form of organized criminality is the unanticipated consequence of state-sponsored societal reaction.

Final Comments

The chief goal of this work has been to reveal that the structuring perspective constitutes a longstanding theoretical paradigm in the field. To be sure, a survey of criminology and deviance texts will not uncover any chapters discussing such an approach. Nonetheless, once the concepts and principles of a structuring perspective are well understood, it is difficult to ignore the many instances in which scholars have pushed beyond the issue of the causation of deviance per se to the question of why a particular kind of deviance transpires. Yet the body of literature that seeks to "account for form" is impressive not merely due to the numbers involved, but also because it encompasses works that focus on divergent realms of crime and deviance, embrace competing theoretical assumptions, and are informed by varying ideological persuasions. Indeed, the theme that wayward conduct is socially structured runs through nearly every theoretical and substantive tradition in the field.

This conclusion assumes importance because it suggests that the issues addressed by the structuring perspective are sufficiently compelling that they cannot be neglected easily or without consequence. What remains, however, is for scholars to embark on structuring analyses that are at once systematic and consciously oriented toward the development of a coherent approach to the study of crime and deviance. Such investigations contain the potential advantages of making the structuring perspective truly manifest and of encouraging additional explorations of the circumstances that account for the forms of deviance people select. Further, if the premises set forth in the current enterprise have merit, these undertakings hold the promise of furnishing fresh insights into the structuring process, and thus of providing a more complete theoretical understanding of the origins of criminal and deviant activity.

Notes

1. Unlike current studies that almost uniformly employ measures of only one deviant form, a research design informed by a structuring perspective would utilize indicators of multiple forms of deviance. Further, such a design would include not only scales tapping motivational states but also measures of variables which might be expected to structure the deviant choices made by the members of the sample.

2. Gove and Tudor observed that "in Western society, as elsewhere, sex acts as a master status, channeling one into particular roles" (1973 : 814). They focused, however, only on the ways in which sex can "channel" men and women into legitimate roles (e.g., housewife vs. member of the work force) that differentially expose them to stress. As such, they did not consider the ways in which sex, as a master status, might determine not only how much stress men and women experience, but also how they can respond to this stress. That is, Gove and Tudor overlook the likely possibility that sex status channels men and women into different kinds of *illegitimate* roles. As discussed in Chapter 5, this oversight is similar to that of Merton, who applied the concept of means to explain the origins of stress but did not examine how the concept might be used to explain how involvement in any form of deviance is socially structured (cf. Cloward 1959). For a more general discussion of this tendency in the deviance and crime literature, see Cullen and Link (1980).

3. The famous critic of Lombroso's theory of the "criminal typè," Charles Goring, also touched upon this very point when he proposed that social class patterns the type of crime committed even though it has no effect on the overall rate of crime. Driver has summarized Goring's views on this issue:

> He did observe that types of crime appeared to be related to certain occupations and social classes. . . . However, Goring felt that type of occupation did not induce criminality but rather different occupations present dissimilar opportunities for committing a particular crime. Among the social classes there was a predominance of: crimes of violence, stealing and burglary in the lower class; sexual offenses in the poor and destitute classes; and fraud in the middle and upper classes. [1972 : 437]

4. These broad structural-historical conditions may work to structure deviant responses in at least two ways. First, they operate to define the range of possible adaptations from which people can select. Second, to the extent that they regulate which illegitimate options are more or less open to people located at various points in the social structure, they constrain deviant choices and thus help to account for variations across social statuses in rates of specific forms of deviance.

References

Adler, Freda. 1975. *Sisters in Crime: The Rise of the New Female Criminal*. New York: McGraw-Hill.

Ageton, Suzanne S., and Delbert S. Elliot. 1974. "The effects of legal processing on self-concept." *Social Problems* 22 (October): 87–100.

Akers, Ronald L. 1968. "Problems in the sociology of deviance: Social definitions and behavior." *Social Forces* 46 (June): 455–65.

Akers, Ronald L., Marvin D. Krohn, Lonn Lanza-Kaduce, and Marcia Radosevich. 1979. "Social learning and deviant behavior: A specific test of a general theory." *American Sociological Review* 44 (August): 636–55.

Aron, Raymond. 1967. *Main Currents in Sociological Thought*. Vol. 2. New York: Basic Books.

Askenasy, Alexander R., Bruce P. Dohrenwend, and Barbara S. Dohrenwend. 1977. "Some effects of social class and ethnic group membership on judgments of the magnitude of stressful life events: A research note." *Journal of Health and Social Behavior* 18 (December): 432–39.

Bales, Robert F. 1946. "Cultural differences in rates of alcoholism." *Quarterly Journal of Studies on Alcohol* 16 (March): 480–99.

Balkan, Sheila, Ronald J. Berger, and Janet Schmidt. 1980. *Crime and Deviance in America: A Critical Approach*. Belmont, CA: Wadsworth Publishing Co.

Barlow, Hugh D. 1978. *Introduction to Criminology*. Boston: Little, Brown & Co.

Barnett, Harold C. 1981. "Corporate capitalism, corporate crime." *Crime and Delinquency* 27 (January): 4–23.

Bayer, Ronald. 1981. "Crime, punishment, and the decline of liberal optimism." *Crime and Delinquency* 27 (April): 169–80.

Beaumont, Gustave de, and Alexis de Toqueville. 1964. *On the Penitentiary System in the United States and Its Application in France*. Dubuque, IA: William C. Brown Co.

Becker, Howard S. 1963. *Outsiders: Studies in the Sociology of Deviance*. Glencoe, IL: The Free Press.

———. 1974. "Labeling theory reconsidered." In *Deviance and Social Control*, edited by Paul Rock and Mary McIntosh, 41–66. London: Tavistock.

Benoit-Smullyan, Emile. 1948. "The sociologism of Emile Durkheim and his school." In *An Introduction to the History of Sociology*, edited by Harry Elmer Barnes. Abr. ed., 205–43. Chicago: University of Chicago Press.

Berger, Peter L. 1979. *The Heretical Imperative: Contemporary Possibilities of Religious Affirmation*. Garden City, NY: Anchor Books.

Berger, Peter L., and Thomas Luckmann. 1966. *The Social Construction of Reality*. Garden City, NY: Anchor Books.

Black, Donald J., and Albert J. Reiss. 1970. "Police control of juveniles." *American Sociological Review* 35 (August): 733–48.

Black, Max. 1961. *The Social Theories of Talcott Parsons*. Englewood Cliffs, NJ: Prentice-Hall.

Blake, Judith, and Kingsley Davis. 1964. "Norms, values, and sanctions." In *Handbook of Modern Sociology*, edited by Robert E.L. Paris, 456–84. Chicago: Rand McNally.

Blau, Peter M. 1960. "Structural Effects." *American Sociological Review* 25 (April): 178–93.

Blumer, Herbert. 1969. *Symbolic Interactionism: Perspective and Method*. Englewood Cliffs, NJ: Prentice-Hall.

Blumstein, Alfred, Jacqueline Cohen, and Daniel Nagin, eds. 1978. *Deterrence and Incapacitation: Estimating the Effects of Criminal Sanctions on Crime Rates*. Washington, D.C.: National Academy of Sciences.

Bollen, Kenneth L., and David P. Phillips. 1981. "Suicidal motor vehicle fatalities in Detroit: A replication." *American Journal of Sociology* 87 (September): 404–12.

———. 1982. "Imitative suicides: A national study of the effects of television news stories." *American Sociological Review* 47 (December): 802–9.

Bonger, Willem. 1969. *Criminality and Economic Conditions*. Bloomington: Indiana University Press.

Bordua, David J. 1961. "Delinquent subcultures: Sociological interpretations of gang delinquency." *Annals of the American Academy of Political and Social Science* 338 (November): 119–36.

Braithwaite, John. 1981. "The myth of social class and criminality reconsidered." *American Sociological Review* 46 (February): 36–57.

Braithwaite, Richard B. 1968. *Scientific Explanation*. Cambridge: Cambridge University Press.

Briar, Scott, and Irving Piliavin. 1965. "Delinquency, situational inducements, and commitment to conformity." *Social Problems* 13 (Summer): 35–45.

Brill, Harry. 1982. "Auto theft and the role of big business." *Crime and Social Justice* 18 (Winter): 62–68.

Burgess, Robert L., and Ronald L. Akers. 1966. "A differential association-reinforcement theory of criminal behavior." *Social Problems* 14 (Fall): 128–46.

Cassell, John. 1975. "Social science in epidemiology: Psychosocial processes and 'stress' theoretical formulation." In *Handbook of Evaluation*, edited by Elmer Struening and Marcia Guttentag, 537–49. Beverly Hills, CA: Sage Publications.

Chambliss, William J. 1964. "A sociological analysis of the law of vagrancy." *Social Problems* 12 (Summer): 67–77.

———. 1975. "Toward a political economy of crime." *Theory and Society* 2 (Summer): 149–70.

Clausen, John A. 1966. "Drug Addiction." In *Contemporary Social Problems*, edited by Robert K. Merton and Robert A. Nisbet. 2d ed., 193–235. New York: Harcourt, Brace and World.

Clinard, Marshall B. 1964. "The theoretical implications of anomie and deviant behavior." In *Anomie and Deviant Behavior*, edited by Marshall B. Clinard, 1–56. New York: The Free Press.

———. 1974. *Sociology of Deviant Behavior*. 4th ed. New York: Holt, Rinehart and Winston.

Clinard, Marshall B., and Peter C. Yeager. 1980. *Corporate Crime*. New York: The Free Press.

Cloward, Richard A. 1959. "Illegitimate means, anomie, and deviant behavior." *American Sociological Review* 24 (April): 164–76.

———. 1960. "Social control in the prison." In *Theoretical Studies in Social Organization of the Prison*. Pamphlet 15. New York: Social Science Research Council.

Cloward, Richard A., and Lloyd Ohlin. 1960. *Delinquency and Opportunity: A Theory of Delinquent Gangs*. New York: The Free Press.

Cloward, Richard A., and Frances Fox Piven. 1979. "Hidden protest: The channeling of female innovation and resistance." *Signs* 4 (Summer): 651–69.

———, with the assistance of Francis T. Cullen and Roslyn Tichen. 1977. *The Structuring of Deviant Behavior: A Preliminary Perspective*. First Year Report to the Law Enforcement Assistance Administration.

Cohen, Albert K. 1955. *Delinquent Boys: The Culture of the Gang*. New York: The Free Press.

———. 1959. "The study of social disorganization and deviant behavior." In *Sociology Today: Problems and Prospects*, edited by Robert K. Merton, Leonard Broom, and Leonard S. Cotrell. Vol. 2, 461–84. New York: Harper & Row.

————. 1966. *Deviance and Control*. Englewood Cliffs, NJ: Prentice-Hall.

Cohen, Albert K., and James F. Short. 1966. "Juvenile delinquency." In *Contemporary Social Problems*, edited by Robert K. Merton and Robert A. Nisbet, 84–135. New York: Harcourt, Brace and World.

Cohen, Lawrence E., and Marcus Felson. 1979. "Social change and crime rate trends: A routine activities approach." *American Sociological Review* 44 (August): 588–608.

Cole, Stephen. 1975. "The growth of scientific knowledge: Theories of deviance as a case study." In *The Idea of Social Structure: Papers in Honor of Robert K. Merton*, edited by Lewis A. Coser, 175–220. New York: Harcourt, Brace, Jovanovich.

Cole, Stephen, and Harriet Zuckerman. 1964. "Appendix." In *Anomie and Deviant Behavior*, edited by Marshall B. Clinard, 243–311. New York: The Free Press.

Collins, Randall, and Michael Makowsky. 1972. *The Discovery of Society*. New York: Random House.

Colvin, Mark. 1982. "The 1980 New Mexico prison riot." *Social Problems* 29 (June): 449–63.

Conklin, John E. 1977. *"Illegal But Not Criminal": Business Crime in America*. Englewood Cliffs, NJ: Prentice-Hall.

Coser, Lewis A. 1956. *The Functions of Social Conflict*. New York: The Free Press.

————. 1962. "Some functions of deviant behavior and normative flexibility." *American Journal of Sociology* 68 (September): 172–81.

————. 1966. "Some functions of violence." *Annals of the American Academy of Political and Social Science* 364 (March): 8–18.

Cressey, Donald R. 1950. "The criminal violation of financial trust." *American Sociological Review* 15 (December): 738–43.

————. 1953. *Other People's Money: A Study in the Social Psychology of Embezzlement*. New York: The Free Press.

————. 1960. "Epidemiology and individual conduct: A case from criminology." *Pacific Sociological Review* 3 (Fall): 47–58.

Cullen, Francis T., and John B. Cullen. 1977. "The Soviet model of Soviet deviance." *Pacific Sociological Review* 20 (July): 389–410.

————. 1978a. *Toward a Paradigm of Labeling Theory*. Monograph No. 58, University of Nebraska Studies. Lincoln: University of Nebraska Press.

————. 1978b. "Labeling theory and the empty castle phenomenon." *Western Sociological Review* 9 (1): 28–38.

Cullen, Francis T., and Karen E. Gilbert. 1982. *Reaffirming Rehabilitation*. Cincinnati: Anderson Publishing Co.

Cullen, Francis T., and Bruce G. Link. 1980. "Crime as an occupation: A new look." *Criminology* 18 (November): 399–410.

Cullen, Francis T., Bruce G. Link, and Craig W. Polanzi. 1982. "The seriousness of crime revisited: Have attitudes toward white-collar crime changed? *Criminology* 20 (May): 83–102.

Cullen, Francis T., Richard A. Mathers, Gregory A. Clark, and John B. Cullen. 1983. "Public support for punishing white-collar crime: Blaming the victim revisited?" *Journal of Criminal Justice*. Forthcoming.

Cullen, Francis T., and John F. Wozniak. 1982. "Fighting the appeal of repression." *Crime and Social Justice* 18 (Winter): 23–33.

Cusky, W.R., T. Premkumar, and L. Sigel. 1972. "Survey of opiate addiction among females in the United States between 1850 and 1970." *Public Health Reviews* 1 : 5–39.

Darrow, Clarence S. 1972. *Resist Not Evil*. Montclair, NJ: Patterson Smith.

Davies, James C. 1962. "Toward a theory of revolution." *American Sociological Review* 27 (February): 5–19.

Davis, Nanette J. 1975. *Sociological Constructions of Deviance: Perspectives and Issues in the Field*. Dubuque, I: Willian C. Brown Co.

DeLamater, John. 1968. "On the nature of deviance." *Social Forces* 46 (June): 445–55.

Dentler, Robert A., and Kai T. Erikson. 1959. "The functions of deviance in groups." *Social Problems* 7 (Fall): 98–107.

Dinitz, Simon, Frank R. Scarpitti, and Walter C. Reckless. 1962. "Delinquency and vulnerability: A cross group and longitudinal analysis." *American Sociological Review* 27 (August): 515–17.

Dohrenwend, Bruce. 1975. "Sociocultural and social-psychological factors in the genesis of mental disorders." *Journal of Health and Social Behavior* 16 (December): 365–92.

Dohrenwend, Bruce P., and Barbara Snell Dohrenwend. 1976. "Sex differences and psychiatric disorders." *American Journal of Sociology* 81 (May): 1447–54.

Driver, Edwin D. 1972. "Charles Buckman Goring." In *Pioneers in Criminology*, edited by Hermann Mannheim. 2nd ed., 429–42. Montclair, NJ: Patterson-Smith.

Dubin, Robert. 1959. "Deviant behavior and social structure: Continuities in social theory." *American Sociological Review* 24 (April): 147–64.

Durkheim, Emile. 1933. *The Division of Labor*. New York: The Free Press.

———. 1938. *The Rules of Sociological Method*. 8th ed. New York: The Free Press.

———. 1951. *Suicide: A Study in Sociology*. New York: The Free Press.

———. 1961. *Moral Education*. New York: The Free Press.

Eaton, William W. 1978. "Life-events, social supports, and psychiatric symptoms: A re-analysis of the New Haven data." *Journal of Health and Social Behavior* 19 (June): 230–34.

Ehrlich, Isaac. 1973. "Participation in illegitimate activities: A theoretical and empirical investigation." *Journal of Political Economy* 65 (June): 397–417.

Empey, LaMar T. 1982. *American Delinquency*. 2nd ed. Homewood, IL: Dorsey Press.

England, Ralph W. 1960. "A theory of middle class juvenile delinquency." *Journal of Criminal Law, Criminology, and Police Science* 50 (March-April): 535–40.

Epstein, Cynthia Fuchs. 1970. *Woman's Place: Options and Limits in Professional Careers*. Berkeley: University of California Press.

Erikson, Kai T. 1964. "Notes on the sociology of deviance." In *The Other Side*, edited by Howard Becker, 9–21. New York: The Free Press.

———. 1966. *Wayward Puritans*. New York: John Wiley & Sons.

Eve, Raymond A. 1978. "A study of the efficacy and interactions of several theories for explaining rebelliousness among high school students." *Journal of Criminal Law and Criminology* 69 (Spring): 115–25.

Faia, Michael A. 1967. "Alienation, structural strain, and political deviancy: A test of Merton's hypothesis." *Social Problems* 14 (Spring): 389–413.

Finestone, Harold. 1976. "The delinquent and society: The Shaw and McKay tradition." In *Delinquency, Crime, and Society*, edited by James F. Short, 23–49. Chicago: University of Chicago Press.

Fischer, Claude. 1973. "On urban alienation and anomie: Powerlessness and social isolation." *American Sociological Review* (June): 311–26.

Fogel, David. 1975. *"We Are the Living Proof": The Justice Model for Corrections*. Cincinnati: Anderson Publishing Co.

Foucault, Michel. 1977. *Discipline and Punish: The Birth of the Prison*. New York: Pantheon Books.

Fox, John W. 1980. "Gove's specific sex-role theory of mental illness: A research note." *Journal of Health and Social Behavior* 21 (September): 260–67.

Freud, Sigmund. 1961. *Civilization and Its Discontents*. New York: W. W. Norton & Co.

Garrett, Gerald R., and Howard M. Bahr. 1973. "Women on skid row." *Quarterly Journal of Studies on Alcohol* 34 (December): 1228–43.

Geis, Gilbert, and Colin Goff. 1982. "Edward H. Sutherland: A biographical and analytical commentary." In *White-Collar and Economic Crime: Multidisciplinary and Cross-National Perspectives*, edited by Peter Wickman and Timothy Dailey, 3–21. Lexington, MA: Lexington Books.

Gersten, Joanne C., Thomas S. Langner, Jeanne G. Eisenberg, and Ora Simcha-Fagan. 1977. "An evaluation of the etiologic role of stressful life-change events in psychological disorders." *Journal of Health and Social Behavior* 18 (September): 228–44.

Giallombardo, Rose. 1966. "Social roles in a prison for women." *Social problems* 13 (Winter): 268–88.

Gibbons, Don C. 1971. "Observations on the study of crime causation." *American Sociological Review* 77 (September): 262–78.

————. 1979. *The Criminological Enterprise: Theories and Perspectives*. Englewood Cliffs, NJ: Prentice-Hall.

————. 1981. *Changing the Lawbreaker: The Treatment of Delinquents and Criminals*. Montclair, NJ: Allanheld, Osmun & Co.

Gibbs, Jack P. 1966. "Suicide." In *Contemporary Social Problems*, edited by Robert K. Merton and Robert A. Nisbet, 281–321. 2nd ed. New York: Harcourt, Brace, and World.

————. 1972. "Issues in defining deviant behavior." In *Theoretical Perspectives on Deviance*, edited by Robert A. Scott and Jack D. Douglas, 39–68. New York: Basic Books.

Gibbs, Jack P., and Walter T. Martin. 1958. "A theory of status integration and its relationship to suidice." *American Sociological Review* 23 (April): 140–47.

————. 1964. *Status Integration and Suicide: A Sociological Study*. Eugene, OR: University of Oregon Books.

Gibbs, Jack P., and James F.Short, Jr. 1974. "Criminal differentiation and occupational differentiation." *Journal of Research in Crime and Delinquency* 11 (July): 89–100.

Giddens, Anthony. 1976. "Classical social theory and the origins of modern sociology." *American Journal of Sociology* 81 (January): 703–29.

Glaser, Daniel. 1956. "Criminality theory and behavioral images." *American Journal of Sociology* 61 (March): 433–44.

————. 1974. "The classification of offenses and offenders." In *Handbook of Criminology*, edited by Daniel Glaser, 45–83. Chicago: Rand McNally.

Glassner, Barry, and Bruce Berg. 1980. "How Jews avoid alcohol problems." *American Sociological Review* 45 (August): 647–64.

Goffman, Erving. 1961. *Asylums: Essays on the Social Situation of Mental Patients and Other Inmates*. Garden City, NY: Anchor Books.

Gordon, David. M. 1973. "Capitalism, class, and crime in America." *Crime and Delinquency* 19 (April): 163–86.

Gore, Susan. 1978. "The effect of social support in moderating the health consequences of unemployment." *Journal of Health and Social Behavior* 19 (June): 157–65.

Gould, Leroy C. 1969. "Juvenile entrepreneurs." *American Journal of Sociology* 74 (May): 710–19.

Gouldner, Alvin W. 1970. *The Coming Crisis of Western Sociology*. New York: Avon Books.

————. 1973. Forward to *The New Criminology: For a Social Theory of Deviance*, by Ian Taylor, Paul Walton, and Jack Young, ix–xiv. London: Routledge and Kegan Paul.

Gove, Walter R. 1975. *The Labelling of Deviance: Evaluating a Perspective*. 1st ed. New York: Halsted Press.

————. 1980. *The Labelling of Deviance: Evaluating a Perspective*. 2nd ed. Beverly Hills, CA: Sage Publications.

Gove, Walter R., and Jeannette F. Tudor. 1973. "Adult sex roles and mental illness." *American Journal of Sociology* 78 (January): 812–35.

Greenberg, David F. 1977. "Delinquency and the age structure of society." *Contemporary Crises* 1 (April): 189–223.

————. 1981. *Crime and Capitalism: Readings in Marxist Criminology*. Palo Alto, CA: Mayfield Publishing Co.

Gusfield, Joseph. 1967, "Moral passage: The symbolic process in public designations of deviance." *Social Problems* 15 (Fall): 175–88.

Hagan, John. 1973. "Labeling and deviance: A case study in the 'sociology of the interesting' " *Social Problems* 20 (Spring): 447–58.

Hagan, John R., John H. Simpson, and A.R. Gillis. 1979. "The sexual stratification of social control: A gender-based perspective on crime and delinquency." *British Journal of Sociology* 30 (March): 24–30.

Hakim, Simon, and George F. Rengert. 1981. *Crime Spillover*. Beverly Hills, CA: Sage Publications.

Halleck, Seymour L. 1967. *Psychiatry and the Dilemmas of Crime: A Study of Causes, Punishment and Treatment*. New York: Harper & Row.

Halleck, Seymour L., and Ann D. Witte. 1977. "Is rehabilitation dead?" *Crime and Delinquency* 23 (October): 372–82.

Harary, Frank. 1966. "Merton revisited: A new classification for deviant behavior." *American Sociological Review* 32 : 693–97.

Harris, Anthony. 1977. "Sex and theories of deviance: Toward a functionalist theory of deviant type-scripts." *American Sociological Review* 42 (February): 3–16.

Hawkins, Gordon. 1976. *The Prison: Policy and Practice*. Chicago: University of Chicago Press.

Henry, Andrew P., and James F. Short. 1954. *Suicide and Homicide: Some Economic, Sociological and Psychological Aspects of Aggression*. New York: The Free Press.

Hepburn, John L. 1977. "The impact of police intervention upon juvenile delinquents." *Criminology* 15 (August): 235–62.

Hill, Robert B. 1968. *Parent and Peer Group Pressures Toward Deviant Student Behavior*. New York: Bureau of Applied Social Research, Columbia University.

Hindelang, Michael J. 1979. "Sex differences in criminal activity." *Social Problems* 27 (December): 142–55.

Hirschi, Travis. 1969. *Causes of Delinquency*. Berkeley: University of California Press.

———. 1973. "Procedural rules and the study of deviant behavior." *Social Problems* 21 (Fall): 159–73.

———. 1975. "Labelling theory and juvenile delinquency: An assessment of the evidence." In *The Labelling of Deviance*, edited by Walter R. Gove, 181–203. New York: Halsted Press.

Hobbes, Thomas. 1964. *Leviathan*. Edited by Francis B. Randall. New York: Washington Square Press.

Hollingshead, August B., and Frederick C. Redlich. 1958. *Social Class and Mental Illness*. New York: John Wiley.

Homans, George C. 1967. *The Nature of Social Science*. New York: Harcourt, Brace, Jovanovich.

Horning, Donald N. M. 1970. "Blue-collar theft: Conceptions of property, attitudes toward pilfering, and work group norms in a modern industrial plant." In *Crimes Against Bureaucracy*, edited by Erwin O. Smigel and H. Lawrence Ross, 46–64. New York: Van Nostrand Reinhold Co.

Horowitz, Ruth, and Gary Schwartz. 1974. "Honor, normative ambiguity and gang violence." *American Sociological Review* 39 (April): 238–51.

Horton, Donald. 1943. "The functions of alcohol in primitive societies: A cross-cultural study." *Quarterly Journal of Studies on Alcohol* 4 (September): 199–320.

House, James S. 1981. *Work Stress and Social Support*. Reading, MA: Addison-Wesley.

House, James S., and Elizabeth B. Harkins. 1975. "Why and when is status inconsistency stressful." *American Journal of Sociology* 81 (September): 395–412.

Humphreys, Laud. 1975. *Tearoom Trade: Impersonal Sex in Public Places*. Chicago: Aldine.

Humphries, Drew, and Don Wallace. 1980. "Capitalist accumulation and urban crime, 1950–1971." *Social Problems* 28 (December): 179–93.

Ianni, Francis A.J. 1974. *Black Mafia : Ethnic Succession in Organized Crime*. New York: Simon & Schuster.

Ignatieff, Michael. 1978. *A Just Measure of Pain: The Penitentiary in the Industrial Revolution, 1750–1850*. New York: Pantheon Books.

Inciardi, James A. 1974. "Vocational crime." In *Handbook of Criminology*, edited by Daniel Glaser, 299–401. Chicago: Rand McNally.

Irwin, John, and Donald Cressey. 1962. "Thieves, convicts, and the inmate culture." *Social Problems* 10 (Fall): 142–55.

Jacobs, James B. 1977. *Stateville: The Penitentiary in Mass Society*. Chicago: University of Chicago Press.

Jankovic, Ivan. 1977. "Labor market and imprisonment." *Crime and Social Justice* 8 (Fall-Winter): 17–31.

Jeffrey, Clarence R. 1972. "The historical development of criminology." In *Pioneers of Criminology*, edited by Hermann Mannheim. 2nd ed., 458–98. Montclair, NJ: Patterson-Smith.

———. 1977. *Crime Prevention Through Environmental Design*. Beverly Hills, CA: Sage Publications.

Jenkins, Philip. 1982. "The radicals and the rehabilitative ideal, 1890–1915." *Criminology* 20 (November): 347–72.

Jensen, Gary F. 1972. "Delinquency and adolescent self-conceptions: A study of the personal relevance of infraction." *Social Problems* 20 (Summer): 84–103.

Johnson, Barcay D. 1965. "Durkheim's one cause of suicide." *American Sociological Review* 30 (December): 875–86.

Kahn, Robert L., Donald M. Wolf, Robert P. Quinn, and J. Diedrick Snoek, in collaboration with Robert A. Rosenthal. 1964. *Organizational Stress: Studies in Role Conflict and Ambiguity.* New York: John Wiley.

Kendall, Patricia L., and Paul F. Lazarsfeld. 1950. "Problems of survey analysis." In *Continuities in Social Research*, edited by Robert K. Merton and Paul F. Lazarsfeld, 133–96. New York: The Free Press.

Kitsuse, John I. 1964. "Societal reaction to deviant behavior: Problems of theory and method." In *The Other Side*, edited by Howard Becker, 87–102. New York: The Free Press.

———. 1975. "The 'new conception of deviance' and its critics." In *The Labelling of Deviance*, edited by Walter Gove, 273–84. New York: Halsted Press.

Kitsuse, John I., and Aaron V. Cicourel. 1972. "A note on the uses of official statistics." In *Faces of Delinquency*, edited by John P. Reed and Fuad Baali, 45–53. Englewood Cliffs, NJ: Prentice-Hall.

Kittrie, Nicholas N. 1971. *The Right to be Different: Deviance and Enforced Therapy.* Baltimore: Penguin Books.

Klemke, Lloyd W. 1978. "Does apprehension for shoplifting amplify or terminate shoplifting activity?" *Law and Society Review* 12 (Spring): 391–403.

Klockars, Carl. 1974. *The Professional Fence.* New York: The Free Press.

Kobrin, Solomon. 1951. "The conflict of values in delinquency areas." *American Sociological Review* 16 (October): 653–61.

Kornhauser, Ruth Rosner. 1978. *Social Sources of Delinquency: An Appraisal of Analytic Models.* Chicago: University of Chicago Press.

Krisberg, Barry. 1975. *Crime and Privilege: Toward a New Criminology.* Englewood Cliffs, NJ: Prentice-Hall.

Kuhn, Thomas S. 1962. *The Structure of Scientific Revolutions.* Chicago: University of Chicago Press.

Lakatos, Imre. 1970. "Falsification and methodology of scientific research programs." In *Criticism and the Growth of Knowledge*, edited by Imre Lakatos and Alan Musgrave, 91–196. London: Cambridge University Press.

Langner, Thomas S., and Stanley T. Michael. 1963. *Life Stress and Mental Health.* New York: The Free Press.

Lemert, Edwin M. 1951. *Social Pathology.* New York: McGraw-Hill.

———. 1972. *Human Deviance, Social Problems, and Social Control.* 2nd ed. Englewood Cliffs, NJ: Prentice-Hall.

Leonard, Eileen B. 1982. *Women, Crime, and Society: A Critique of Theoretical Criminology.* New York: Longman.

Letkemann, Peter. 1973. *Crime as Work.* Englewood Cliffs, NJ: Prentice-Hall.

Liem, Ramsay, and Joan Liem. 1978. "Social class and mental illness reconsidered: The role of economic stress and social support." *Journal of Health and Social Behavior* 19 (June): 139–56.

Light, Ivan. 1977. "The ethnic vice industry, 1880–1944." *American Sociological Review* 42 (June): 464–79.

Lindesmith, Alfred R., and John R. Gagnon. 1964. "Anomie and drug addiction." In *Anomie and Deviant Behavior*, edited by Marshall B. Clinard, 158–88. New York: The Free Press.

Lindesmith, Alfred, and Yale Levin. 1937. "The Lombrosian myth in criminology." *American Journal of Sociology* 42 (March): 653–71.

Linsky, Arnold S., and Murray A. Straus. 1982. "Crime and other maladaptive responses to stress in American states and regions." Paper presented at the annual meeting of the American Sociological Association.

Lisansky, Edith. 1968. "Drinking and alcoholism: Psychological aspects." *International Encyclopedia of the Social Sciences*, Vol. 4 : 264–68. New York: The Free Press.

Liska, Allen E. 1981. *Perspectives on Deviance.* Englewood Cliffs, NJ: Prentice-Hall.

Lolli, Giorgio, Emidio Serianni, Grace Golder, and Claudia Balboni. 1953. "Further observations on the use of wine and other alcohol beverages by Italians and Americans of Italian extraction." *Quarterly Journal of Studies on Alcohol* 14 (September): 395–405.

Lombroso-Ferrero, Gina. 1972. *Criminal Man According to the Classification of Cesare Lombroso*. Montclair, NJ: Patterson Smith.

Lopreato, Joseph. 1971. "The concept of equilibrium: Sociological tantalizer." In *Institutions and Social Exchange: The Sociologies of Talcott Parsons and George C. Homans*, edited by Herman Turk and Richard L. Simpson, 309–43. New York: Bobbs-Merrill.

Lottier, Stuart. 1942. "A tension theory of criminal behavior." *American Sociological Review* 7 (December): 840–48.

Maris, Ronald W. 1969. *Social Forces in Urban Suicide*. Homewood, IL: Dorsey Press.

Marks, Alan. 1977–1978. "Sex differences and its affect upon cultural evaluations of methods of self-destruction." *Omega* 8 (1): 65–70.

Marks, Alan, and Thomas Abernathy. 1974. "Toward a sociocultural perspective on means of self-destruction." *Life-Threatening Behavior* 4 (Spring): 3–17.

Marks, Alan, and C. Shannon Stokes. 1976. "Socialization, firearms, and suicide." *Social Problems* 23 (June): 622–29.

Marks, Stephen. 1974. "Durkheim's theory of anomie." *American Journal of Sociology* 80 (September): 329–63.

Marx, Gary T. 1981. "Ironies of social control: Authorities as contributors to deviance through escalation, nonenforcement and covert facilitation." *Social Problems* 28 (February): 221–46.

Masaryk, Thomas G. 1970. *Suicide and the Meaning of Civilization*. Chicago: University of Chicago Press.

Matza, David. 1964. *Delinquency and Drift*. New York: John Wiley.

———. 1969. *Becoming Deviant*. Englewood Cliffs, NJ: Prentice-Hall.

McCloskey, David. 1976. "On Durkheim, anomie, and the modern crisis." *American Journal of Sociology* 81 (May): 1481–88.

McClosky, Herbert, and John R. Schaar. 1965. "Psychological dimensions of anomy." *American Sociological Review* 30 (February): 14–40.

McCord, Joan. 1978. "A thirty year follow-up of treatment effects." *American Psychologist* 33 (March): 284–89.

———. 1981. "Consideration of some effects of a counseling program." In *New Directions in the Rehabilitation of Criminal Offenders*, edited by Susan E. Martin, Lee B. Sechrest, and Robin Redner, 394–405. Washington, D.C.: National Academy Press.

Mead, George H. 1918. "The psychology of punitive justice." *American Journal of Sociology* 23 (March): 577–602.

Meier, Robert F. 1977. "The new criminology: Continuity in criminological theory." *Journal of Criminal Law and Criminology* 67 (December): 460–69.

Merton, Robert K. 1936. "The unanticipated consequences of purposive social action." *American Sociological Review* 1 (December): 894–904.

———. 1938. "Social structure and anomie." *American Sociological Review* 3 (October): 672–82.

———. 1948a. "Social structure and anomie." In *Social Theory and Social Structure*, 131–60. Glencoe, IL: The Free Press.

———. 1948b. "Social structure and anomie: Revisions and extensions." In *The Family: Its Function and Destiny*, edited by Ruth Anshen, 226–57. New York: Harper & Row.

———. 1955. "The socio-cultural environment and anomie." In *New Perspectives for Research on Juvenile Delinquency*, edited by H. L. Witmer and R. Kotinsky, 24–50. Washington, D.C.: U.S. Government Printing Office.

———. 1957. "Priorities in scientific discovery: A chapter in the sociology of science." *American Sociological Review* 22 (December): 635–59.

———. 1959. "Social conformity, deviation, and opportunity structures: A comment on the contributions of Dubin and Cloward." *American Sociological Review* 24 (April): 177–89.

———. 1964. "Anomie, anomia, and social interaction: Contexts of deviant behavior." In *Anomie and Deviant Behavior*, edited by Marshall B. Clinard, 213–42. New York: The Free Press.

———. 1968a. "Manifest and latent functions: Toward the codification of functional analysis in sociology." In *Social Theory and Social Structure*. Enlarged ed., 73–138. New York: The Free Press.

———. 1968b. "Social structure and anomie." In *Social Theory and Social Structure*. Enlarged ed., 185–214.

————. 1968c. "Continuities in the theory of social structure and anomie." In *Social Theory and Social Structure*. Enlarged ed., 215–48. New York: The Free Press.

Merton, Robert K., and M.F. Ashley Montague. 1940. "Crime and the anthropologist." *American Anthropologist* 42 (July-September): 384–408.

Miller, Martin B. 1980. "Sinking gradually into the proletariat: The emergence of the penitentiary in the United States." *Crime and Social Justice* 14 (Winter): 37–43.

————. 1982. "Rothman revisited." *Crime and Social Justice* 17 (Summer): 98–103.

Mills, C. Wright. 1942. "The professional ideology of social pathologists." *American Journal of Sociology* 49 (September): 165–80.

Mizruchi, Ephraim H. 1964. *Success and Opportunity: A Study of Anomie*. New York: The Free Press.

Nettler, Gwynn. 1978. *Explaining Crime*. 2nd ed. New York: McGraw-Hill.

Nisbet, Robert A. 1966. *The Sociological Tradition*. New York: Basic Books.

————. 1974. *The Sociology of Emile Durkheim*. New York: Oxford University Press.

Norland, Stephen, and Neal Shover. 1977. "Gender roles and female criminality: Some critical comments." *Criminology* 15 (May): 87–104.

Nye, F. Ivan. 1958. *Family Relationships and Delinquent Behavior*. New York: John Wiley.

O'Connor, Gerald B. 1970. "The impact of initial detention upon male delinquents." *Social Problems* 18 (Fall): 194–99.

Office of Policy Planning and Research. 1965. *The Negro Family: The Case for National Action*. Washington, D.C.: U.S. Government Printing Office.

O'Malley, Pat. 1979. "Class conflict, land and social banditry: Bushranging in nineteenth century Australia." *Social Problems* 26 (February): 271–83.

Orcutt, James D. 1972. "Societal reaction and the response to deviation in small groups." *Social Forces* 52 (December): 259–67.

Palamara, Frances, Joanne C. Gersten, and Francis T. Cullen. 1983. "The effect of police and mental health intervention on juvenile deviance: Specifying contingencies in the impact of formal reaction." Unpublished paper, Columbia University.

Palmore, Erdman B., and Phillip E. Hammond. 1964. "Interacting factors in juvenile delinquency." *American Sociological Review* 29 (December): 848–54.

Parsons, Talcott. 1937. *The Structure of Social Action*. Two vols. New York: The Free Press.

————. 1947. "Certain primary sources and patterns of aggression in the social structure of the western world." *Psychiatry* 10 (May): 167–81.

————. 1951. *The Social System*. New York: The Free Press.

————. 1954a. "Age and sex in the social structure." In *Essays in Sociological Theory*. Rev. ed., 89–103. New York: The Free Press.

————. 1954b. "Psychoanalysis and the social structure." In *Essays in Sociological Theory*. Rev. ed., 336–47. New York: The Free Press.

————. 1954c. "Democracy and social structure in pre-Nazi Germany." In *Essays in Sociological Theory*. Rev. ed., 104–23. New York: The Free Press.

————. 1954e. "Propaganda and social control." In *Essays in Sociological Theory*. Rev. ed., 142–76. New York: The Free Press.

Parsons, Talcott, and Robert F. Bales, in collaboration with James Olds, Morris Zelditch, and Philip E. Slater. 1955. *Family, Socialization and Interaction Process*. New York: The Free Press.

Parsons, Talcott, and Gerald M. Platt, with Neil J. Smelser. 1973. *The American University*. Cambridge, MA: Harvard University Press.

Parsons, Talcott, and Dean R. Gerstein. 1977. "Two cases of social deviance: Addiction to heroin, addiction to power." In *Deviance and Social Change*, edited by Edward Sagarin, 19–57. Beverly Hills, CA: Sage Publications.

Pearce, Frank. 1976. *Crimes of the Powerful: Marxism, Crime and Deviance*. London: Pluto Press.

Pearlin, Leonard I., and Clarice W. Radabaugh. 1976. "Economic strains and the coping functions of alcohol." *American Journal of Sociology* 82 (November): 652–63.

Pearlin, Leonard I., and Carmi Schooler. 1978. "The structure of coping." *Journal of Health and Social Behavior* 19 (March): 2–21.

Phillips, David P. 1979. "Suicide, motor vehicle fatalities, and the mass media: Evidence toward a theory of suggestion." *American Journal of Sociology* 94 (March): 1150–74.

Piven, Frances Fox, and Richard A. Cloward. 1977. *Poor People's Movements: Why They Succeed, How They Fail*. New York: Pantheon Books.

Platt, Anthony M. 1969. *The Child Savers: The Invention of Delinquency*. Chicago: University of Chicago Press.

———. 1974. "The triumph of benevolence: The origins of the juvenile justice system in the United States." In *Criminal Justice in America: A Critical Understanding*, edited by Richard Quinney, 356–89. Boston: Little, Brown & Co.

———. 1975. "The prospects for a radical criminology in the U.S.A." In *Critical Criminology*, edited by Ian Taylor, Paul Walton, and Jock Young, 95–112. London: Routledge and Kegan Paul.

———. 1982. "Crime and punishment in the United States: Immediate and long-term reforms from a Marxist perspective." *Crime and Social Justice* 18 (Winter): 38–45.

Pope, Whitney. 1976. *Durkheim's Suicide: A Classic Analyzed*. Chicago: University of Chicago Press.

Popper, Karl R. 1959. *The Logic of Scientific Discovery*. New York: Harper & Row.

Quicker, John C. 1974. "The effect of goal discrepancy on delinquency." *Social Problems* 22 (October): 76–86.

Quinney, Richard. 1970. *The Social Reality of Crime*. Boston: Little, Brown & Co.

———. 1973. "Crime control in capitalist society: A critical philosophy of legal order." *Issues in Criminology* 8 (Spring): 75–99.

———. 1977. *Class, State, and Crime: On the Theory and Practice of Criminal Justice*. New York: David McKay Co.

Rabkin, Judith G., and Elmer L. Struening. 1976. "Life events, stress, and illness." *Science* 194 (December): 1013–20.

Radzinowicz, Leon. 1966. *Ideology and Crime: A Study of Crime in Its Social and Historical Context*. New York: Columbia University Press.

Rahav, Michael. 1979. "Age, Sex, and the Social Structuring of Deviant Behavior." Unpublished Ph.D. dissertation, Columbia University.

Reckless, Walter C. 1961. *The Crime Problem*. 3d ed. New York: Appleton-Century-Crofts.

Reckless, Walter C., and Simon Dinitz. 1967. "Pioneering with self-concept as a vulnerability factor in delinquency." *Journal of Criminal Law, Criminology and Police Science* 58 (December): 515–23.

Reckless, Walter C., Simon Dinitz, and Barbara Kay. 1957. "The self component in potential delinquency and potential non-delinquency." *American Sociological Review* 22 (October): 566–70.

Reckless, Walter C., Simon Dinitz, and Ellen Murray. 1956. "Self concept as an insulator against delinquency." *American Sociological Review* 21 (December): 744–46.

———. 1957. "The 'good boy' in a high delinquency area." *Journal of Criminal Law, Criminology and Police Science* 48 (May–June): 18–25.

Redl, Fritz, and David Wineman. 1951. *Children Who Hate: The Disorganization and Breakdown of Behavior Controls*. New York: The Free Press.

Reiman, Jeffrey H. 1979. *The Rich Get Richer and the Poor Get Prison: Ideology, Class, and Criminal Justice*. New York: John Wiley & Sons.

Reiss, Albert J. 1951. "Delinquency as the failure of personal and social controls." *American Sociological Review* 16 (April): 196–207.

Robins, Lee N. 1975. "Alcoholism and labelling theory." In *The Labelling of Deviance*, edited by Walter R. Gove, 21–33. New York: Halsted Press.

Robinson, W.S. 1950. "Ecological correlations and the behavior of individuals." *American Sociological Review* 15 (June): 351–57.

Rodgers, Glennda J. 1975. "Deviance: An ethnomethodological account." *Graduate Faculty Journal of Sociology* 1 (Winter): 37–56.

Rose, Jerry D. 1982. *Outbreaks: The Sociology of Collective Behavior*. New York: The Free Press.

Rosenblum, Karen E. 1975. "Female deviance and the female sex role: A preliminary investigation." *British Journal of Sociology* 26 (June): 169–85.

Ross, E.A. 1907. *Sin and Society: An Analysis of Latter-Day Iniquity*. New York: Harper & Row.

Rossi, Peter H., Emily Waite, Christine E. Bose, and Richard E. Berk. 1974. "The seriousness of crimes: Normative structure and individual differences." *American Sociological Review* 39 (April): 224–37.

Rothman, David J. 1971. *The Discovery of the Asylum: Social Order and Disorder in the New Republic*. Boston: Little, Brown & Co.

———. 1978. "The state as parent: Social policy in the Progressive era." In *Doing Good: The Limits of Benevolence*, by Willard Gaylin, Ira Glasser, Steven Marcus, and David Rothman, 67–96. New York: Pantheon Books.

———. 1980. *Conscience and Convenience: The Asylum and Its Alternatives in Progressive America*. Boston: Little, Brown & Co.

Rubington, Earl. 1958. "The chronic drunkeness offender." *Annals of the American Academy of Political and Social Science* 315 (January): 65–72.

Rusche, Georg, and Otto Kirchheimer. 1939. *Punishment and Social Structure*. New York: Columbia University Press.

Ryan, William. 1971. *Blaming the Victim*. New York: Vintage Books.

Sagarin, Edward. 1975. *Deviants and Deviance: An Introduction to the Study of Disvalued People and Behavior*. New York: Praeger.

Sadoun, Roland, Giorgio Lolli, and Milton Silverman. 1965. *Drinking in French Culture*. New Brunswick, NJ: Rutgers Center of Alcohol Studies.

Sampson, Harold, Sheldon L. Messinger, Robert D. Towne, et al. 1964. "The mental hospital and marital family ties." In *The Other Side*, edited by Howard Becker, 139–62. New York: The Free Press.

Scarpitti, Frank R., Ellen Murray, Simon Dinitz, and Walter C. Reckless. 1960. "The 'good' boy in a high delinquency area: Four years later." *American Sociological Review* 25 (August): 555–58.

Schervish, Paul G. 1973. "The labeling perspective: Its bias and potential in the study of political deviance." *American Sociologist* 8 (May): 47–57.

Schuessler, Karl. 1962. "Components of variation in city crime rates." *Social Problems* 9 (Spring): 314–23.

Schur, Edwin M. 1965. *Crimes Without Victims: Deviant Behavior and Public Policy*. Englewood Cliffs, NJ: Prentice-Hall.

———. 1971. *Labeling Deviant Behavior: Its Sociological Implications*. New York: Harper & Row.

———. 1973. *Radical Non-Intervention: Rethinking the Delinquency Problem*. Englewood Cliffs, NJ: Prentice-Hall.

Schwendinger, Herman, and Julia Schwendinger. 1975. "Defenders of order or guardians of human rights?" In *Critical Criminology*, edited by Ian Taylor, Paul Walton, and Jock Young, 113–46. London: Routledge and Kegan Paul.

———. 1976. "The collective varieties of youth." *Crime and Social Justice* 5 (Spring–Summer): 7–25.

———. 1982. "The paradigmatic crisis in delinquency theory." *Crime and Social Justice* 18 (Winter): 70–78.

Scull, Andrew T. 1977. *Decarceration: Community Treatment and the Deviant—A Radical View*. Englewood Cliffs. NJ: Prentice-Hall.

Sechrest, Lee, Susan O. White, and Elizabeth D. Brown, eds. 1979. *The Rehabilitation of Criminal Offenders: Problems and Prospects*. Washington, D.C.: National Academy of Sciences.

Sellin, Thorsten. 1938. *Culture Conflict and Crime*. Bulletin 41. New York: Social Science Research Council.

———. 1976. *Slavery and the Penal System*. New York: Elsevier.

Serrill, Michael S. and Peter Katel. 1980. "New Mexico: The anatomy of a riot." *Corrections Magazine* 6 (April): 6–16, 20–24.

Shannon, Lyle W. 1982. *Assessing the Relationship of Adult Criminal Careers to Juvenile Careers: A Summary*. Washington, D.C.: U.S. Department of Justice.

Shaw, Clifford R. 1930. *The Jack-Roller: A Delinquent Boy's Own Story*. Chicago: University of Chicago Press.
Shaw, Clifford R., and Henry D. McKay. 1929. *Delinquency Areas*. Chicago: University of Chicago Press.
———. 1972. *Juvenile Delinquency and Urban Areas: A Study of Rates of Delinquency in Relation to Differential Characteristics of Local Communities in American Cities*. Rev. ed. Chicago: University of Chicago Press.
Shaw, Clifford R., with the assistance of Henry D. McKay and James F. McDonald. 1938. *Brothers in Crime*. Chicago: University of Chicago Press.
Shaw, Clifford R., in collaboration with Maurice E. Moore. 1931. *The Natural History of a Delinquent Career*. Chicago: University of Chicago Press.
Shaw, George Bernard. 1946. *The Crime of Imprisonment*. New York: The Philosophic Library.
Short, James F. 1963. "Introduction to the abridged edition of *The Gang: A Study of 1,313 Gangs in Chicago*, by Frederic M. Thrasher," xv–liii. Chicago: University of Chicago Press.
———. 1975. "The natural history of an applied theory: Differential opportunity and 'Mobilization for Youth'." In *Social Policy and Sociology*, 193–210. New York: Academic Press.
Short, James F., and Fred L. Strodtbeck. 1965. *Group Process and Gang Delinquency*. Chicago: University of Chicago Press.
Simon, Rita J. 1975. *Women and Crime*. Lexington, MA: D.C. Health.
Simon, William, and John H. Gagnon. 1976. "The anomie of affluence: A post-Mertonian conception." *American Journal of Sociology* 82 (November): 356–78.
Singer, Jerome L., and Marvin K. Opler. 1956. "Contrasting patterns of fantasy and motility in Irish and Italian schizophrenics." *Journal of Abnormal and Social Psychology* 53 (July): 42–47.
Smart, Carol. 1977. *Women, Crime and Criminology: A Feminist Critique*. Boston: Routledge and Kegan Paul.
Smelser, Neil J. 1962. *Theory of Collective Behavior*. New York: The Free Press.
———. 1973. "Epilogue: Social-structural dimensions of higher education." In *The American University*, by Talcott Parsons and Gerald M. Platt, 389–422. Cambridge, MA: Harvard University Press.
Smelser, Neil J., and R. Stephen Warner. 1976. "Talcott Parsons' theory of deviance and social control." In *Sociological Theory: Historical and Formal*, by Neil J. Smelser and R. Stephen Warner, 179–204. Morristown, NJ: Silver Burdett Co.
Snyder, Charles R. 1956. "Studies of drinking in Jewish culture. IV. Culture and sobriety." *Quarterly Journal of Studies on Alcohol* 17 (March): 124–43.
———. 1958. *Alcohol and the Jews: A Cultural Study of Drinking and Sobriety*. New Haven: Yale Center of Alcohol Studies
———. 1962. "Culture and Jewish sobriety: The ingroup-outgroup factor." In *Society, Culture, and Drinking Patterns*, edited by David J. Pittman and Charles R. Snyder, 188–225. New York: John Wiley & Sons.
Snyder, Charles R., and David J. Pittman. 1968. "Drinking and alcoholism: Social aspects." In *International Encyclopedia of the Social Sciences*, Vol. 4, 268–75. New York: The Free Press.
Social Forces. 1981. "Special issue: Durkheim lives!" Vol. 59 (June).
Spergel, Irving. 1964. *Racketville, Slumtown, Haulburg*. Chicago: University of Chicago Press.
Srole, Leo. 1956. "Social integration and certain corollaries: An exploratory study." *American Sociological Review* 21 (December): 709–16.
Steffensmeier, Darrell J. 1978. "Crime and the contemporary woman: An analysis of changing levels of female property crime, 1960–75." *Social Forces* 57 (December): 566–84.
———. 1980. "Sex differences in patterns of adult crime, 1965–77 : A review and assessment." *Social Forces* 58 (June): 1080–1108.
———. 1982. "Organization properties and sex-segregation in the underworld: Building a sociological theory of sex differences in crime." *Social Forces* 61 (June): 1010–32.
Steffensmeier, Darrell J., and Michael J. Cobb. 1981. "Sex differences in urban arrest patterns, 1934–79." *Social Problems* 29 (October): 37–50.
Steffensmeier, Darrell, and Renee Hoffman Steffensmeier. 1980. "Trends in female delinquency:

An examination of arrest, juvenile court, self-report, and field data." *Criminology* 18 (May): 62–85.

Stein, Harman D., and John D. Martin. 1962. " 'Swastika offenders': Variations in etiology, behavior and psycho-social characteristics." *Social Problems* 10 (Summer): 56–70.

Stinchcombe, Arthur L. 1975. "Merton's theory of social structure." In *The Idea of Social Structure: Papers in Honor of Robert K. Merton*, edited by Lewis A. Coser, 11–33. New York: Harcourt, Brace, Jovanovich.

Stone, Christopher D. 1975. *Where the Law Ends: The Social Control of Corporate Behavior.* New York: Harper & Row.

Stone, W.G. 1982. *The Hate Factory*. Agoura, California : Paisano Publications.

Sutherland, Edwin H. 1937. *The Professional Thief: By a Professional Thief.* Chicago: University of Chicago Press.

———. 1949. *White Collar Crime*. New York: Holt, Rinehart and Winston.

———. 1973a. "Development of the theory." In *On Analyzing Crime*, edited by Karl Schuessler, 13–29. Chicago: University of Chicago Press.

———. 1973b. "Critique of the theory." In *On Analyzing Crime*, edited by Karl Schuessler, 30–41. Chicago: University of Chicago Press.

———. 1973c. "Crime and the conflict process." In *On Analyzing Crime*, edited by Karl Schuessler, 99–111. Chicago: University of Chicago Press.

———. 1973d. "Wartime crime." In *On Analyzing Crime*, 120–28. Chicago: University of Chicago Press.

Sutherland, Edwin H., and Donald R. Cressey. 1970. *Criminology*. 8th ed. Philadelphia : J.B. Lippincott Co.

Sykes, Gresham, M. 1974. "The rise of critical criminology." *Journal of Criminal Law and Criminology* 65 (June): 206–13.

———. 1978. *Criminology*. New York: Harcourt, Brace, Jovanovich.

Sykes, Gresham M., and David Matza. 1957. "Techniques of neutralization." *American Sociological Review* 22 (December): 664–70.

Szasz, Thomas S. 1960. "The myth of mental illness." *American Psychologist* 15 (February): 113–18.

———. 1970. *The Manufacture of Madness*. New York: Dell.

Takagi, Paul. 1975. "The Walnut Street Jail: A penal reform to centralize the powers of the state." *Federal Probation* 39 (December): 18–26.

Tannenbaum, Frank. 1938. *Crime and the Community*. New York: Columbia University Press.

Taylor, Ian, Paul Walton, and Jock Young. 1973. *The New Criminology: For a Social Theory of Deviance*. London: Routledge and Kegan Paul.

Thio, Alex. 1973. "Class bias in the sociology of deviance." *American Sociologist* 8 (February): 1–12.

———. 1975. "A critical look at Merton's anomie theory." *Pacific Sociological Review* 18 (April): 139–58.

Thrasher, Frederic M. 1963. *The Gang: A Study of 1,313 Gangs in Chicago*. Abridged ed. Chicago: University of Chicago Press.

Timasheff, Nicholas S. 1955. *Sociological Theory: Its Nature and Growth*. New York: Random House.

Tiryakian, Edward A. 1981. "Sexual anomie, social structure, societal change." *Social Forces* 59 (June): 1025–53.

Tittle, Charles R. 1975. "Deterrents or labeling?" *Social Forces* 53 (March): 399–410.

Tittle, Charles R., Wayne J. Villemez, and Douglas A. Smith. 1978. "The myth of social class and criminality." *American Sociological Review* 43 (October): 643–56.

Toby, Jackson. 1974. "The socialization and control of deviant motivation." In *Handbook of Criminology*, edited by Daniel Glaser, 85–100. Chicago: Rand McNally.

Toqueville, Alexis de. 1945. *Democracy in America*. Vol. 2. New York: Vintage Books.

Turk, Austin T. 1966. "Conflict and criminality." *American Sociological Review* 31 (June): 338–52.

Turk, Herman, and Richard L. Simpson, eds. 1971. *Institutions and Social Exchange: The Sociologies of Talcott Parsons and George C. Homans*. New York: Bobbs-Merrill.

van den Haag, Ernest. 1975. *Punishing Criminals: Concerning a Very Old and Painful Question*. New York: Basic Books.

Vold, George B. 1958. *Theoretical Criminology*. New York: Oxford University Press.

Waldorf, Dan. 1973. *Careers in Dope*. Englewood Cliffs, NJ: Prentice-Hall.

Wallace, Anthony F.C. 1961. "Mental illness, biology, and culture." In *Psychological Anthropology: Approaches to Culture and Personality*, edited by Francis L.K. Hsu, 225–95. Homewood, IL: Dorsey Press.

———. 1970. *Culture and Personality*. 2d ed. New York: Random House.

Waller, Willard. 1932. *The Sociology of Teaching*. New York: John Wiley & Sons.

Warren, Carol A.B. and John M. Johnson. 1972. "A critique of labeling theory from the phenomenological perspective." In *Theoretical Perspectives on Deviance*, edited by Robert A. Scott and Jack D. Douglas, 69–92. New York: Basic Books.

Webb, Stephen, and John Collette. 1977. "Rural-urban differences in the use of stress-alleviative drugs." *American Journal of Sociology* 83 (November): 700–7.

Weis, Joseph G. 1976. "Liberation and crime: The invention of the new female criminal." *Crime and Social Justice* 6 (Fall–Winter): 17–27.

Wellford, Charles. 1975. "Labelling theory and criminology: An assessment." *Social Problems* (February): 332–45.

Wheeler, Gerald R. 1978. *Counter-Deterrence: A Report on Juvenile Sentencing and Effects of Prisonization*. Chicago: Neison-Hall.

Wheeler, Stanton. 1976. "Trends and problems in the sociological study of crime." *Social Problems* 23 (June): 525–34.

Whyte, William F. 1943a. *Street Corner Society: The Social Structure of an Italian Slum*. Chicago: University of Chicago Press.

———. 1943b. "Social organization in the slums." *American Sociological Review* 8 (February): 34–39.

Wilson, Nanci Koser. 1981. "The masculinity of violent crime: Some second thoughts." *Journal of Criminal Justice* 9 (No. 2): 111–23.

Winick, Charles. 1959–1960. "The use of drugs by jazz musicians." *Social Problems* 7 (Winter): 240–54.

———. 1961. "Physician narcotic addicts." *Social Problems* 9 (Fall): 174–86.

Wolfe, Nancy T., Francis T. Cullen, and John B. Cullen. 1982. "Describing the female offender: A demographic analysis of arrest patterns." Paper presented at the annual meeting of the Academy of Criminal Justice Sciences.

Wolfgang, Marvin E. 1980. "On an evaluation of criminology." In *Handbook of Criminal Justice Evaluation*, edited by Malcolm W. Klein and Katherine S. Teilmann, 19–52. Beverly Hills, CA: Sage Publications.

Wood, Arthur L. 1961. "A socio-structural analysis of murder, suicide, and economic crime in Ceylon." *American Sociological Review* 26 (October): 744–53.

Zuckerman, Harriet. 1977. "Deviant behavior and social control in science." In *Deviance and Social Change*, edited by Edward Sagarin, 87–138. Beverly Hills, CA: Sage Publications.

Index